Lords of the Western Bench

A Biographical History of the Supreme and District Courts of Alberta, 1876-1990

Lords of the Western Bench

*A Biographical History of the Supreme and
District Courts of Alberta, 1876-1990*

Louis Knafla
Richard Klumpenhouwer

The —
**Legal
Archives
Society**
— of —
Alberta

Copyright 8 1997 by the Legal Archives Society of Alberta
Printed in Canada

Printed on acid-free paper

Canadian Cataloguing in Publication Data

Knafla, Louis, 1935 -
Klumpenhouwer, Richard, 1959 -

Lords of the western bench: a biographical history of the supreme and
district courts of Alberta, 1876-1990

Includes bibliographical references and index.
ISBN 0-9681939-0-0

1. Judges -- Alberta -- Biography -- Dictionaries.
2. Alberta. Supreme Court -- Officials and employees -- Biography -- Dictionaries.
3. Alberta. District Courts -- Officials and employees -- Biography -- Dictionaries.
I. Knafla, Louis A., 1935 - II. Legal Archives Society of Alberta. III. Title.

KE396.A4K58 1997   347.7123'014   C97-900301-6

To the memory of Orrin H.E. Might, QC

The grant made by The Nat Christie Foundation in support of this publication is in memory of the late Orrin Henry Eyres Might, QC (1918-1973), who was a brother-in-law of the late Nat Christie, and who, during the course of his practice in Calgary, 1920 to 1962, would have known a great number of the judges included in this publication.

The publisher and authors gratefully acknowledge
the following for their support of this volume:

Contents

The Hon. Mr. Justice J.W. McClung

Foreword

Alberta's substantial contribution to the development of Canadian law has been unique and colourful. Beginning with the first summary trials by NWMP Justice of the Peace James F. Macleod in 1874, the region's courts would witness an ongoing accommodation between the ponderous, yet adaptable British traditions of jurisprudence and the uneven demands of a new and rapidly expanding frontier. The Stipendiary Magistrates, followed by the Supreme and District Court judges, would take the lead in establishing and protecting the authority of law in Alberta by their collective intelligence and resourcefulness. They met this immense challenge, not in spite of, but by their passion and humanity. In this way, the lives and careers of Alberta's judiciary chronicled here help us to gain a greater appreciation of and to celebrate the rule of law in Alberta's rich history. The authors, Louis Knafla and Richard Klumpenhouwer, are to be congratulated on their conception and development of this remarkable collection.

The Hon. Mr. Justice J.W. McClung
Court of Appeal of Alberta, Edmonton
February, 1997

Preface

This work had its inception in a series of lists of federally appointed judges in Alberta completed by the Calgary Courthouse Library between 1981 and 1988. Researchers who contributed to this publication were Henry A. Berg, Anne Retzer, Keith Brown, and Richard Klumpenhouwer. Building on this foundation, the Legal Archives Society of Alberta began constructing a database of biographical information on Alberta judges in 1990. As the database grew and its value as a reference tool became evident, the idea of publishing a biographical history of federally appointed Alberta judges seemed simply a natural extension of this work. After almost five years of research and revisions to the biographies, however, it is clear that we underestimated the extent of the task of bringing this formidable work to publication. As a result, many hands have contributed to shaping its multiple facets.

Those who contributed as researchers at the Legal Archives Society include Scott Clapperton, Jacqueline Juselius, and Susan Pepper. Special recognition is reserved for Archival Assistants Leanne Wescott-Henry, Jill Clayton, and Kirsten Olson. Kirsten was indefatigable in hunting down photographs, and Jill was instrumental in bringing the text into final production. The Hon. Mr. Justice J.W. McClung and Hon. J.H. Laycraft, QC, read the manuscript and provided useful comments.

The authors would like to thank those students in Prof. Knafla's Canadian legal history seminars at The University of Calgary who completed term paper assignments on a number of the major judges, including discussions of their jurisprudence: James Brown, Ted Coderre, Robert Constantinescu, Sean Furlong, Jane Griffith, Joel Hodorek, Roderick Martin, Heather McFarquhar, Brad Mustard, Karen Myrheim, Joy Otelaar, Bruce Pollock, Allison Rankin, Robert Virdis, Darren Wagner, Kim Williams and Todd Wytrychowski. They also wish to thank his graduate students Rod Martin, Paul Nigol, Robert Omura, and Allison Rankin for their assistance in the later stages of the work, and Maggie Watson for her help in indexing.

In addition, Joyce Langevin of Alberta Justice Communications, Jeannie Ellingson of the Court of Appeal, Calgary, Evelyn Schwabe of the Court of Queen's Bench, Edmonton, and Wayne Schafer helped in the collection of photographs. Finally, the authors wish to acknowledge the valuable assistance of the courts, archives and libraries in bringing this work to fruition: The Court of Appeal and Court of Queen's Bench, Justice Canada, the Glenbow-Alberta Institute Archives, the Provincial Archives of Alberta, the Calgary Courthouse Library, and the University of Calgary Law Library.

Louis Knafla
Richard Klumpenhouwer
Hilary, 1997

President's Acknowledgments

A "book" on the judges is an exciting prospect for practising lawyers. To know some of their interests and tendencies permits lawyers to put their arguments in a receptive way. But this book is more. It marks LASA's second publication. We hope there are many more! It strives to capture something of the essence of those who played their part in legal developments in Alberta. We hope we have done that. It also recognizes women and men who, true to their oath, in thousands of cases "did justice" between the parties.

On behalf of the Board and members of the Legal Archives Society of Alberta, I wish to acknowledge the support of the Law Society of Alberta, the legal profession, the Nat Christie Foundation, and the Alberta Historical Resources Foundation in this project.

Graham Price, President
The Legal Archives Society of Alberta
February, 1977

Table of Abbreviations

AD	Appellate Division, Supreme Court of Alberta
AG	Attorney General
AJ	Alberta Justice Communications
ALR	*Alberta Law Reports*
AR	*Alberta Reports*
B.A.	Bachelor of Arts degree
B.C.L.	Bachelor of Civil Laws degree
CA	Court of Appeal of Alberta
CANT	Court of Appeal of the Northwest Territories
CAYT	Court of Appeal of the Yukon Territory
CCC	*Canadian Criminal Cases*
CLA	City of Lethbridge Archives
DC	District Court
DLR	*Dominion Law Reports*
GAI	Glenbow-Alberta Institute
JCPC	Judicial Committee of the Privy Council, Great Britain
JP	Justice of the Peace
KC	King's Counsel
LASA	Legal Archives Society of Alberta
LL.B.	Bachelor of Laws degree
LL.D.	Doctor of Laws degree
M.A.	Master of Arts degree
MLA	Member of the Legislative Assembly of Alberta
MP	Member of Parliament of Canada
NWMP	North-West Mounted Police
NWT	North-West Territories (1870-1905)
PAA	Provincial Archives of Alberta
PC	Provincial Court, Alberta
QB	Queen's Bench, Court of, Alberta
QC	Queen's Counsel
RCMP	Royal Canadian Mounted Police
RDA	Red Deer and District Archives
RFL	*Reports on Family Law*
RNWMP	Royal North-West Mounted Police
SA	*Statutes of Alberta*
SAB	Saskatchewan Archives Board
SCA	Supreme Court of Alberta
SCC	Supreme Court of Canada
SCNT	Supreme Court of the Northwest Territories
SCNWT	Supreme Court of the North-West Territories (1887-1907)
SCR	*Supreme Court Reports*
SCYT	Supreme Court of the Yukon Territory
SG	Solicitor General
SM	Stipendiary Magistrate

TD	Trial Division, Supreme Court of Alberta
TLR	*Territories Law Reports*
WWR	*Western Weekly Reports*

List of Entries

Agrios, John Andrew
Allen, Gordon Hollis
Andrekson, Alexander
Beaumont, Arthur
Beck, Nicholas Du Bois Dominic
Belzil, Roger Hector
Berger, Ronald Leon
Bielby, Myra Beth
Bowen, Donald Haines
Boyle, John Robert
Bracco, John David
Brennan, William Robert
Buchanan, Nelles Victor
Bury, Ambrose Upton Gledstanes
Cairns, James Mitchell
Cairns, Laurence Yeomans
Carpenter, Arthur Allan
Cavanagh, James Creighton
Cawsey, Robert Alan
Chrumka, Paul Stephen
Clarke, Alfred Henry
Clement, Carlton William
Conrad, Carole Mildred
Cooke, Alan Thomas
Cormack, John Spiers
Côté, Jean Edouard Leon
Crawford, John Lyndon
Cross, Thomas Lynde
Crossley, Arthur William
Cullen, Alan Joseph
Dea, John Berchmans
Dechene, André Miville
Decore, John Nickolas
Decore, Lionel Leighton
Deyell, Roy Victor
Dixon, Russell Armitage
Dubuc, Lucien
Edmanson, Roy Manning
Edwards, Manley Justin
Egbert, William Gordon
Egbert, William Gordon Neil
Ewing, Albert Freeman
Fairbairn, Lynden Eldon

Farthing, Hugh Cragg
Feehan, Joseph Bernard
Feir, Elmor Best
Foisy, René Paul
Ford, Clinton James
Ford, Frank
Forsyth, Gregory Rife
Foster, Nina Leone
Fraser, Catherine Anne
Fraser, Harry Blackwood
Gallant, Tellex William
Gardiner, Duncan McIntyre
Gariepy, Charles Edouard
Girgulis, William James
Greene, George Wellington
Greschuk, Peter
Haddad, William Joseph
Harradence, Asa Milton
Harvey, Horace
Hetherington, Mary Margaret
    McCormick
Holmes, Jack Kenneth
Hope, John McIntosh
Howson, William Robinson
Hutchinson, Ernest Arthur
Hyndman, James Duncan
Irving, Howard Lawrence
Ives, William Carlos
Jackson, John Ainslie
Jennison, John Leslie
Johnson, Horace Gilchrist
Johnstone, Thomas Cooke
Kane, Edward William Scott
Kerans, Roger Philip
Kerr, Stanley Chandos Stavely
Kidd, James George
Kirby, William John Cameron
Kryczka, Joseph Julius
Laycraft, James Herbert
Lees, William Andrew Dickson
Legg, Sidney Vincent
Lieberman, Samuel Sereth
Lomas, Melvin Earl

Lunney, Henry William
Lutz, Arthur Morton
MacCallum, Edward Patrick
MacDonald Angus Marcellus
MacDonald, Hugh John (1944-1965)
MacDonald, Hugh John (1968-1986)
MacDonald, William Alexander
MacKenzie, John Horace
MacLean, Lawrence David
MacLeod, Donald Ingraham
Macleod, James Farquharson
MacNaughton, Frederick Richards
MacPherson, Jack Leon
Mahaffy, James Jeffers
Manning, Marshall Edward
Marshall, Ernest Arthur
Mason, David Blair
Matheson, Douglas Randolph
Matheson, Joseph Duncan
McBain, Ross Thomas George
McBride, James Boyd
McCarthy, Maitland Steward
McClung, John Wesley
McDermid, Neil Douglas
McDonald, David Cargill
McDonald, John Cameron
McDonald, John Walter
McFadyen, Elizabeth Ann
McGillivray, Alexander Andrew
McGillivray, William Alexander
McGuire, Thomas Horace
McIsaac, Joseph Patrick
McLaurin, Colin Campbell
McNeill, Edward Peel
Medhurst, Donald Herbert
Miller, Tevie Harold
Milvain, James Valentine Hogarth
Mitchell, Charles Richmond
Moir, Arnold Fraser
Montgomery, Robert Archibald
    Fraser
Moore, William Kenneth
Morrison, Frederic Augustus
Morrow, William George
Moshansky, Virgil Peter

Murray, Alec Thirlwell
Newlands, Henry William
Noel, Joseph Camillien
O'Byrne, Michael Brien
O'Connor, George Bligh
O'Leary, Willis Edward
Parlee, Harold Hayward
Patterson, Henry Stuart
Perras, Delmar Walter Joseph
Picard, Ellen Irene
Porter, Marshall Menzies
Power, Peter Charles Garneau
Prendergast, James Emile Pierre
Primrose, Neil Phillip
Prowse, David Clifton
Prowse, Hubert Samuel
Purvis, Stuart Somerville
Quigley, Francis Hugh
Rawlins, Bonnie Leigh
Richardson, Hugh
Riley, Harold William
Roslak, Yaroslaw
Rouleau, Charles Borromée
Rowbotham, Henry Slater
Ryan, Matthew
Scott, David Lynch
Sellar, William
Shannon, Melvin Earl
Shepherd, Simpson James
Sifton, Arthur Lewis
Simmons, William Charles
Sinclair, William Robert
Sissons, John Howard
Smith, Sidney Bruce
Smith, Vernor Winfield MacBriare
Stack, Luke Hannon
Steer, George Alexander Cameron
Stevenson, William Alexander
Stewart, John Douglas Reginald
Stratton, Joseph John
Stuart, Charles Allan
Sulatycky, Allan Borislaw Zenoviy
Tavender, Edward Rusling
Taylor, Hedley Clarence
Travis, Jeremiah

Trussler, Marguerite Jean
Turcotte, Louis Sherman
Tweedie, Thomas Mitchell March
Veit, Joanne Barbara
Virtue, Charles Gladstone
Wachowich, Allan Harvey Joseph
Waite, John Hilary
Walsh, William Legh
Wetmore, Edward Ludlow
Whittaker, Bruce Cavanagh
Wilson, Ernest Brown
Winter, William Roland
Yanosik, Clarence George

Introduction

Judicial Histories

The history of judges in Canada is a subject that has been sketched in its broadest outlines at the national level, and haphazardly at the provincial. The leading historical survey of our national judiciary, so to speak, is the classic study of James Snell and Frederick Vaughan, which brought together the interests of a historian and a political scientist to write a history of the Supreme Court of Canada that combines biography with institutional history and the larger regional and political contexts.[1] What was left undone in this national survey, was a closer examination of the jurisprudence of the Court, of the history of its decisions. Thus it was Ian Bushnell, a lawyer, who brought the impressive case law history of the Court to bear in a study that broke up its history into five historical eras and examined the judgments of the Court on the major issues which confronted it in each of those periods.[2] The touchstone of this work was the published views of former Chief Justices Bora Laskin and Brian Dickson that the Court had, up until the abolition of appeals to the Judicial Committee of the Privy Council in 1949,[3] been captive to English jurisprudence and therefore absent of an interactive academic environment and an independent legal tradition;[4] further, that it took the *Canadian Charter of Rights and Freedoms* in 1982 to allow such an environment and tradition to emerge.

Bushnell's study of the Supreme Court of Canada's sixty-seven judges over the course of its first 115 years highlights some of the quintessential elements of judicial history in Canada which are relevant not only to the Supreme Court of Canada, but also to the judiciary of any one of its territories or provinces. What Bushnell, and other authors of judges in Great Britain and the United States have been concerned with, is what we might call the "life of the law": what goes into the making of judicial decisions, and the extent to how that reflects, works with, and influences the social, economic, cultural, and religious customs of society; a recognition that the fundamental principles of the law are not static and unchanging, but continuously in flux; and that the job of the historian is to hoe the furrows of this landscape in order to harvest the yield which emerges.

With regard to judicial biography, there have been a number of biographies of major Canadian judges that have gone beyond the basic narrative of life and times to an exploration of their ideas, jurisprudence, and mindset. These include, for the early period, Upton's study of William Smith of New York and Quebec,[5] Brode's now classic biography of John Beverly Robinson of Ontario,[6] and Williams' duet of British Columbia's twin towers, Sir Matthew Begbie and Sir Lyman Duff.[7] Later, we have Boyer's elegant portrait of James McRuer of Ontario,[8] and Bale's not so elegant study of New Brunswick's William Ritchie.[9] Apart from Wilbur Bowker's solid study of the case law of Chief Justice Harvey,[10] Alberta, let alone the other prairie provinces, have no tradition of judicial biography even though they have spawned some of the best judges in the country.

Too often judges are seen as anonymous law-makers. C.C. McCaul observed, when writing from personal experience in 1925 about the early judges of the North-

West Territories, that a judge's most prized possession is "a solid sense of justice and a fund of sound common sense; [he is] above all, a gentleman and very human, the best of all qualities in a judge."[11] What this biographical collection aspires to achieve is that they should be seen as real persons dealing with real issues, and that a knowledge of who they are, where they come from, and what they have done in life, as well as in their careers, sheds light on their minds, judicial acts, and decisions which shape much of the world that touches upon the law. Combining the skills of the legal archivist and the legal historian, this work is designed to bring that record into the public theatre where it can enrich our understanding of the past.

The Judicial History of Alberta

Alberta was not without its key moments in the history of the growth of Canadian jurisprudence. On several occasions, legal crises in the province have surfaced on the national scene. Perhaps the first prominent one was the problem of conscription during World War One. Parliament passed the *Military Service Act* in 1917 for the Dominion government to bolster recruitment for the war effort. An exemption for persons in essential occupations was removed the next spring by Order in Council under the *War Measures Act*. In Alberta, a farmer named Lewis who had been exempted was called up, and his counsel R.B. Bennett applied for a writ of *habeas corpus* for his release. The Supreme Court of Alberta held that the Dominion government had no power under the Act to cancel exemptions, and ordered the farmer's release.[12] The Dominion Cabinet then directed its Orders to be applied across the country irrespective of the decision, while back in Alberta another twenty conscripts appealed for *habeas corpus* for their release. The Calgary Barracks refused to accept the writs, and a writ of attachment was issued against the commanding officer. Ottawa, meanwhile, instructed the military to oppose any service of the writs with force, and the Alberta Minister of Justice applied to the Supreme Court of Canada. Meanwhile, Chief Justice Harvey delivered judgment on a second case *Re. Norton*, holding that while the Court was sympathetic to the Dominion government and its prosecution of the war effort, court decisions must be obeyed.[13] As the fear of violence gripped the city, the Supreme Court of Canada reversed the Lewis decision on a similar application from Ontario, and held the Order valid in Council.[14]

The second major event was the "Persons" case of 1928. Women gained the right to vote in 1918, and Agnes Macphail was elected from Ontario as the first female Member of Parliament in 1921. Since membership in the Senate was by appointment of the Dominion government, Alberta's Emily Murphy was chosen for a reference case to the Supreme Court of Canada. Murphy was an interesting choice.[15] Appointed Police Magistrate for Edmonton in 1916, she was the first female magistrate in the British Empire. She was also a reputable writer under the pen name of "Janey Canuck".[16] Challenged in her first day in court by a lawyer who claimed that women were not "persons" for the purpose of government appointment under the *British North America Act* of 1867, the death of an Alberta senator in 1922 allowed her to challenge such an interpretation and apply for the senate

The Supreme Court of the North-West Territories, Regina, 1887 *(LASA)*
L-R (behind bench): E.L. Wetmore, J.F. Macleod, Hugh Richardson,
C.B. Rouleau, T.H. McGuire

Supreme Court Alberta, Appellate Division, ca. 1935 *(LASA)*
L-R (behind bench): H.W. Lunney, A.H. Clarke, Chief Justice
Horace Harvey, C.R. Mitchell, A.A. McGillivray

appointment. Since Prime Minister Mackenzie King had promised to support women for the Senate, Murphy used a procedure never used before or after: a five-person petition to the federal government requesting a reference to the Supreme Court of Canada. The 1927 petition was submitted by five prominent Alberta women[17] in 1927, Murphy, Nellie McClung, Louise McKinney, Irene Parlby, and Henrietta Muir Edwards, and directed by the King government to the Supreme Court.[18]

The reference was heard on March 14, 1928 by a panel of five judges, in what would become the highest profiled case in the history of the Court to date. It was supported by the government of Alberta, and opposed by the government of Quebec. The Court decided against the petitioners in a decision that fit well with its conservative standing. It had ruled on the narrow ground that Senate membership was a political matter, and that judges were only concerned with the language of the constitution. Chief Justice Anglin's judgment was lacking in credible authorities and earmarked by judicial diarrhea. Only the learned Justice Sir Lyman Duff of British Columbia dissented. While the federal government announced immediately an amendment to the constitution to allow women to be Senators, the petitioners launched an appeal to the Judicial Committee of the Privy Council.[19] Heard on October 18, 1929, the Lord delivered a judgment which mirrored social reality by finding for the appellant and allowing for Murphy's appointment. Although Anglin's judgment was butchered, the mechanical jurisprudence of the Supreme Court of Canada shouldered on.[20]

While the Persons case revealed the Supreme Court of Canada at its nadir, the Alberta Legislation case of 1938 revealed its first crest. On August 22, 1935, William Aberhart's Social Credit Party swept to power with an economic program based on Major C.H. Douglas' new economic theory. Promising just prices, debt-free government, and a financial dividend, two years later the new provincial government enacted three statutes which struck at the heart of the banking and free enterprise system. Ottawa disallowed the statutes on the ground that they infringed upon federal powers, the legislature passed three new statutes, and in October 1938 the two governments agreed to have the validity of the statutes determined by a reference to the Supreme Court of Canada. Earlier, the Court had overturned some of Prime Minister Richard Bennett's "New Deal" legislation of 1935, and the Judicial Committee reversed much of the rest of it.[21] Presided over by Chief Justice Duff, the Supreme Court was emerging as a new judicial force in the country.

The Supreme Court held all three statutes invalid as an infringement on federal authority[22] and affirmed the Dominion's authority to set aside provincial legislation.[23] Duff opined that provincial legislatures lacked the authority to impose limits on the freedom of public interests, which was reserved to the Dominion. The Court's decision was seen not only as a vote for the judiciary as an instrument of government, but also as stamping authority on a more modern notion of the federal state. The decision also had an impact on the future of the Judicial Committee of the Privy Council, which had in the past upheld, and been a stalwart of, much provincial legislation. This marked the beginning of the drive to end appeals to England and they were abolished by statute on December 10, 1949.[24] Thus Alberta's

The Courthouse at Edmonton, constructed in 1913, demolished in 1973 *(LASA)*

The Courthouse at Calgary, now the Court of Appeal, constructed in 1914

(CA)

"matter" contributed in no small part to the creation of a more activist jurisprudence at the federal level, and jurisprudential attitudes that would be more conducive to upholding the more instrumental role which provincial judiciaries such as Alberta's had exercised since the turn of the century.

This more activist judicial tradition came into play on the national scene once again in 1950, when the Alberta government appealed *Huggard Assets v. AG of Alberta*. The Dominion government had granted to Huggard's predecessor in 1913 oil and gas rights to land near Fort McMurray. The grant included words that allowed the collection of royalties as prescribed from time to time. The federal government had never imposed one, and when the natural resources were transferred to the province in 1930, the grant went with it. The province later claimed the right to impose such a royalty, and Huggard brought an action against the claim. The Supreme Court of Alberta held that the collection was operative only at the time of the grant, and that the company was free from the province.[25] The Appeal brought a split vote, confirming the trial decision on the ground that the royalty was vague and ambiguous,[26] and the province appealed to the Supreme Court of Canada in 1950. The question arose there as to whether the law of Alberta included the English *Statute of Tenures* of 1660, which converted land to free and common socage tenure with duties payable to the Crown. Charles II granted Rupert's Land to the Hudson's Bay Company in 1670 with this tenure, which was transferred to Canada in 1870, and to Alberta in 1930. The Supreme Court dismissed the Province's appeal,[27] and it was then appealed to the Judicial Committee, which could sit on any case still in progress. Therefore, in one of the last decisions of the Judicial Committee on a Canadian matter, the Supreme Courts of Alberta and Canada were reversed; the *Statute of Tenures* was deemed not to apply to Rupert's Land, and the province was free to collect variable royalties and thereby gain control over its natural resources.[28]

Whereas the Alberta courts have often been viewed in a light commensurate with the province's conservative political ideology, this has not always been an accurate reflection. Its judges have often been at the cutting edge of shaping the law to fit the larger socio-economic concerns of society. This is well evidenced in the judicial biographies which follow in this volume, and it has existed since the earliest days of the Supreme Court of the North-West Territories. Moreover, the large number of challenging legal minds in the province have set the stage for the evaluation of judicial doctrines old and new on an almost annual basis. This has also been demonstrated most recently in *Vriend v. Alberta*.[29]

Mr. Vriend went to the Queen's Bench at Edmonton in 1992 to appeal his dismissal as a lab assistant at a private Christian college. The college argued that Vriend, as a gay person, violated the college's prohibition against homosexual practices; Vriend argued his rights under the *Charter of Rights and Freedoms*. Justice Anne Russell held that while Alberta's human rights legislation did not extend to protect gay rights, it must be interpreted to do so. On appeal, that decision was reversed three to two. Justice John W. McClung, grandson of pioneer suffragette Nellie McClung, held for the Court of Appeal that the legislature had sole authority to add, or not to add, the protection of gay rights to its human rights legislation. These two judgments reflect a Court deeply steeped in the historic common law tradition of independent judges making law based on their vision of the customs of their society.

Biographical Judicial Histories

One of the early attempts at provincial judicial biography was Clara Greco's summary analysis of the superior court judges of Nova Scotia, 1754-1900.[30] Greco, a lawyer, was the first scholar to apply the discipline of prosopography to the study of a Canadian judiciary. She examined the profile of their ages and tenure in office, places of birth, social status, religion, education, legal training, political activities, and "the spoils of office". Unfortunately, no one has done anything similar for any other jurisdiction or region of the country.

An exception is a slim hagiography of the judges of British Columbia written by the Honourable David Verchere.[31] Based on a few reported cases, statutes, and newspaper articles, it suggests perhaps that judges should not write history, just as historians and archivists should not judge cases. In this respect, Canada trails all other common law countries in the history of its judges.[32]

The authors of this volume are attempting to build a platform on which a history of the judges of Alberta can some day be written. Thus the individual biographies should be seen as gathering the biographical information from the original sources upon which the collective judicial history of the province, studies of judges in any historical aspect, as well as of the history of the case law and jurisprudence of the region, can be written. Since no such history has been written for a province in the country, it is also proffered that this can serve as a model for the judicial history of other provinces.[33]

The Biographical Judicial History of Alberta

The current work is an inaugural history of the federally-appointed judges of Alberta. Geographically, it includes the land which now comprises the province from the creation of the North-West Territories in 1870 down to the founding of the Province of Alberta in 1905. For the Territorial period, this includes Stipendiary Magistrates appointed under Section 59 of the *North-West Territories Act* of 1875 to sit in judicial districts of the later district of Alberta created in 1884, and subdivided into Southern and Northern Alberta in 1887; and the Judges of the North-West Territories for the two Alberta districts created under the *North-West Territories Act* of 1886. For the provincial period, it includes all Judges of the Supreme Court, Trial and Appellate Divisions, and the District Courts of Alberta since 1907, and of the later Courts of Queen's Bench and Appeal.

The biographies are presented in three parts. First, we have identified all 187 federally-appointed judges who were appointed from 1876 through 1990. This includes the titles, places, and dates of all the courts to which they were appointed.

Second, we have identified certain key biographical information for each person, including: date and place of birth, academic degrees, date of call to the bar, and date of retirement and death as appropriate. This information has been gathered and checked as to historical accuracy. Third, we have obtained biographical information to the best of our abilities. This information, which is not always complete, includes the following: primary, secondary, university and post-graduate education, law schools, and degrees; pre-legal/judicial work experience; articling firm, and legal practices; government and royal commissions, community organizations, and memberships in public and private clubs and associations; political affiliation, and public offices locally, provincially, and nationally; and honourary degrees and distinctions.

Fourth, we have tried to create a section on the judicial activities and jurisprudence of each judge. We have concentrated on those judges who served in the superior courts, and whose decisions and judgments have been reported in the various law reports. We have also consulted judicial notebooks where they are extant and have been preserved in an Archives. The purpose of this section is to obtain some historical vision of what kinds of cases a judge offered written judgements, what kinds of sources he/she used in making judgments, and what attitudes were revealed towards the law and legal issues in those writings within their historical context. This is the perhaps the least developed section of some of the biographies. Judges who served on superior courts, and especially in the appellate division, for long periods of time, are covered more fully here than others. Likewise, judges who have ended their service on the bench receive more attention than those who are still sitting. It should be made clear that there is no necessary connection between the length of any one biography and the significance of the judge's career. Finally, we have managed to collect and reproduce 161 photographs of the 187 judges, and these are included in three insert sections of the text in alphabetical order. In the end, it is our hope that the second edition will provide a much more complete account of all the judges biographical information, the judges' leading decisions, and the law espoused therein than is contained in this volume.

The Judicial Districts of Alberta

The history of courts is a subject that has never moved off the ground in Canada. Most common law countries have numerous histories, both general and particular. In Canada, apart from the history of the Supreme Court of Canada, and studies of individual courts in time, few provinces have any narrative account of the history of their court systems or of their judiciaries. An initial project that lost its way was the projected series on private law in Canada. Only one volume was published.[34] However, as an outline of all the Canadian courts for civil actions derived meticulously from statutory legislation and orders in council, it remains an important relic. The leading study remains that of the late law librarian Margaret Banks who wrote a history of the courts of Ontario.[35] Banks provided diagrammed charts with a full narrative to present the history of the courts from the relevant legislation with additional commentary from legislative journals and selected judges papers.

Court of Queen's Bench of Alberta, 1984

In Alberta, the history of the courts remains to be reconstructed, and the various judicial districts to which judges were assigned has not yet been compiled. Originally, the first judges of the newly created North-West Territories were appointed in 1876, following the surrender of the Charter of the Hudson's Bay Company to the British Crown in 1869, and the subsequent transfer of its lands and authority under the Royal Charter of 1670 to the Dominion of Canada in 1870. Thus the *Dominion Act* of 1870 and 1871 designated the lands between Manitoba and British Columbia, which with Manitoba had comprised Prince Rupert's Land, as the North-West Territories.[36] The power to administer law in the Territories was delegated by the Governor General of Canada to the Lieutenant Governor in Council, and the Act of 1873 created the North-West Mounted Police to serve as constables and JPs, and in the following year as its officers were authorized to serve as Stipendiary Magistrates.[37] The Lieutenant Governor was given control over these officials in the administration of justice by the *North-West Territories Act* of 1875.[38] It was under this Act that the first Stipendiary Magistrates were appointed for the Territories.

Stipendiary Magistrates were paid Justices of the Peace, descendants of that honourary English institution dating from the fourteenth century, who presided over District Courts. The law which they administered was English law as of 1870,[39] including law and equity as provided by the *English Judicature Act* of 1873.[40] They were succeeded in 1887 by the Supreme Court of the North-West Territories, which was created by Dominion legislation.[41] Assize circuits were instituted the same year, bringing the administration of justice up to date with that of England. Judges heard cases in the districts over which they presided, and sat together as a full court to hear reserved cases and appeals. Stipendiary Magistrates were abolished, replaced with paid Justices of the Peace and attended by the North-West Mounted Police. It was this structure, apart from the creation later of new districts and subdivisions, that lasted through the establishment of the provinces of Saskatchewan and Alberta in 1905 down into the twentieth century.[42]

In Alberta, the new legislation creating the court system went into force in 1907,[43] establishing the Supreme Court of Alberta and several District Courts with limited jurisdiction in minor cases. This structure lasted until 1921, when the Supreme Court was divided into Trial and Appellate Divisions.[44] In 1935, the various District Courts were amalgamated to form the District Court of Northern Alberta and Southern Alberta[45] and in 1975, the two District Courts were merged into one District Court of Alberta.[46] The entire federal court system was restructured on June 30, 1979. The District Court of Alberta was abolished and the judges assigned to the Court of Queen's Bench, which replaced the Trial Division. The Court of Appeal of Alberta replaced the Appellate Division.[47] The judges of these various courts, from 1876 to 1990, have been listed by court in the appendix of Court Lists at the end of this volume.

Conclusion

The current book can be considered a work in progress. We plan to publish a new edition after the year 2000, which will fill out and update all the biographies contained herein to that year, and include all the judges federally appointed to the year 2000. Therefore, it is hoped that this work will provide some of the raw material by which the courts and their districts eventually may be fully reconstructed, and integrated with the context of the men and women who served in them as well as the legal issues and problems which emerged. In the end, the life of the law can be no richer than the people, events, and ideas which nurtured it.

Notes

1. James G. Snell and Frederick Vaughan, *The Supreme Court of Canada. History of the Institution* (Toronto: The Osgoode Society, 1985).
2. Ian Bushnell, *The Captive Court. A Study of the Supreme Court of Canada* (Montreal & Kingston: McGill-Queen's University Press, 1992).
3. Bora Laskin, "The Supreme Court of Canada: A Final Court of and for Canadians," *Canadian Bar Review* 29 (1951): 138-140.
4. For a lament from the Northwest Territories, see W. G. Morrow, "The Last Case," *Alberta Law Review* 16 (1978): 1-19.
5. L.F.S. Upton, *The Loyal Whig. William Smith of New York and Quebec* (Toronto: University of Toronto Press, 1969).
6. Patrick Brode, *Sir John Beverley Robinson: Bone and Sinew of the Compact* (Toronto: The Osgoode Society, 1984).
7. Williams, David R. *". . . The Man for a New Country": Sir Matthew Baillie Begbie* (Sidney: Gray's Publishing, 1977; and his *Duff: A Life in the Law* (Vancouver: University of British Columbia Press, 1984.
8. Patrick Boyer, *A Passion for Justice. The Legacy of James Chalmers McRuer* (Toronto: The Osgoode Society, 1994).
9. Gordon Bale, *Chief Justice William Johnstone Ritchie* (Ottawa: Carleton University Press, 1991). Unfortunately, this first volume of the new Supreme Court of Canada Historical Society has not been succeeded by any others to date.
10. W.F. Bowker, "The Honourable Horace Harvey, Chief Justice of Alberta," *Canadian Bar Review* 32 (1954): 933-981, 1118-1139.
11. C.C. McCaul, "Precursors of the Bench and Bar in the Western Provinces," *Canadian Bar Review* 3 (1925): 38.
12. *Re Lewis* ([1918] 2 WWR 287).
13. *Re. Norton* ([1918] 2 WWR 865).
14. *Re. Gray* ([1918] 57 SCR 150. See also Wilbur Bowker, "The Honourable Horace Harvey, Chief Justice of Alberta," in Bowker, *A Consolidation of Fifty Years of Legal Writings by Wilbur F. Bowker 1938-1988* (Edmonton: University of Alberta, 1989), at pp. 59-62.
15. See her book, *The Black Candle* (Toronto: Thomas Allen 1922; repr. Edmonton 1973).
16. Donna James, *Emily Murphy* (Toronto: Fitzhenry and Whiteside, 1977).
17. See, for example, Edwards' *Legal Status of Women in Alberta* (Fort Macleod, 1921).

18. *Reference as to Meaning of the Word "Persons" in Section 24 of the British North America Act, 1867* ([1928] SCR 276).

19. *Edwards v. Attorney General for Canada* ([1930] AC 124).

20. For a contemporary scholarly view of the significance of the case for the future of Canadian law, see W.P.M. Kennedy, *The Canadian Constitution as interpreted by the Judicial Committee, 1916-1929* (Toronto: Carswell Co., 1930).

21. W.H. McConnell, "The Judicial Review of Prime Minister Bennett's 'New Deal'," *Osgoode Hall Law Journal* 6 (1968): 39-68.

22. *In the Matter of Three Bills passed by the Legislative Assembly of the Province of Alberta* ([1938] SCR 100.

23. *Reference re. the Power of the Governor General in Council to Disallow Provincial Legislation and the Power of reservation of a Lieutenant Governor of a Province* ([1938] SCR 71.

24. Bushnell, *The Captive Court*, pp. 243-277. This is also a sure guide to the Court's history on the matters discussed above.

25. *Huggard Assets v. AG of Alberta and Minister of Lands and Mines* ([1949] 2 WWR 370).

26. *AG for Alberta v. Huggard Assets and Minister of Lands and Mines* ([1950] 1 WWR 69).

27. *Ibid.* ([1951] SCR 427).

28. *Ibid.* ([1953] AC 420). See also for context, Wilbur Bowker, "Fifty-Five Years at the Alberta Bar: George Hobson Steer, Q.C.", in his *A Consolidation of Fifty Years of Legal Writings by Wilbur F. Bowker 1938-1988* (Edmonton: University of Alberta, 1989), at pp. 563-567.

29. *Vriend v. Alberta* ([1996] 161 AR 16; 184 AR 351).

30. Clara Greco, "The Superior Court Judiciary of Nova Scotia, 1754-1900: A Collective Biography," in *Essays in the History of Canadian Law, Volume III,* Nova Scotia, eds. Philip Girard and Jim Phillips (Toronto: The Osgoode Society, 1900), 42-79.

31. David R. Verchere, *A Progression of Judges. A History of the Supreme Court of British Columbia* (Vancouver: University of British Columbia Press, 1988).

32. One should mention here the valuable work of Peter H. Russell, *The Judiciary in Canada: The Third Branch of Government* (Toronto: McGraw-Hill Ryerson Ltd., 1987. This book has an excellent description and analysis of the civil and criminal courts, superior and inferior, and their judges, with some historical perspective and considerable analysis.

33. The *Dictionary of Canadian Biography* is becoming a genuine source for the history of judges and lawyers in Canada. Although extending now only to 1910, and proceeding at approximately the rate of a decade once every four years, it will not unfortunately be of much value to Western Canada until at least another decade or two. An example of how full biographical accounts can illuminate the history of a province, the law, and the courts, is the seventy collected biographies in *Provincial Justice. Upper Canadian Legal Portraits from the Dictionary of Canadian Biography*, ed. Robert Fraser

(Toronto: The Osgoode Society, 1992).

34. J.A. Clarence Smith and Jean Kerby, *Private Law in Canada. A Comparative Study* (Ottawa: University of Ottawa Press, 1975).

35. Margaret Banks, "The Evolution of the Ontario Courts 1788 -1981," in *Essays in the History of Canadian Law, Volume II*, ed. David Flaherty (Toronto: The Osgoode Society, 1983), 492-572.

36. *Manitoba Act, 1870* (32 & 33 Victoria c. 3); and the *British North America Act, 1871* (34 & 35 Victoria, c. 28).

37. *An Act respecting the Administration of Justice, and for the establishment of a Police Force in the North-West Territories* (1873), c. 35.

38. (1875), c. 49.

39. *North-West Territories Act* (1875), c. 49

40. *North-West Territories Act, R.S.C.* (1886), c. 50, s. 48.

41. *Administration of Justice Act* (1885), c.51; and *An Act further to amend the law respecting the North-West Territories* (1886), c. 25 (proclaimed February 18, 1887).

42. The records of these courts have been preserved in the Provincial Archives of Alberta, and most of them have been microfilmed.

43. *An Act respecting the Supreme Court, S.A.* (1907), c.3; *An Act respecting the District Courts*, S.A. (1907), c.4.

44. *An Act respecting the Supreme Court, S.A.* (1919), c.3, s.8.

45. *District Courts Amendment Act, S.A.* (1933), c.15.

46. *District Courts Amendment Act, S.A.* (1974), c.68.

47. *Court of Appeal Act, S.A.* (1978), c. 50; *Court of Queen's Bench Act*, c.51.

Judges Biographies

Agrios, John Andrew

Court of Queen's Bench of Alberta,
Edmonton, July 3, 1980 -

The Honourable Justice John Andrew Agrios was born in Edmonton, Alberta, on October 30, 1932. He is the son of Andrew J. Agrios, a prominent Edmonton hotel proprietor and a leader in Edmonton's Greek-Canadian community. Agrios attended the University of Alberta, graduating with a B.A. in 1955 and an LL.B. in 1956. He was admitted to the Alberta bar on June 28, 1957. Agrios practiced with the Edmonton firm of Emery Jamieson from 1957 until his appointment to the bench at Edmonton in 1980.

On the bench, Agrios specialized in commercial law. While few of his decisions were reported, a number of his judgments on loan guarantees, mortgages, and foreclosures were published. In *Alberta Housing Corporation v. Orysiuk, and Alberta Housing Corporation v. Toshack* ([1982] 117 ALR 2d 60), Orysiuk, an executive director of the plaintiff, was held negligent for concealing the terms of a loan; and in a similar scenario with a different agent, he was found liable for fraud and misrepresentation: *Alberta Housing Corporation v. Orysiuk, and Alberta Housing Corporation v. Achtem* ([1982] 18 ALR 2d 56). Agrios laid out the facts in a clear manner, reciting the relevant Canadian case law on the subject. And in *Credit Foncier Trust Company v. Hornigold, etc.* ([1985] 35 ALR 2d 341), he awarded costs and charges on a solicitor-client bill that was prepared in a mortgage foreclos-ure action. Again, Agrios defined the issue clearly, and presented a simplified account of the problems and his resolution with a schedule of the allowables.

Allen, Gordon Hollis

Supreme Court of Alberta, Appellate
Division, Calgary, May 12, 1966 -
May 28, 1978

The Honourable Gordon Hollis Allen was born in Chesterton, New York on May 28, 1901, and came to western Canada as a boy with his family in 1912. He attended Crescent Heights Collegiate in Calgary and began his five-year articles in 1918 while still in high school with Bill Lent, H.C.B. Forsyth, and the Calgary firm of Taylor, Allison, Moffat and Wetham. He attended the University of Alberta, graduating with an LL.B. in 1923. After being admitted to the Alberta bar on November 27, 1923, Allen practiced law in Calgary with the firm of Lent, MacKay and Mann, then Brownlee, Porter, Goodall and Rankin, and finally formed a firm with the prominent litigator Marshall M. Porter in 1932. Allen was named KC on December 29, 1945 and was President of the Law Society of Alberta, 1959-1961. Active in the areas of commercial, and oil and gas, law during World War II, he was counsel for the Emergency Coal Production and Oil Boards under C.D. Howe. He was a senior partner in the firm of Allen, MacKimmie, Matthews, Wood, Phillips, and Smith when he was appointed to the bench at Calgary in

1966. He was appointed to the CANT in 1971. Allen retired on May 28, 1978, and died in Calgary on July 30, 1995.

Allen adjudicated many cases involving oil and gas matters. Replacing Hugh J. MacDonald on the AD, his appointment ended the tradition of maintaining a Roman Catholic "seat" on the Alberta court.

Andrekson, Alexander

Court of Queen's Bench of Alberta,
    Edmonton, August 22, 1985 -
Supernumerary Justice, Edmonton,
    February 21, 1996 -

The Honourable Justice Alexander Andrekson was born in Parnu, Estonia, on November 13, 1923, and immigrated to Canada in 1926. He attended the University of Alberta, receiving a B.Sc. in 1947, a M.Sc. in 1949, and an LL.B. in 1954. Andrekson was admitted to the Alberta bar on June 10, 1955, and was named QC on December 19, 1973. He was President of the Law Society of Alberta, 1982-1983. Andrekson was a senior partner in the Edmonton firm of Bryan Andrekson when he was appointed to the bench at Edmonton in 1985.

Andrekson gave a number of decisions on matters concerning administrative law, insurance, and contracts. In *Alberta Agricultural Development Corporation v. Tiny Tym's Poultry Ltd. et. al.* ([1989] 66 ALR 2d 279), the defendant company applied for a loan to consolidate debts and construct a building. The plaintiff company took a promissory note and a mortgage, and later sued to determine whether the covenant on the mortgage was a guarantee under the *Guarantees Ac-*

knowledgement Act. Andrekson held for the plaintiff in an opinion that linked a string of cases and statutes with lengthy quotations. In the *Province of Alberta Treasury Branches v. Smith* ([1989] 67 ALR 2d 357), the defendant again obtained a loan from the plaintiff to consolidate debts for her farming business. The defendant claimed that the note was void because she did not receive the interest shielding program for farmers. Andrekson held for the plaintiff on the grounds that it had all been explained to her. Setting out the cases fully, he set the case in writing to in effective story format. And in *Modern Livestock Ltd. v. Elgersma and Elgersma* ([1989] 69 ALR 2d 20), a religious colony's hog herd became infected with haemophilus pneumonia, a highly contagious disease that was lethal to hogs. The hogs were sold by an agent to a buyer for slaughter. When the hogs began dying soon after purchase, autopsies revealed the disease. In a complex case, Andrekson held the liability of the colony at sixty per cent, of the agent at thirty per cent, and the plaintiff ten per cent. Compiling a formidable collection of case law from England and Canada, together with statutory regulations and treatises on tort law, Andrekson presented the narrative of the case as an interesting story.

Beaumont, Arthur

District Court of Southern Alberta,
    Lethbridge, December 24, 1958 -
    March 17, 1964

His Honour Arthur Beaumont was born on December 25, 1891, at Ballinrobe, Mayo County, Ireland. He was educated at St. Andrew's College, Dublin, Ireland, and he took his examination for the entrance into the Law Society of Ireland at the age of sixteen. He was called to the Irish bar in December 1913, but he immigrated to Canada the following year. In 1915, Beaumont enlisted in the 4th Canadian Mounted Rifles as a Private, and he served in France with the Canadian Expeditionary Force. He returned to Canada as a Lieutenant in 1919 and was admitted to the Alberta bar on March 19 that year. Beaumont set up a sole practice in Killam until 1922, and in Ponoka, 1922-1929. He then settled in Lethbridge, where he remained until his appointment to the DC in 1958. He acted as defence counsel for many of his files, and was known for his generosity and sociability. Beaumont was named KC on December 24, 1936 and was a Police Magistrate in Lethbridge, 1936-1948. As a judge, he was considered somewhat defence-oriented, reflecting his experience as a lawyer. He died in Calgary on March 17, 1964.

Beck, Nicholas Du Bois Dominic

Supreme Court of Alberta, Edmonton, September 23, 1907 - September 15, 1921
Supreme Court of Alberta, Appellate Division, Edmonton, September 15, 1921 - May 14, 1928

The Honourable Nicholas Du Bois Dominic Beck was born in Cobourg, Ontario, on May 4, 1857. He attended the University of Toronto, and Osgoode Hall Law School, graduating with an LL.B. in 1881. Called to the

Ontario bar in 1879, he began his professional career in Peterborough, Ontario. In 1883, Beck moved to Winnipeg and was admitted to the Manitoba bar. He relocated to Calgary and was admitted to the North-West Territories bar on November 18, 1889. Beck was a member of the firm of Lougheed, McCarthy and Beck in Calgary from 1889 to 1891. He moved to Edmonton in 1891 to form the new firm of Beck, Emery, Newell and Boulton, and became Crown Prosecutor in Edmonton the same year. He was named QC in 1893. Beck was President of the Law Society of the North-West Territories, 1901-1907, and Editor of the *Territories Law Reports*, 1883-1907. He became a Roman Catholic in 1883 and was a strong advocate for the Catholic community in Alberta: he was an active political supporter of separate schools, he served as Chairman of the Catholic section of the Education Council for the North-West Territories, and he was Editor of the *North-West Catholic Review.* Beck was active in the Conservative Party for a while, but by 1900 he was a strong Liberal Party supporter since that party recognized some status for separate schools in a new province. His appointment to the bench in 1907 filled the "Catholic seat" on the Alberta court left by James E.P. Prendergast, who became a Justice of the Supreme Court of Saskatchewan. Beck died in Seattle, Washington on honeymoon with his third wife, Jeanne Tilley, on May 14, 1928.

Beck's judicial career was marked by a willingness to make new law for the new Canadian west, and his work on the court covered the entire ambit of jurisprudence. Many of Beck's major judgments, however, were concerned with financial law and liability. Beck was always ready to debate points of law with colleagues. For example, in *R. v. The Canadian Pacific Railroad Company* ([1912] 5 ALR 1st 341), his broad interpretation of a party's claim to privilege in refusing to produce documents for an examination on damages stemming from an accident was restricted by the court*en banc*. In *Canadian Pacific Railroad Company v. Meadows* ([1908] 1 ALR 1st 344) the court*en banc* debated his interpretation of rescission under English law. And in *Vanstone and Rogers v. Scott* ([1908] 1 ALR 1st 462 at 471), Beck dissented strongly to the majority's interpretation of territorial ordinances. More frequently, however, major figures on the bench such as Harvey, Sifton, and Stuart would agree with him. Beck's expertise in financial and commercial law made him the obvious choice for Chairman of a Royal Commission in 1910 to investigate alleged government corruption in financing the Alberta and Great Waterways Railway. His report absolved then-Premier Alexander Rutherford from blame, but Beck's revelations about the financial bungling of the Liberal government nevertheless prompted the Premier to resign. A meticulous and mathematically-minded judge, his bench notes are filled with his numeric calculations. He also revisited his original notes, making additional comments across the tops and down the margins of his pages. Beck enjoyed playing Poker, and according to his colleagues one could never read his hand from his face. He did not possess an overactive sense of humour, becoming almost totally absorbed in his work. It is perhaps partly for this reason that he was so despised by Bob Edwards, who criticized him mercilessly in the *Calgary Eye Opener* as harsh, rigid, and officious. Beck remained active on the bench until his death at age seventy-one. His judgments were often cited in the superior courts of western and central Canada, as well as at the SCC.

Belzil, Roger Hector

District Court of Northern Alberta, Edmonton, June 5, 1969 - October 1, 1975
District Court of Alberta, Edmonton, October 1, 1975 - June 30, 1979
Court of Queen's Bench of Alberta, Edmonton, June 30, 1979 - June 18, 1981
Court of Appeal of Alberta, Edmonton, June 18, 1981 - December 26, 1996
Supernumerary Justice, January 1, 1987 - December 26, 1996

The Honourable Roger Hector Belzil was born in St. Paul, Alberta on December 26, 1921. He received his B.A. from Laval University in 1942 and his LL.B. from the University of Alberta in 1945. Belzil articled with Ronald Martland, QC and was admitted to the Alberta bar on October 31, 1946. He set up practice in St. Paul. When he was appointed to the DC at Edmonton in 1969, Belzil was practicing there with the firm of Belzil and Swist.

Belzil wrote judgments on a number of cases concerning property law, debtor-creditor relations, mechanics liens, municipal corporations, labour law, and criminal law procedures. *Calgary City Council v. Hartel*

Holdings Ltd. ([1982] 18 ALR 2d 1) brought to fruition years of struggle for residents of northern Calgary to have Nose Hill Park become a reality. The City applied to have the land purchased as agricultural by its by-law, while the defendant company wanted it zoned for its commercial value. Belzil held that provincial legislation did not intend to prohibit municipalities from freezing land values for municipal purposes, and upheld the City's municipal plan for acquisition. In *R. v. Hughes* ([1982] 21 ALR 2d 253), a conviction for drunk driving on the evidence of a breath-alyzer test was overturned for a new trial on appeal where the evidence of the defendants's previous simulated events was deemed insufficient. Belzil wrote a long dissent, opining that no simulation was capable of real evidence, and presented a number of legal writings in support of his position. He also wrote a long dissent in *Reference Re. Public Service Employees Relations Act, Labour Relations Act and Police Officers Collective Bargaining Act* ([1985] 35 ALRT 2d 124), concerning strikes and lockouts. Where the majority of the Court held that the *Charter of Rights and Freedoms* altered some legal rights, but not others, Belzil argued that it did not alter any. If someone refuses to fulfil a contract, and it is breached, then he/she is subject to dismissal.

Berger, Ronald Leon

Court of Queen's Bench of Alberta, Edmonton, August 22, 1985 - June 20, 1996
Court of Appeal of Alberta, June 20, 1996 -

The Honourable Justice Ronald Leon Berger was born in Montreal, Quebec, on October 26, 1943. He attended McGill University in Montreal, receiving his B.A. in 1964 and his B.C.L. in 1967. He was articled to William Henkel, QC, at the AG's Department in Edmonton, and was admitted to the Alberta bar on February 3, 1969. Berger began practicing law with Norman Silverman, QC, in Edmonton before moving to the law firm of Hill, Starkman and Berger where he specialized in criminal and civil litigation. He was named QC on January 18, 1980. Berger was working in Edmonton as a sole practitioner in 1985 when he was appointed to the bench. He was the supervising judge at the provincial inquiry into the collapse of the Principal Group of companies. Berger is also Justice of CANT since 1996.

Bielby, Myra Beth

Court of Queen's Bench of Alberta, Edmonton, December 24, 1990 -

The Honourable Justice Myra Beth Bielby was born in Edmonton, Alberta on July 8, 1951. She graduated from the University of Alberta with a B.A. in History in 1971, and an LL.B. in 1974. As a law student, she was awarded the Horace Harvey Gold Medal in Law. Bielby was admitted to the Alberta bar on July 14, 1975, and to the bar of the Northwest Territories in 1976. She was a partner in the firm of Field and Field in Edmonton when she was appointed to the bench in 1990. Named QC in 1990, Bielby has served as Director of the Institute of Law Research and Reform. She has also lectured at the University of Al berta Faculty of Law and for the Alberta Bar Admissions Course.

Bowen, Donald Haines

Supreme Court of Alberta, Trial
    Division, Edmonton, January 20,
    1972 - June 30, 1977
Court of Queen's Bench of Alberta,
    Edmonton, June 30, 1979 -
    September 14, 1986

The Honourable Donald Haines Bowen was born in Edmonton, Alberta on March 31, 1923. In 1943, he left his studies at the University of Alberta to enlist in the Canadian Navy, where he served for two years before being discharged with the rank of Lieutenant. He returned to complete his studies at the University of Alberta, graduating with a LL.B. in 1949. Admitted to the Alberta bar on June 9, 1951, Bowen became a member of the Edmonton firm of Duncan, Miskew, Dechene specializing in negligence and contract law. Named QC on December 30, 1965, he was appointed to the Bench in 1972. Bowen was an Edmonton School Board Trustee, 1954-1955, and served on Edmonton City Council as an Alderman, 1956-1960. Bowen was also appointed Deputy Judge of the SCNT on October 6, 1977. He died on September 14, 1986.

Bowen had only a few of his decisions published in the law reports, and they were primarily on family law, labour relations, and debts. In *Helstein v. Helstein* ([1980] 11 ALR 2d 56), a wife who was granted a divorce applied for a division of property under the *Matrimonial Property Act*. Since she had helped to build their house, and had been assaulted by her husband, Bowen held for her in a close analysis of the personal facts of their relationship. In *Carwold Concrete and Gravel Company Limited v. General Security Insurance Company of Canada et. al.* ([1985] 36 ALR 2d 283), the plaintiff was hired to deliver concrete and install it for a gas plant. The concrete was inadequate, and the plaintiff removed and restored it, then suing the insurer for costs. Bowen dismissed this claim because the policy did not cover these expenses, and the insurer was never notified to participate. The judgment was made, again, on a close reading of the facts in the case. And in *Adler Furman & Associates Ltd. v. Owners, Condominium Plan CDE 13442* ([1985] 37 ALR 2d 338), condominium fees were owing when a property was sold, and the plaintiff filed a caveat for their collection before the funds were transferred. The defendant appealed the caveat, and was dismissed. Again, Bowen made his decision on the facts presented, and upheld the right of condominium associations to control the common property.

Boyle, John Robert

Supreme Court of Alberta, Trial
    Division, Edmonton, August 27,
    1924 - February 15, 1936

The Honourable John Robert Boyle was born in Sykeston, Ontario, on February 3, 1871, the son of a Scottish farmer, and was educated at the Sarnia Collegiate Institute in Ontario. Entering Osgoode Hall, he found it too expensive and moved west to Regina in 1894, articling with the firm of Mackenzie and Brown. He moved to Edmonton in 1896 and was admitted to the North-West Territories bar on August 10, 1899. Boyle began practice with H.G. Taylor, and was with the successor firm of Boyle, Parlee, Freeman, Abbot, and Mustard when he left practice in 1912. He was named KC on May 4, 1912. The firm grew so rapidly that its new building, constructed in 1913, was named The Lambton Block after the county near Sarnia, Ontario where he was born. Nicknamed "J.R.", Boyle was elected Alderman on the first City Council of the newly-incorporated City of Edmonton in 1904. He was President of the Young Liberals Association in 1900, and in 1905 Boyle was elected Liberal MLA for Sturgeon of the first Alberta legislature, serving as Deputy Speaker. As a politician, he developed a close friendship with Bob Edwards of the *Calgary Eye Opener* and openly attacked his Liberal government's actions in the Alberta and Great Waterways Railway scandal, which led to the resignation of Premier Alexander Rutherford. He was Minister of Education, 1912-1918, and AG, 1918-1921. As AG, he was a diligent enforcer of Alberta's *Liquor Act*, enacted in 1915. With the defeat of the Liberal government in the 1921 election, Boyle served as Leader of the Liberal opposition in the Legislative Assembly, 1922-1924. Appointed to the bench at Edmonton in 1924, Boyle died in Ottawa on February 15, 1936. The town of Boyle, 75 kilometres northeast of Edmonton, was named after him for his work in politics, the church, and the law.

Boyle had a reputation for fairness in both civil and criminal cases before the TD. He would reprimand jurors for not heeding the evidence presented to them, and was particularly atten-

tive to the clarity of the evidence in his written judgments. His active political career, however, came back to haunt him on the bench: as AG between 1919 and 1921, he refused to draft legislation to reinstate Horace Harvey as Chief Justice of Alberta in the newly-formed Trial and Appellate divisions of the SCA. The Dominion government appointed David Lynch Scott instead and Harvey never forgave his Liberal colleague Boyle. More than a few of Boyle's trial judgments were overturned by Harvey on appeal. Nonetheless, Boyle's precedent-setting ruling in *Wilson v. Ward* ([1929] 2 WWR 122) that a mortgage created a binding contract for an agreement of sale, overturned by Harvey, was reinstated by the SCC. While Boyle heard a wide number of matters as a trial justice, his most notable judgments were in the areas of contract and tort. A keen observer of the judgments of the English high courts, he was active on the bench until his death.

Bracco, John David

District Court of Northern Alberta, Edmonton, July 31, 1975 - October 1, 1975
District Court of Alberta, Edmonton, October 1, 1975 - June 30, 1979
Court of Queen's Bench of Alberta, Calgary, June 30, 1979 - December 31, 1987
Court of Appeal of Alberta, Calgary, December 31, 1987 -
Supernumerary Justice, Calgary, August 3, 1991 -

The Honourable Justice John David Bracco was born in Edmonton, Alberta, on March 31, 1925, and spent his childhood on a farm near Redwater, Alberta. He received his B.Ed. from the University of Alberta in 1949 and, after working as a teacher for several years, he returned to the University of Alberta and received his LL.B. in 1956. Bracco maintained his interest in education, however, serving on the Edmonton Public School Board. Admitted to the Alberta bar on June 13, 1957, he practiced in Edmonton with the firm of Stack, Smith, Bracco and Irwin until he was appointed to the DC there in 1975. In addition to serving on the Alberta bench, Bracco was Deputy Judge of the SCYT in 1976 and 1978-1983. In addition, he was appointed Deputy Judge on the SCNT in 1979, and to the CANT in 1987. Bracco was awarded the honorary degree of Doctor of Divinity for his services on behalf of St. Stephen's College at the University of Alberta. In 1992, the Edmonton Public School Board named the John D. Bracco Junior High School in his honour.

Bracco's judgments on the bench have dealt with the areas of contracts, energy and natural resources, judicial administration, family law, and human rights. In *Zaplotinsky v. Zaplotinsky* ([1980] 14 ALR 2d 6), he ruled on the distribution of property under the *Family Relief Act*. In *Solomon & Southam Inc. v. McLaughlin & R. in Right of Alberta* ([1982] 20 ALR 2d 63), he held that the public has unrestricted access to the records of the courts unless specifically precluded by a ruling of the court. Access to court records, subject to statutory restrictions, ensures the protection of social values and the proper administration of justice. Finally, in *Re. Pannu, Kang and Gill* ([1986]

45 ALR 2d 289), Bracco upheld the right of Sikhs under the *Individual's Rights Protection Act* to wear beards and headgear without discrimination from their employers.

Brennan, William Robert

Supreme Court of Alberta, Trial Division, Calgary, April 8, 1976 - June 30, 1979
Court of Queen's Bench, Calgary, June 30, 1979 - November 7, 1995
Supernumerary Justice, Calgary, April 8, 1991 - November 7, 1995

The Honourable Justice William Robert Brennan was born on August 17, 1922 in Veteran, Alberta. He was educated at St. Mary's Boys School in Calgary. From 1941 to 1945, Brennan served as a pilot with the Royal Canadian Air Force, earning the distinguished Flying Cross. Following his discharge from the Air Force, he attended the University of Alberta, graduating with a B.A. in 1949 and an LL.B. in 1950. He was admitted to the Alberta bar on June 6, 1951 and began practice with the Calgary firm of Fenerty Fenerty McGillivray and Robertson. He was named QC on December 30, 1965. When he was appointed to the bench in 1976, Brennan was practicing with the Calgary firm of Fenerty McGillivray Robertson Prowse Brennan Fraser Bell and Code, where he specialized in civil litigation and insurance law.

Brennan's written decisions are concerned chiefly with contract and company law. *R. v. Cominco Ltd.* ([1980] 2 WWR 693) was one of the longest trials in Alberta's history, lasting 150 days. Cominco was found not guilty of conspiring to monopolize the fertilizer market under the *Combines Investigation Act* of 1970 in this landmark commercial monopoly case. In *Nathu v. Imbrook Properties Ltd.* ([1990] 107 AR 336 and [1992] 125 AR 34), the plaintiff, a fast food restaurant operator, sued for losses when the defendant leased space for an almost identical business. Brennan held that Nathu's interest in the contract was harmed by the uses put to the lease. Throughout his career on the bench, Brennan applied a close reading of the law to the evidence presented.

Buchanan, Nelles Victor

District Court of Northern Alberta, Edmonton, March 4, 1952 - October 14, 1953
District Court of Northern Alberta, Chief Judge, Edmonton, October 14, 1953 - January 23, 1965

His Honour Nelles Victor Buchanan was born in Crystal City, Manitoba in 1890, and came to Alberta with his parents in 1899. He received his B.A. from Victoria College at the University of Toronto in 1915, and enlisted immediately with the 38th Regina Battery of the Canadian Expeditionary Force. He fought at Cambrai, Vimy, Passchendale, and the Somme, and he was awarded the Military Cross in 1917. Buchanan returned to Canada and attended the University of Alberta, graduating with an LL.B. in 1921. He was called to the Alberta bar on February 12 the same year. Buchanan began practicing law in Edmonton where he joined the firm of Wood and Buchanan, and was a partner in the firm of Wood Buchanan and

Campbell when he was appointed to the DC at Edmonton in 1952. Buchanan served five terms as President of the Alberta Hospital Association and was awarded the George Findlay Stephens Memorial Award in 1965 for his contributions. He retired on January 23, 1965, and died at the age of 96 in Edmonton on November 26, 1986.

Bury, Ambrose Upton Gledstanes

District Court of Northern Alberta, Edmonton, August 3, 1935 - December 19, 1944

His Honour Ambrose Upton Gledstanes Bury was born on August 1, 1869, in County Kildare, Ireland. He received his B.A. in 1890 and his M.A. in 1893 at Trinity College, Dublin University, and was distinguished in his academic performance both at school and university. He was admitted to the Irish bar and King's Inn in 1906. Bury immigrated to Canada in 1912 and was admitted to the Alberta bar on January 21, 1913. He began practice with the firm of Dickie and Wilson in Edmonton, and was a partner in Harvie, Bury and Yanda there for fifteen years. He was named KC on June 4, 1928. Active in civic politics, Bury served as an Alderman on Edmonton City Council, 1922-1925, and was elected Mayor of Edmonton for three terms in 1927, 1928 and 1929. A Conservative provincially in his early years, he was elected to the Federal House of Commons as a Liberal Member for East Edmonton in 1925, but lost his seat in 1926. In 1930, he was re-elected to the House of Commons and served until 1935, when he lost his seat once more. He was immediately thereafter appointed to the DC. From 1919 to 1951, he served as Chancellor of the Anglican Diocese of Athabasca and was an active Freemason. Bury retired on December 19, 1944, grieving the loss of his son who had been killed in Sicily serving with the Loyal Edmonton Regiment. He moved to Ottawa in 1951 to live with his daughter-in-law and died on March 29.

Cairns, James Mitchell

Supreme Court of Alberta, Trial
    Division, Calgary, March 4, 1952 -
    February 15, 1965
Supreme Court of Alberta, Appellate
    Division, Calgary, February 15,
    1965 - October 25, 1977

Born in Edinburgh, Scotland, on October 25, 1902, the Honourable James Mitchell Cairns immigrated to Canada in 1910. The family settled in Nelson, British Columbia, and became fruit farmers. He received his early education at Nelson and Trail, B.C. Cairns went to Edmonton to study law at the University of Alberta, earning a B.A. in 1925 and his LL.B. in 1927. Articling with Alexander Macleod Sinclair of Lougheed, McLaws, Sinclair and Redman, he was admitted to the Alberta bar on June 28, 1928. Cairns practiced with a number of Calgary law firms: McLaws, Redman, Lougheed and Cairns, 1929-1935; Goodall and Cairns, 1935-1939; as a sole practitioner, 1939-1942; McLaws, Cairns and McLaws, 1942-1946; and Cairns and Howard, 1946-1952. He was named KC in December, 1945. At the time of his appointment to the bench in 1952, Cairns was a senior partner in the Calgary firm of Cairns and Howard, where he specialized in corporate and commercial law and held directorships in a number of major businesses. He was elected Alderman on Calgary City Council, 1945-1946, and was active in the local Liberal Party. In addition to serving on the Alberta bench, he was a Judge of the CANT, 1971-1973. Cairns was a passionate golfer and curler into his retirement on October 25, 1977, and died in Calgary on December 13, 1978.

Cairns' practice in commercial law provided a unique working background for the bench. He made many notable judgments on the law of contracts, property, and fraud, and was a no-nonsense judge. He had a fiery temperament and was known within the legal community as a popular judge renowned for his sharp wit, keen sense of humour, and quick grasp of the facts. He was also meticulous in the use of precedent, and a fearless critic of error when he found it. Prior to being appointed to the CA, he was called by the Court to sit with it in an appeal of his conviction of a barrister for fraudulent activity in *Jonas et al. v. Pennock* ([1962] 37 WWR 134). In an unusual event, the Court also asked him to write their judgment in support of their majority decision confirming his previous one. Heading a Royal Commission to investigate the Alberta Housing Corporation in 1973, whose public officials were implicated in fraudulent loans and land sales in the Fort MacMurray area, he frequently berated both legal counsel and witnesses for their delays and their refusal to testify. In the end, he was regarded by practitioners as one of the best trial judges of his era.

Cairns, Laurence Yeomans

District Court of Northern Alberta,
    Edmonton, September 24, 1957 -
    September 1, 1965

His Honour Laurence Yeomans
Cairns was born in Winnipeg, Manitoba on May 19, 1891, and came to
Alberta in 1905. He graduated from
the University of Alberta in 1912, with
a B.A.. He began his articles with James
E. Wallbridge, KC, of the firm of
Wallbridge, Henwood and Gibson, and
studied law at the University of Alberta. He enlisted for service during
World War I on August 18, 1916 after
being called to the Alberta bar on August 8, 1916. After the war, Cairns
taught law and commerce at the University of Alberta from 1919 until 1939.
He also practiced with the firm of
Wallbridge, Cairns and Company in
Edmonton, where he remained until
his appointment to the DC in 1957. He
was named KC in 1934 and was President of the Law Society of Alberta,
1950-1951. Cairns was Chancellor of
the University of Alberta, 1958-1964,
and received an honorary LL.D. in
1955. He retired on September 1, 1965,
and died in Edmonton on July 28,
1967.

Carpenter, Arthur Allan

District Court of Macleod, Fort
    Macleod, November 21, 1907 -
    November 12, 1910
District Court of Calgary, Calgary,
    November 12, 1910 - November 15,
    1915

His Honour Arthur Allan Carpenter was born in Hamilton, Ontario, on
September 3, 1873. He received his
B.A. from the University of Toronto in
1894, his LL.B. from Osgoode Hall in
1897, and was admitted to the Law
Society of Upper Canada that same
year. He practiced law in Hamilton
for the next six years. In 1903, Carpenter came west and was admitted to the
North-West Territories bar on April
16, 1903. He set up practice in Innisfail,
where he remained until appointed to
the DC at Fort Macleod in 1907. Carpenter moved to the DC at Calgary in
1910, and resigned his position there
in 1915 to sit on the Board of Public
Utilities Commissioners in Edmonton. He was later appointed Chairman of the Board. Carpenter was
named KC on February 4, 1919. He
died in Edmonton on February 17,
1949.

Cavanagh, James Creighton

Supreme Court of Alberta, Trial
    Division, Edmonton, May 18, 1973
    - June 30, 1979
Court of Queen's Bench of Alberta,
    Edmonton, June 30, 1979 -
    December 31, 1990
Supernumerary Justice, Edmonton,
    June 16, 1986 - December 31, 1990

The Honourable James Creighton
Cavanagh was born in Ernford, Saskatchewan on June 15, 1916 and was
raised in Aneroid, Saskatchewan. He
served as a Flying Officer in World
War II in England and in the North
African theatre. Cavanagh graduated
from the University of Saskatchewan
with a B.A. in 1950 and an LL.B. in
1949, and was admitted to the Alberta
bar on May 31, 1951. He had a high-
profile criminal law practice and was

appointed QC in 1964. At the time of his appointment to the bench in 1973, he was with the Edmonton firm of Parlee Cavanagh Irving Henning Mustard and Rodney. In addition to serving on the Alberta bench, Cavanagh was appointed Deputy Judge of the SCNT, 1980-1990. He retired on December 31, 1990, and died on January 17, 1991.

Cavanagh delivered judgments on some notable and curious criminal trials. One of the most notable is *International Society for Krishna Consciousness (Iskon Canada) v. City of Edmonton and Attorney General of Alberta* ([1979] 8 ALR 2d 375), in which the plaintiff claimed that the city was discriminating against its right to solicit funds as a charitable organization. Cavanagh held that in spite of its status as a religious group, Iskon was required to follow municipal by-laws and dismissed its application. In *R. v. Burchnall and Dumont* ([1980] 24 ALR 2d 17), the accused had cannabis surgically removed from his stomach and was prosecuted for trafficking in drugs. Cavanagh was sympathetic to Burchnall's condition and gave a suspended sentence for three years in part because the accused had a pregnant wife and Cavanagh believed he could reform himself. Finally, in *R. v. James and Svidal* ([1991] 120 AR 333) the accused were charged with fraud. Cavanagh denied their applications for legal aid because they had transferred title to the property they owned to their wives. Cavanagh's judgments ranged from strong sympathy to stout moralism, especially in narcotics cases. He was a judge whose decisions reflected his feelings on the human circumstances arraigned before him.

Cawsey, Robert Allan

Court of Queen's Bench of Alberta, Edmonton, November 27, 1979 - Supernumerary Justice, Edmonton, November 11, 1992 -

The Honourable Justice Robert Allan Cawsey was born in Wetaskiwin, Alberta, on November 11, 1922. He received his B.A. and LL.B. from the University of Alberta. Admitted to the Alberta bar on June 23, 1952, he was named QC in 1966. Cawsey practiced in Wetaskiwin, Alberta, with the firm of Manley, Cawsey, and Vickerson, where he was a general practitioner with an emphasis on criminal, probate, and litigation. Appointed to the PC at Edmonton in 1973, he moved to the QB in 1979. One of his major special tasks was service on the Native Justice Commission in the 1980s.

Cawsey gave numerous judgments on administrative and corporate law, the law of evidence, and securities, energy and natural resources law. In *Von Thurn und Taxis (Johannes Prinz) v. Edmonton* ([1982] 20 ALR 2d 135), he held that actions in tort against a municipal corporation was a citizen's right not restricted by the Alberta *Municipal Government Act*. In *R. v. Raymond and Maloney* ([1985] 39 ALR 2d 104), he allowed an expert's evidence on using crazy glue to enhance a set of fingerprints without clinical technique on the basis that the opinion was restricted to physically observable evidence. And in *Central Western Railway Corporation v. Surface Rights Board and Signalta Resources Ltd* ([1988] 56 ALR 2d 115), Cawsey ruled that the province's Surface Rights Board was required to give all affected parties the right to be heard on application for an entry order according to the rules of natural justice and administrative procedures.

Chrumka, Paul Stephan

Court of Queen's Bench of Alberta, Calgary, January 28, 1982 -

The Honourable Justice Paul Stephan Chrumka was born on September 19, 1932, on a farm in Tilley, Alberta. He was educated at the University of Alberta, receiving a B.A. in 1955, and an LL.B. in 1958. After graduating from law school, Chrumka came to Calgary and articled with Edward J. McCormick, QC. He was admitted to the Alberta bar on June 5, 1959 and became a Crown Prosecutor in April, 1961. Specializing in criminal law, Chrumka became Chief Crown Prosecutor for Calgary in 1975. He was appointed QC on January 27, 1976. Chrumka was Regional Agent for Southern Alberta, and a lawyer with the Alberta AG's Department in Calgary when he was appointed to the bench there in 1982. In addition to serving in Alberta, Chrumka was appointed Deputy Judge to both the SCNT and the SCYT in 1991.

Chrumka has rendered judgments in the areas of bankruptcy, corporate and commercial law, and employer/employee relations. In *Re. Amonson* ([1985] 39 ALR 2d 307), he upheld the duties and powers of trustees in waiving solicitor-client privilege if the property of the debtor can not be determined in any other way. And in *Wilson v. Newell No. 4 Board of Education* ([1985] 37 ALR 2d 44), he upheld the school board's transfer of a teacher following allegations of misconduct in order to give the teacher a fresh start in a new school. Chrumka brought his careful examinations as Crown Prosecutor to bear on his work as a judge in assessing lawful and wrongful liability in civil cases.

Clarke, Alfred Henry

Supreme Court of Alberta, Appellate Division, Calgary, September 15, 1921 - January 30, 1942

The Honourable Justice Alfred Henry Clarke was born in Manilla, Ontario, on October 25, 1860. He attended Osgoode Hall, receiving his LL.B. in 1880. He was admitted to the Law Society of Upper Canada in 1883, and he practiced law in Windsor, Ontario, for the next thirty years. He served there as County Attorney, Clerk of the Peace, and local master of the Supreme Court, respectively. He was also a Liberal M.P. for South Essex in 1904 and was re-elected in 1908 and 1911. Clarke decided to move to Alberta following the defeat of Laurier's government the next year. He was admitted to the Alberta bar on March 12, 1912, and was a member of the firm of Clarke, McCarthy, Carson, and Macleod from then until his appointment as one of the first members of the AD at Calgary in 1921. He was named KC on March 19, 1913. Clarke served as a Bencher of the Law Society of Alberta, and was an active member of the United Church. He died in Calgary on January 30, 1942 from a heart attack shortly after being carried home from the bench by two associate justices.

Clarke wrote many judgments for the Court, particularly on procedural questions, corporate and criminal law, and negligence and liability. One of his more interesting initial judgments was *R. v. Read* ([1921] 3 WWR 403), in which he quashed a conviction of prostitution on the grounds that a woman going to a particular house to have sex was insufficient evidence to determine the keeping of a bawdy house. If she confessed under duress, the confession would not stand in law.

Clarke authored a series of judgments which defined the boundaries of administrative and judicial procedures in the 1920s and 1930s. In this regard he showed himself as a strict constructionist. The earliest in this vein was *Colpman v. Canadian National Railways* ([1921] 3 WWR 420) in which a railway was not held directly liable for killing cattle at a railroad crossing because the cattle's safety was the responsibility of their owner. As in one of his last opinions, *Lindev v. Stead* ([1942] 2 DLR 918), he dissented to a court clerk paying a sheriff without a court order to uphold the sanctity of legislative prescription.

Clement, Carlton Ward

Supreme Court of Alberta,
    Appellate Division, Edmonton,
    February 12, 1970 - June 30,
    1979
Court of Appeal of Alberta,
    Edmonton, June 30, 1979 -
    January 7, 1982

The Honourable Carlton Ward Clement was born in Waterloo, Ontario on January 7, 1907. He was educated at St. John's College in Winnipeg, and attended the University of Manitoba. He completed his studies at the University of Alberta, where he received his B.A. in 1928 and his LL.B. in 1931. Articling with George H. Steer, he was admitted to the Alberta bar on April 12, 1932. Clement was a sole practitioner in Peace River, Alberta, 1932-1933. When he returned to Edmonton in 1933, he joined George Van Allen in partnership. After Van Allen's death, Clement joined the Parlee firm and, when Harold H. Parlee was appointed to the bench in 1944, Clement became the senior partner in the firm. He remained there until his appointment directly to the AD in 1970 and was named KC on January 26, 1943. Clement was very active in both the law profession and the community. He served as President of the Law Society of Alberta, 1968-1969, and was President of the Edmonton Chamber of Commerce and the Alberta and North West Chamber of Mines. Clement also served as Justice of the CANT, 1971-1982. He retired on January 7, 1982.

As an appeal judge, Clement combined scholarship with practicality to make rulings which were consistent with precedent, yet eminently practical. He authored a number of judgments on the parameters of jurisdiction in the province and the requirements for appeals. For example, in *Absand Holdings Ltd. and Williams v. R. in Right of Alberta* ([1980] 14 ALR 2d 59), he confirmed that Appeal Courts will not interfere with trial decisions unless the weight of evidence shows otherwise. In *Burns v. Alberta Chiropractic Association* ([1980]

16 ALR 2d 120), a chiropractor who performed acupuncture did not inform the patient that the procedure was not part of allowable practice under bylaws of the Association. The trial verdict finding the chiropractor guilty of misconduct was dismissed, but the portion of the appeal concerning excessive fees was allowed. Finally, in *Haugen v. County of Camrose and Agriculture Services Board* ([1979] 9 ALR 2d 40), Clement quashed a county by-law because the Council's view that it could enact provisions in the DC against individuals without their notification was unjudicial. The Appeal Court, in finding a minor local by-law null and void, was exercising a judicial activism that was somewhat notable at this level.

Conrad, Carole Mildred

Court of Queen's Bench of Alberta,
    Calgary, November 10, 1986 -
    June 24, 1992
Court of Appeal of Alberta, Calgary,
    June 24, 1992 -

The Honourable Justice Carole Mildred Conrad was born on September 30, 1943. She graduated from the University of Alberta with a B.A. in 1964 and an LL.B. in 1967. Conrad was called to the Alberta bar on June 14, 1968, and was named QC on January 18, 1980. Prior to her appointment to the bench in 1986, she practiced law in Calgary with Conrad Bloomenthal Carruthers. She also served as Vice-Chairman of the Rent Control Board in Calgary. Conrad was appointed Deputy Judge of the SCYT and the SCNT in 1991, and Justice of the CANT in 1992.

Cooke, Alan Thomas

Court of Queen's Bench of Alberta,
Edmonton, November 10, 1986 -

The Honourable Justice Alan Thomas Cooke was born in Edmonton, Alberta, on March 30, 1930. He received his B. Comm. from the University of Alberta in 1954, and his LL.B. from the University of Alberta in 1957. Cooke was admitted to the Alberta bar on June 16, 1958, and was named QC on December 19, 1973. Prior to his appointment to the bench in 1986, he practiced with Cooke Shandling in Edmonton where he specialized in the marketing of agricultural products and administrative law. In addition to serving on the Alberta bench, Cooke was appointed Deputy Judge of the SCNT on May 18, 1989.

Cormack, John Spiers

District Court of Northern Alberta,
    Edmonton, March 19, 1963 -
    October 1, 1975
District Court of Alberta, Edmonton,
    October 1, 1975 - June 30, 1979
Court of Queen's Bench of Alberta,
    Edmonton, June 30, 1979 -
    February 21, 1985
Supernumerary Justice, Edmonton,
    October 1, 1979 - February 21, 1985

The Honourable Justice John Spiers Cormack was born in Edmonton, Alberta, on February 21, 1910. He was educated at the University of Alberta, where he received his LL.B. in 1932. Unable to find immediate employment in the legal field during the depression years, Cormack accepted a teaching position and maintained a life-long interest in education. He was admitted to the Alberta bar on May 14, 1945, and became a senior partner in the Edmonton firm of Cormack, Dantzer and Kerans in 1958 where he practiced until his appointment to the DC in 1963. Cormack was named QC in 1958. He served as a member of the Alberta Royal Commission on Education in 1959 and was Secretary-Treasurer of the Law Society of Alberta, 1957-1961. Cormack retired on February 21, 1985, and died in Edmonton in 1991.

Cormack had several of his decisions published in the law reports, and most of them concerned matrimonial causes, property law, debt and bankruptcy, and landlord-tenant relations. In *Provincial Treasurer of Alberta v. Lafrance* ([1980] 13 ALR 2d 142), the land of the respondent and her husband was sold, and the applicant sought a property division for his promissory notes. Cormack held for the Treasury Branch, opining that it could claim from either party. He compiled a wide range of case law across the country, and explored the complex evidence and its circumstances with dexterity. *Boland v. Boland (Trachuk); Boland v. Boland and Craig* ([1980] 14 ALR 2d 154), involved a division of matrimonial property. The wife destroyed and moved assets physically, claiming mental cruelty on behalf of her husband, and sued for half the estate. The husband wished to restore his business, and applied for a divorce. Cormack awarded the divorce, and dismissed the claim for mental cruelty on grounds that she knew his traits before their marriage. The judge's decision was composed of a large number of cases, a long

disquisition on the evidence pleaded, and a treatise on matrimonial law. And in *Chieftain Development Co. Ltd. v. Lachowich* ([1982] 17 ALR 2d 106), the evidence of the province's Surface Rights Board was deemed insufficient, and Cormack, hearing the case on appeal, allowed a partial recovery of compensation to the defendant landowner. In another long judgment, Cormack organized a very large number of cases, statutes, and rules to explain the effects of such a decision had it been or not been given.

Côté, Jean Edouard Leon

Court of Appeal of Alberta,
    Edmonton, October 30, 1987 -

The Honourable Justice Jean Edouard Leon Côté was born in Edmonton, Alberta, on August 14, 1940. He attended McGill University, graduating with a B.A. in 1961. Côté received his first law degree from the University of Alberta, where he was the Gold Medallist in 1964. On a Viscount Bennett Scholarship, Côté studied at Oxford University in England, graduating in 1966 with a B.C.L.. Returning to Canada, he was a law clerk to Justice Ronald Martland at the SCC. He was admitted to the Alberta bar on January 9, 1968 and practiced law with the firm of Hulburt Reynolds Stevenson and Agrios in Edmonton. Côté became a noted legal author, writing *An Introduction to the Law of Contract* in 1974. Beginning in 1981, he co-authored with William A. Stevenson the *Annotations of the Alberta Rules of Court*, later called the *Civil Procedure Guide*, which became a standard legal text. Côté was also a sessional lecturer at the University of Alberta Faculty of Law for many years. He was named QC on December 30, 1984. Côté practiced litigation in Edmonton with the firm of Reynolds, Mirth and Côté prior to his appointment to the CA at Edmonton in 1987. In addition to serving on the Alberta bench, Côté was appointed to the CANT in 1987.

Côté has delivered many civil appeal judgments since his relatively recent appointment. His cases involve commercial law, administrative law, court procedures, contracts, and torts. His judgments are lively explorations of logic and legal questions. In *Can-Air Services Ltd. v. British Aviation Insurance Company Ltd. et al.* ([1989] 63 ALR 2d 61), Côté allowed an appeal based on his assessment that the examination of discovery used reliance questions that went beyond seeking facts. In *Nova, an Alberta Corporation v. Guelph Engineering Company* ([1990] 70 ALR 2d 97), a company negligence case relating to a gas compressor explosion, Côté dissented from the majority judgment, emphasizing that the trial judgment relied solely on expert opinions and did not explore the facts of the case sufficiently. Côté also differed partly with the opinion of the Court in *Reference re. Bill C-62, an Act to amend the Excise Tax Act* (Canada) ([1991] 82 ALR 2d 289), which upheld the constitutional right of the federal government to institute and administer the GST in Alberta. Côté contended that certain services of the Alberta government may not be subject to tax and that the federal government does not have clear authority to apply the GST in all circumstances.

Crawford, John Lyndon

District Court of Macleod, Fort Macleod, November 25, 1910 - March 19, 1913
District Court of Edmonton, Edmonton, March 19, 1913 - August 3, 1935
District Court of Northern Alberta, Edmonton, August 3, 1935 - September 2, 1946

His Honour John Lyndon Crawford was born in Aylmer, Ontario on August 3, 1868. He received a B.A. from the University of Toronto in 1890, and an LL.B. from Osgoode Hall in 1894. He was admitted to the Ontario bar in his graduating year and began practicing law with his father's firm in Aylmer where he remained for four years. In 1903, Crawford settled in Red Deer, Alberta. He was admitted to the North-West Territories bar on March 10, 1903. He was a Crown Prosecutor in Red Deer when he was appointed to the DC at Fort Macleod in 1910, moving to the DC at Edmonton in 1913. Crawford retired from the bench in 1946 as one of the longest-serving DC judges in the province, and died in Calgary on September 2, 1946.

Cross, Thomas Lynde

District Court of Northern Alberta, Edmonton, February 24, 1948 - September 30, 1975
District Court of Alberta, Edmonton, October 1, 1975 - July 1, 1977

His Honour Thomas Lynde Cross was born in Edmonton, Alberta, on November 14, 1900. He was the son of

Charles Wilson Cross, former AG of Alberta. He attended Osgoode Hall Law School in Toronto, but received his LL.B. from the University of Alberta in 1928. He was admitted to the Alberta bar on June 11, 1928. With the exception of the period between 1931 and 1933, when he served as a Crown Prosecutor in Edmonton, Cross practiced with the firm of Duncan, Cross and Johnson until his appointment to the DC in 1948. He retired on November 14, 1975 and died in Edmonton on July 1, 1977.

Several of Cross' DC judgments have been reported and cover a very diverse range of the law, from property to employment and municipal by-laws. In *Burkard v. Municipal District of Camrose* ([1953] 8 WWR 401), he found a municipality not responsible for the negligent performance of a weed inspector because the inspector was not enforcing municipal by-laws and statutes. And in *R. v. Hayduk* ([1955] 16 WWR 112), he heard the Crown's appeal against an acquittal for impaired driving by a police magistrate. Cross found that the Crown had an automatic interest in private prosecutions, and the right to appeal decisions in civil actions, and convicted the accused.

Crossley, Arthur William

District Court of Northern Alberta, Edmonton, November 1, 1973 - October 1, 1975
District Court of Alberta, Edmonton, October 1, 1975 - June 30, 1979
Court of Queen's Bench of Alberta, Edmonton, June 30, 1979 - September 9, 1991
Supernumerary Justice, Edmonton, November 1, 1988 - September 9, 1991

The Honourable Arthur William Crossley was born in Edmonton, Alberta, on September 29, 1920. He attended the University of Alberta, where he earned a B.Sc. in 1945, a B.A. in 1948, and an LL.B. in 1949. He was admitted to the Alberta bar on May 31, 1951, and was named QC on December 29, 1967. Crossley practiced with the firm of Stuart Campbell in Edmonton prior to his appointment to the DC in 1973. He died in Edmonton on September 9, 1991.

Crossley's reported judgments deal with municipalities, taxes, schools, zoning and planning authority, and insurance, banking, builder's liens, and conditional sales. *Melcor Developments Ltd. v. Edmonton and Edmonton Development Officer* ([1982] 20 ALR 2d 179) was a civic authority case where the plaintiff challenged the conditions contained in a final development agreement. Crossley dismissed the application on the grounds that the Court's prerogative allowed him the discretion to refuse an intervention when an alternative remedy is available to the plaintiff. A similar situation occurred in *Northern Alberta Agribusiness Ltd. v. Town of Falmer* ([1980] 14 ALR 2d 97), where an abatement of taxes granted to the plaintiff company was ruled *ultra vires*. In *Can-Air Services Ltd. v. British Aviation Insurance Co. Ltd. et al.* ([1988] 55 ALR 2d 42), he ruled that, in an examination for discovery, the persons examined must answer requests for facts upon which the allegations in the pleadings are based.

Cullen, Alan Joseph

District Court of Southern Alberta,
     Lethbridge, August 1, 1964 -
     February 12, 1970
Supreme Court of Alberta, Trial
     Division, Calgary, February 12,
     1970 - April 23, 1975

The Honourable Alan Joseph
Cullen was born in Fort Macleod, Alberta, on December 25, 1916. He was
educated in Bow Island, Saskatchewan, and attended Campion College
in Regina. After receiving his B.A.
from the University of Manitoba in
1936, Cullen articled with G.R.A. Rice
of Lethbridge. He was admitted to the
Alberta bar on June 11, 1940. He was
the last Albertan to be admitted to the
bar as an articling student without a
law degree. Enlisting in the Canadian
Army during World War II, Cullen
served as a Captain with the 39th
Battalion in northwest Europe. Following the war, he returned to
Lethbridge where he practiced law for
the next eighteen years. Cullen was
named QC on December 31, 1957. He
was a member of the firm of Rice
Patterson when he was appointed to
the DC at Lethbridge in 1964. Cullen
was active in the Lethbridge community and with the Alberta Liberal Association. Cullen died in Calgary on
April 23, 1975.
     Cullen was renowned on the bench
for his diligence and thoroughness
and for his highly articulate judgments. He had a keen interest of Canadian law as an evolutionary form of
English common law. He would often
present precedents from Canadian
jurisdictions within the context of previous English law. For example, in

*Heintzman & Company Ltd. v. Hashman
Construction Ltd.* ([1973] 1 WWR 202),
Cullen made liberal use of the treatises and texts in Canadian and
English tort law before marshalling
the case law which brought him to
judgment. In a more direct use of the
historical argument, *Kreway v. Ren-
frew Chrysler Plymouth Ltd. et al. and
Chrysler Canada Ltd. et al.* ([1973] 1
WWR 447), he interpreted the Canadian case law within the context of the
British Summary Jurisdiction Act of
1895. In these judgments, as in others,
Cullen compiled the material for his
judicial reasoning from a wide range
of legal sources. Well read and highly
articulate, he made himself available
freely to young lawyers to assist them
in their careers, and was considered a
font of common sense spiced with a
sense of humour.

Dea, John Berchmans

District Court of Alberta, Edmonton,
     February 2, 1978 - June 30, 1979
Court of Queen's Bench of Alberta,
     Edmonton, June 30, 1979 -

The Honourable Justice John
Berchmans Dea was born in Edmonton, Alberta, on March 11, 1932. He
attended the University of Alberta,
where he obtained his B.A. in 1952
and his LL.B. in 1955. After being
admitted to the Alberta bar on May
31, 1955, Dea joined the Edmonton
law firm of Field and Company. He
was practicing with the successor firm
of Field Hyndman and Company
when he was appointed to the bench
in 1978. He was named QC on January
30, 1978. Dea was a special lecturer in
civil procedure at the Faculty of Law

at the University of Alberta during the 1980s. In addition to serving on the Alberta bench, he was appointed Deputy Judge of the SCYT on December 2, 1982.

Dea had several decisions published in the law reports, including cases on mortgage law, contracts, family law, divorce, labour relations, professional organizations, and jurisdictional and procedural matters. In *Alberta Pork Producers Marketing Board et al. v. Swift Canadian Co. Ltd. et al.* ([1981] 16 ALR 2d 313), the plaintiff brought a class action against the defendant, and the latter sought to strike out parts of the claim alleging insufficient cause. Dea dismissed the defendant's allegation, and presented a large number of cases from England and Canada which he weaved into a discourse on the complex facts of the case. *Broddy and Broddy v. Director of Vital Statistics* ([1982] 17 ALR 2d 208), concerned the applicant's request for a marriage license where his bride was, by adoption, the daughter of his brother. Dea refused the application, holding that *Lord Lyndhurst's Act* was still the law of Alberta on acceptable degrees in marriage. In *United Nurses of Alberta, Local No. 17 and Paish v. High Prairie General Hospital and Nursing District No. 98* ([1985] 37 ALR 2d 25), a nurse refused compulsory retirement and sued her employer on their bargaining agreement, which prohibited discrimination based on age after having her claim rejected by the Board of Arbitrators. Dea allowed her request under the *Labour Relations Act*, opining that the Board's ruling was "patently unreasonable", as well as "in error", and that the QB had the right to interfere in the Board's decision.

Dechene, André Miville

District Court of Northern Alberta, Edmonton, August 21, 1963-February 15, 1965
Supreme Court of Alberta, Trial Division, Edmonton, February 15, 1965 - June 30, 1979
Court of Queen's Bench, Edmonton, June 30, 1979 - March 25, 1987
Supernumerary Justice, August 22, 1978 - March 25, 1987

The Honourable André Miville Dechene was born in Edmonton, Alberta, on March 25, 1912. Following his graduation from Jesuit College in Edmonton in 1932, he received his B.A. from Laval University, Quebec, in 1935. He then worked for Imperial Oil and sold fire and life insurance, before choosing a career in law. Dechene received his LL.B. from the University of Alberta in 1939. He articled under George B. O'Connor and was admitted to the Alberta bar on July 29, 1940. Dechene opened his first practice in Bonnyville and enlisted in the Canadian Army in 1942, attaining the rank of Captain when he was discharged in 1945. Named QC on December 31, 1953, he was a partner in the Edmonton firm of Duncan, Miskew, Dechene, Bowen, Craig and Brosseau from 1952 until his appointment to the DC in 1963. Dechene was a litigator and travelled often to act as Counsel on many cases in the Northwest Territories. Dechene was active in local politics. He was President of the Young Liberals Association and contested three elections as a Liberal candidate for the Alberta legislature in the 1950s and early 1960s, all unsuccessful. From 1950 to 1957 he was

President of the French Canadian Association of Alberta, and from 1953 to 1957 he was Chairman of the Edmonton Separate School Board. Elevated to the SCA in 1965, he also served as Deputy Judge of the SCNT, 1971-1975 and 1980-1987. Dechene retired on March 25, 1987, and died in Edmonton on May 21, 1992.

A patient and compassionate judge with an even temperament and warm, engaging personality, Dechene was respected as a judge who kept to the reasoning and spirit, if not necessarily the exact letter, of the law. For example, in *General Tire and Rubber Company of Canada Ltd. v. Finkelstein* ([1968] 62 WWR 380), there were many minor acts not properly executed for an obligation under the *Guarantees Acknowledgement Act*. A careful reading of the case law on each point however, brought Dechene to rule that the defendant guarantor was in fact liable in law. In *Palinko (Palinka) v. Bower* ([1975] 1 WWR 756), he researched the judgments cited in the briefs submitted by legal counsel, and concluded that the case before him should be decided upon the reasoning used in the judgments of those cases.

Decore, John Nickolas

District Court of Northern Alberta, Chief Judge, Edmonton, March 29, 1965 - October 1, 1975
District Court of Alberta, Chief Judge, Edmonton, October 1, 1975 - June 30, 1979
Court of Queen's Bench of Alberta, Edmonton, June 30, 1979 - April 9, 1984
Supernumerary Justice, Edmonton, August 31, 1979 - April 9, 1984

The Honourable John Nickolas Decore was born on April 9, 1909 in Andrew, Alberta. He attended Normal School in Edmonton, qualifying as a teacher in 1930. After teaching school in rural Alberta for several years, Decore attended the University of Alberta, graduating with a B.A. in 1937 and an LL.B. in 1938. He was called to the Alberta bar on June 19, 1939. Decore served as a Liberal MP for Vegreville from 1949 to 1957, when he became President of the Liberal Association. He was also Parliamentary Advisor to the Canadian Delegation to the United Nations in 1950. Named QC on December 30, 1963, he was practicing in Edmonton with Decore and Decore when he was appointed to the DC in 1965. Decore received an Honorary LL.D. from the University of Alberta in 1980. He retired on April 9, 1984 and died on November 11, 1994.

As a judge, Decore had several reported judgments in both the DC and the QB. These were primarily in the areas of criminal law, mortgages, foreclosures, and mineral and gas rights. His criminal cases dealt largely with criminal negligence as a result of impaired driving, such as *R. v. Pilling* ([1972] 4 WWR 334). On the civil side, he dismissed several applications for the sale of automobiles by sheriffs seizures under writs of execution. Finally, in the mineral and gas rights area, he held several times for landowners seeking compensation for their surface rights from major corporations, such as *Haukedal v. Dome Petroleum* ([1984] 30 ALR 2d 217). The author of brief, terse judgments, Decore demonstrated on the bench the attributes of a general practitioner sensitive to the rights of individuals.

Decore, Lionel Leighton

Court of Queen's Bench of Alberta, Edmonton, August 1, 1983 - March 5, 1984

The Honourable Lionel Leighton Decore was born in Edmonton, Alberta on May 16, 1941, and grew up in Vegreville. A member of a prominent family of Liberal Party politicians and officials, he received his B.A. in Philosophy in 1962 and his LL.B. in 1965 from the University of Alberta. Before being admitted to the bar on December 19, 1966, Decore articled with Morrow, Hurlburt, Reynolds and Company in Edmonton. Decore was with the firm of Decore and Company in Edmonton when he was appointed to the bench in 1983. He resigned shortly afterwards in 1984 to practice with the firm of Biamonte, Cairo and Shortreed in Edmonton. Decore has been a member and Vice-Chairman of the Edmonton Housing Authority.

Deyell, Roy Victor

Court of Queen's Bench of Alberta, Calgary, December 31, 1987 -

The Honourable Roy Victor Deyell was born in Frobisher, Saskatchewan, on April 23, 1925. During World War II, he served in the Royal Canadian Navy's Volunteer Reserves. Deyell received his B.A. in 1948 and his LL.B. in 1950 from the University of Saskatchewan. Upon graduation, he was articled with Donald P. McLaws, QC, before being admitted to the Alberta

bar on June 6, 1951. He practised with McLaws and Company in Calgary until his appointment to the bench in 1987. Deyell was named QC on December 30, 1967. From 1963 to 1965, he served as an Alderman on Calgary City Council. He has also served as a Trustee for the Calgary General Hospital, a Director of the Heritage Park Society, Director and later President of the Alberta Hospital Association, Chairman of the Mount Royal College Board of Governors, President of the Progressive Conservative Association of Alberta, and member of the University of Calgary Law College Development Committee. In 1993, Justice Deyell was made Director of the Canadian Judges Conference.

Dixon, Russell Armitage

Court of Queen's Bench of Alberta, Calgary, October 23, 1980 - Supernumerary Justice, Calgary, April 27, 1995 -

The Honourable Justice Russell Armitage Dixon was born in Medicine Hat, Alberta, on November 14, 1924. His grandfather, John Dixon, settled in Maple Creek, North-West Territories in 1883, and his father was born there in 1885. Dixon joined the Canadian Army in 1943, and served with the 1st Canadian Parachute Battalion of the 6th British Airborne Division in Belgium, Holland, and Germany. After discharge from the army, Dixon enrolled at the University of Alberta, where he received a B.Sc. in 1948 and an LL.B. in 1951. He was admitted to the Alberta bar on June 13, 1952 and named QC on December 19, 1973. Dixon was a senior partner in the Calgary firm of Howard, Dixon, and Mackie when he was appointed to the bench in 1980. He was also President of the Law Society of Alberta at the time of his appointment in 1980.

Many of Dixon's reported cases were in commercial and matrimonial law. In *Goetjen v. Goetjen* ([1981] 41 AR 269), a divorce case, the wife brought an action for matrimonial property in spite of an award for maintenance. Dixon held that the real property should be divided equally, but the two quarter sections of farmland should be divided sixty percent for the husband and forty percent for the wife. In *Kaminsky v. Kaminsky* ([1982] 48 AR 164), the wife sought an annulment for bigamy after ten years of marriage. Dixon awarded her $6000 under the *Matrimonial Property Act.* And in other judgments such as *Odegaard Estate v. Canadian Pacific Ltd. and Alberta* ([1984] 54 AR 69), and *Hammel v. Anderson* ([1985] 57 AR 109), Dixon navigated the shoals of negligence and liability, using the skills as he had learned as a leading practitioner.

Dubuc, Lucien

District Court of Peace River, Peace River, October 6, 1920 - January 25, 1922
District Court of Edmonton, Edmonton, January 25, 1922 - August 3, 1935
District Court of Northern Alberta, Edmonton, August 3, 1935 - September 13, 1949
District Court of Northern Alberta, Chief Judge, Edmonton, March 18, 1944 - September 13, 1949

His Honour Lucien Dubuc was born in Winnipeg, Manitoba, in 1874. He was the son of Sir Joseph Dubuc who was the Chief Justice of Manitoba, 1903-1909. Educated at the University of Manitoba, Dubuc went west in 1900, settling in Edmonton. He became an advocate of the Law Society of the North-West Territories on April 26, 1901, and was called to the Alberta bar on September 16, 1907. He was practicing in Edmonton with the firm of Dubuc and Dubuc when he was appointed to the DC at Peace River in 1920. In 1922, he moved to the DC at Edmonton. Dubuc retired on September 13, 1949, and died on March 5, 1956.

Dubuc became a pioneer in the establishment of Canadian justice among Aboriginals in the North when he presided as trial judge over judicial expeditions to the Yukon and the Northwest Territories between 1921 and 1932. The expeditions heard a number of civil and criminal cases, including the murder trials of seven Inuit at Herschel Island.

Edmanson, Roy Manning

District Court of Southern Alberta, Calgary, March 18, 1944 - September 5, 1960

His Honour Roy Manning Edmanson was born in Brantford, Ontario, on September 12, 1885. He graduated from the University of Toronto in 1912 with a B.A. He served with the Canadian Expeditionary Force in World War I and, after his return, Edmanson moved to Calgary. He articled with the firm of Clarke, Carson, Macleod and Company and was admitted to the Alberta bar on July 13, 1915. He was named KC on June 1, 1939. Prior to his appointment to the DC in 1944, he practiced with the firm of Macleod Edmanson. Active in local politics, Edmanson was President of the Alberta Liberal Association, 1934-1937. He also served on the Calgary Public School Board, the Wartime Prices and Trade Board, and the Calgary Police Commission. Edmanson retired on September 15, 1960, and died in Calgary on March 29, 1966.

Edwards, Manley Justin

District Court of Southern Alberta, Calgary, January 1, 1951 - May 28, 1962

His Honour Manley Justin Edwards was born in Caisterville, Ontario, on February 18, 1892. He was admitted to the Alberta bar on October 10, 1922. Edwards was elected Liberal Member of Parliament for Calgary Southwest in 1942. When he was appointed to the DC in 1951, Edwards was with the Calgary firm of Edwards and Cromarty. He died in Calgary on May 28, 1962.

Egbert, William Gordon

Supreme Court of Alberta, Trial Division, Calgary, January 25, 1950 - February 8, 1960

The Honourable William Gordon Egbert was born in Milverton, Ontario on February 11, 1892. He moved with his family from Ontario to Calgary in 1904 and his father, the Honourable William Egbert, was Lieu-

tenant-Governor of Alberta, 1925-1931. Egbert graduated from the University of Toronto in 1913 with a B.A. in Political Science and was the recipient of the P.W. Ellis Award. He studied law at Osgoode Hall for one year, and then returned to Calgary when finances became a problem. Egbert completed his legal education by attending lectures from prominent Calgary barristers, and received an LL.B. from the University of Alberta in 1916. He was admitted to the Alberta bar on October 31, 1916, and in that same year he won the Law Society Gold Medal. Specializing in corporate law, Egbert began his career with the Calgary firm of Clarke, Carson and Macleod. He remained there until 1925, when he became a partner in the firm of Smith, Egbert and Smith. He continued with this firm until his appointment to the bench in 1950. Egbert was named KC on January 7, 1930. He was one of the founders of the Calgary Junior Chamber of Commerce in 1927, a member of the Calgary Board of Trade, and became a director of many Calgary oil companies. A Liberal, and a member of the United Church, he belonged to the Ranchmen's and the Calgary Golf and Country Club. When he died in Calgary on February 8, 1960, flags on many buildings flew at half mast in honour of this popular jurist.

Egbert specialized in corporate law as a practitioner, and in ten years on the bench wrote many judgments in contract and tort law, and wills and estates. These judgments are notable for their erudition and their length. Egbert quoted extensively from British, American, and Canadian law in writing his decisions, and often went beyond the point at issue to answer ancillary or abstract questions. For example, in *Re. Webster Estate* ([1951] 1 WWR 721), he mentions several cases where judges would not give advice on particular questions, and then goes on to say that if he were asked, he would answer as follows, in the form of an *obiter dicta*.

Egbert delivered the critical trial judgment in *Turta v. Canadian Pacific Railway and Imperial Oil* ([1952] 5 WWR NS 529) in a landmark case dealing with ownership of petroleum rights. The Registrar of Lands had attempted to "correct" land registry documents which had incorrectly left out a clause reserving petroleum rights for the Canadian Pacific Railway when the land was sold in 1908. After the Leduc oil discovery in 1947, the financial stakes in such a case were extremely high, but Egbert voided the Registrar's corrections and gave the petroleum rights to the landowner. Both the AD and the SCC upheld his decision. His judgment was a thorough, scholarly review of case law and statutory authority and has served as a textbook decision affirming the indefeasability of the Torrens system of land registration.

Finally, in a number of criminal cases, such as *Kellie v. Calgary* ([1950] 3 WWR 691) and *R. v. Dreher* ([1952] 5 WWR 337), he took an activist stand with respect to civil liberties by disallowing questionable or improperly obtained evidence. In an age where lawyers could choose their judge by agreement, Egbert was one who, with Justice James M. Cairns, was generally preferred for the more difficult and complex legal cases.

Egbert, William Gordon Neil

Court of Queen's Bench of Alberta, Calgary, November 27, 1979 - Supernumerary Justice, Calgary, April 27, 1995 -

The Honourable Justice William Gordon Neil Egbert was born in Calgary, Alberta on December 21, 1928, the son of Justice William Gordon Egbert of the SCA. He earned his B.A. in 1951 and his LL.B. in 1952 from the University of Alberta. Articling with the Calgary firm of Porter, Allen, and Mackimmie, he was admitted to the Alberta bar on June 21, 1953. He practiced with Macleod Riley McDermid Bessemer and Dixon where he specialized in corporate law. In 1948, Egbert became general counsel and Secretary for Alberta Coal Limited, a Mannix subsidiary. In 1969, he formed a firm with Melvin Shannon and Harry Rowbotham which later amalgamated with the firm Gill Cook. He was named QC on December 31, 1969, and appointed to the bench at Calgary in 1979. Egbert served as Director of the Calgary Stampede from 1967 to 1971. A Fellow of London's Royal Academy, he was Director of the Calgary Philharmonic Orchestra, 1970-1971.

Egbert's most prominent decisions were in the areas of contracts and corporate law, and matrimonial and divorce. In *Denys v. Denys* ([1990] 106 AR 259), he gave the first summary divorce judgment in Alberta. He held that, once reasonable arrangements had been made, a divorce could be granted without legally dictated provisions. In *Organic Research Inc. and Wilder v. Minister of National Revenue*

([1990] 111 AR 336), the corporation's documents were seized from a law firm under the *Income Tax Act*. The corporation applied to exclude certain documents from disclosure on the basis of solicitor-client privilege. Denied at the QB, Egbert on appeal found for the plaintiff, holding that such indiscriminate seizures were unlawful. Egbert's judgments were erudite, succinct and elegantly written, citing a wide range of sources from statutes and case law to legal treatises.

Ewing, Albert Freeman

Supreme Court of Alberta, Trial
   Division, Edmonton, January 27,
   1931 - January 13, 1941
Supreme Court of Alberta, Appellate
   Division, Edmonton, January 13,
   1941 - August 21, 1946

The Honourable Albert Freeman Ewing was born in Elora, Ontario, on June 29, 1871. He was educated in Elora and at the Toronto School of Pedagogy and taught in Milverton, Ontario. In 1899, he came to Calgary, and studied law under Arthur L. Sifton, later Chief Justice of Alberta and Premier. Ewing was admitted as an advocate to the Law Society of the North-West Territories on August 6, 1902, and to the Law Society of Alberta on September 16, 1907. Practicing first with James Short, he then moved to Edmonton where he was a partner with Alan D. Harvie. He was named KC on March 19, 1913. From 1913 to 1921, Ewing was elected Conservative MLA for Edmonton in the Alberta Legislature, becoming House Leader. Ewing was practicing with the firm of Ewing Harvie and Bury in Edmonton when he was appointed to the bench in 1931. He was Chairman of the Farmers Creditors Arrangement Act Board, and chaired the Commission appointed to investigate the Nordegg mine disaster of 1941 which resulted in the deaths of twenty-nine miners after a devastating explosion. He recommended the abolition of explosives in mines and the enforcement of more rigorous compliance with the safety provisions of the *Mines Act*. He was a member of the Presbyterian Church of Canada. Ewing died in Edmonton on August 28, 1946, one week after his resignation from the CA.

Ewing was a respected and influential judge. Replacing Justice Walsh on the SCA, members of the bench often relied on him to write majority opinions for the Court as a whole. Perhaps his earliest prominent judgment was *Shilleto Drug Company v. the Town of Hanna* ([1931] 3 WWR 108), in which the plaintiff refused to pay taxes paid to the town, and sought to have the by-law which enacted them repealed. In spite of a number of flaws in the by-laws and the tax collection process, Ewing denied the claim because the flaws were minor in law. One of his major precedents was given in *Spooner Oils Limited and Spooner v. Turner Valley Gas Conservation Board and the Attorney-General of Alberta* ([1932] 2 WWR 454), where he upheld the constitutionality of the government's conservation board and its actions. This judgment was cited as precedent, as well as judicially noted, down into the 1950s, both within the province and in other jurisdictions.

Fairbairn, Lynden Eldon

District Court of Southern Alberta,
    Lethbridge, April 19, 1945 -
    January 23, 1946

His Honour Lynden Eldon Fairbairn was born on a farm near
Napanee, Ontario, on July 27, 1897.
He moved to Saskatchewan with his
parents, where he lived for several
years before settling in Victoria, British Columbia. Fairbairn enlisted in
the Canadian Expeditionary Force in
1915, serving in France with the 2nd
Canadian Mounted Rifles and with
the Royal Flying Corps. In 1919, he
returned to Canada, and in 1920 completed his matriculation at the University of Alberta. He then articled in
Lethbridge with James Shepherd of
the firm of Shepherd, Dunlop, and
Rice, and was admitted to the Alberta
bar on September 29, 1924. Fairbairn
was named KC on December 31, 1941.
He was practicing in Lethbridge when
he was appointed to the DC in 1945.
He died on January 23, 1946.

Farthing, Hugh Cragg

District Court of Southern Alberta,
    Calgary, February 1, 1958 - April 7,
    1960
Supreme Court of Alberta, Trial
    Division, Calgary, April 7, 1960 -
    July 18, 1967

The Honourable Hugh Cragg Farthing was born in Woodstock, Ontario, on July 17, 1892. His father was
the Right Reverend J.C. Farthing, later
Lord Bishop of Montreal. He received
his B.A. from McGill University in
Montreal in 1914. After serving as a

Lieutenant in the Canadian Expeditionary Force in World War I between
1915 and 1918, Farthing obtained his
LL.B. from Osgoode Hall Law School
in Toronto. He was admitted to the
Ontario bar in 1919, and began his
practice in Toronto. He moved to
Calgary and was admitted to the Alberta bar on June 11, 1923. Farthing
was elected to the Alberta Legislature
as a Conservative MLA from 1930 to
1935, but was defeated as a Conservative candidate in the federal election
of 1940. He was named KC on January
3, 1935. Farthing was a partner in the
Calgary firm of Farthing and Tavender
when he was appointed to the DC in
1958. He was active with the Red Cross,
serving as President of the Calgary
Branch in 1928 as well as President of
the Alberta Division in 1947. He retired on July 18, 1967, and died in
Calgary on June 8, 1968.

Feehan, Joseph Bernard

District Court of Northern Alberta,
    Edmonton, September 13, 1973 -
    October 1, 1975
District Court of Alberta, Edmonton,
    October 1, 1975 - June 30, 1979
Court of Queen's Bench of Alberta,
    Edmonton, June 30, 1979 -
Supernumerary Justice, Edmonton,
    February 11, 1994 -

The Honourable Justice Joseph
Bernard Feehan was born in Saskatoon, Saskatchewan, on February
11, 1929. He attended the University
of Alberta and articled with the Edmonton firm of Amerongen and
Berger before being admitted to the
Alberta bar on June 25, 1954. An active
member of the Liberal Party, he con-

tested unsuccessfully the Edmonton West seat in the 1967 provincial election, losing to Louis D. Hyndman, Jr.. Feehan practised law in Edmonton with the firm of Feehan and Remesz prior to his appointment to the DC in 1973. He was a Sessional Lecturer at the University of Alberta Faculty of Law from 1979 to 1984.

As a trial judge, Feehan heard a wide range of cases. One of his most media-worthy decisions was *Sykes v. Southam Inc., et al.* ([1991] 115 AR 100). in which the former Calgary mayor Rod Sykes brought an action of defamation against the *Calgary Herald* for an editorial. Feehan upheld the lower court's verdict of not guilty, holding that the essence of the story of impaired driving was proven as true. In *Robertson v. Edmonton* ([1990] 104 AR 374), the plaintiff was successful in quashing two city by-laws which would have established a land-fill site in his locality. Feehan took a strong view of the rights of community interests. In *Kozina and Kozina v. Trans-Alta. Mortgage & Financial Services Ltd.* ([1979] 24 AR 405), he allowed the plaintiffs' claim against a mortgage company that did not meet their demands because of their problems with the English language. A compassionate judge on the bench, Feehan became well known for his common sense in applying the rule of law. In addition to serving on the Alberta bench, Feehan was appointed Deputy Judge of the SCYT in 1978.

Feir, Elmor Best

District Court of Southern Alberta, Lethbridge, October 2, 1945 - August 17, 1969

District Court of Southern Alberta, Chief Judge, Lethbridge, September 16, 1955 - August 17, 1969

His Honour Elmor Best Feir was born on August 17, 1894, at Ops township near Omemee, Ontario. He matriculated at the University of Manitoba in 1911, and attended the Normal School at Brandon for his teachers training. He then spent two years teaching at Manyberries before moving to Lethbridge, where he taught at Lethbridge High School from 1914 to 1915. In 1916, Feir served in World War I with the 44th Battalion and 4th Division Wing of the Canadian Expeditionary Force. He fought at Vimy Ridge and spent the rest of the war as a gun instructor. Following the war, he articled with C.V. Bennett in Stettler, and was admitted to the Alberta bar on July 13, 1921. Feir practiced with Bennett in Stettler until World War II, when he organized and commanded B. Squadron, Calgary Tank Regiment, and later became a member of the Canadian Mobilization Board in Alberta. After the war, he returned to his practice until he was appointed to the DC in 1945. He was a member of the Royal Commission on Child Welfare in Alberta in 1947, and in April 1963 he was named to the Royal Commission to inquire into the Crossbow and Sarcee Auxiliary Hospitals. In addition, he was a Freemason, Legionnaire, member of the United Church, and was Secretary of the Stettler Board of Trade. Feir retired on August 17, 1969, and died on April 10, 1973.

Feir's reported judgments deal mainly with contracts, and a few of them were upheld on appeal, forming precedents. His style was concise, and his citations were few, brief, and to the point. Concerned with balance in heading his court, he gave equal treatment to lawyers, litigants, and witnesses. Feir prided himself on being well informed on current legal developments, and believed that the main qualification for a local judge was to be a gentleman.

Foisy, René Paul

District Court of Alberta, Edmonton, March 26, 1979 - June 30, 1979
Court of Queen's Bench of Alberta, Edmonton, June 30, 1979 - January 1, 1987
Court of Appeal of Alberta, Edmonton, January 1, 1987 -

The Honourable Justice René Paul Foisy was born in St. Paul, Alberta, on September 12, 1939. He attended the University of Alberta, where he received his B.A. in 1959, and his LL.B. in 1961. He articled with Roger Belzil before being admitted to the Alberta bar on September 14, 1962. In 1963, Foisy returned to his home town of St. Paul and set up a law practice. In 1973, he joined Richard R. Holeton and formed the firm of Foisy and Holeton, where he remained until he was appointed to the DC at Edmonton in 1979. He was named in 1988 to the Pension Appeal Board, a Federal Appeal Tribunal established under the Canada Pension Plan. In addition to serving on the Alberta bench, Foisy served as Deputy Judge of the SCNT, 1979-1985, and was appointed to the CANT in 1987.

Foisy's reported judgments reveal a strong sense of proper human conduct. In *Muttart Industries Ltd. v. Edmonton et al.* ([1982] 48 AR 321), after very careful discernment he allowed an action in negligence against the City because of its faulty design of the electrical supply system to the plaintiff's premises. In *Christie v. Geiger and the Edmonton Sun* ([1984] 58 AR 168), perhaps his most famous judgment, he made precedent on libel and the law of slander. Finally, in one of his last judgments on appeal, *R. v. Horseman* ([1987] 78 AR 351], he convicted a Treaty Indian for killing a grizzly bear and selling the hide without a licence contrary to the *Wildlife Act* on the grounds that the general protection afforded wildlife took precedence over sport or commerce.

Ford, Clinton James

District Court of Southern Alberta, Calgary, May 6, 1942 - April 19, 1945
Supreme Court of Alberta, Trial Division, Calgary, April 19, 1945 - January 25, 1950
Supreme Court of Alberta, Appellate Division, Calgary, January 25, 1950 - March 1, 1967
Chief Justice of Alberta, January 17, 1957 - March 1, 1961

The Honourable Clinton James Ford was born on a farm near Corinth, Ontario, on March 29, 1882. Attending schools in Tillsonburg and Aylmer for two years, he went on to teach for three years. He matriculated to Victoria College, Toronto, in 1904 and graduated from the University of Toronto in 1907, winning the Prince of Wales medal. He spent the following two years at Osgoode Hall, and moved to Edmonton in 1909 where he completed his LL.B. at the University of Alberta in 1910, winning the Chief Justice's medal. Ford articled with the firm of Reilly and McLean in Calgary and was admitted to the Alberta bar on October 31, 1910. He practiced law with the same firm until 1913 when he was appointed a City Solicitor for Calgary. Ford was named KC on June 23, 1921 and entered into practice with Leo H. Miller of the Calgary firm of Ford, Miller and Harvie in 1922. He was still with them when he was appointed to the DC in 1942. Ford possessed a strong sense of civic duty. In his early years he was active in the business community, helping to organize and becoming President of the Alberta Poultry Federation and serving on the Council of the Calgary Board of Trade, 1921-1932. He was on the Board of Governors of Mount Royal College, 1932-1964 and was Chairman, 1955-1961. Ford was Chair of the Institute of Family and Personal Counselling and heavily involved with the YMCA at both the local and national levels, serving as President of the former and Vice-President of the latter, and assisted with the establishment of Camp Chief Hector. He was an active member of the Central United Church and politically he was President of the Alberta Liberal Association. Ford was the first Chief Justice of Alberta to reside in Calgary, and served simultaneously as the Chief Justice of the CANT from 1957 to 1961. In 1957, the Clinton Ford School was named in his honour. Ford retired on March 1, 1961, and died in Calgary on November 16, 1964.

Ford was an extremely prolific judge, producing hundreds of reported decisions. While he wrote on virtually every legal subject, he was particularly concerned with criminal matters, rules of evidence, estates, torts, and municipalities. His judgments were clear and concise, drawing from legal doctrines in jurisprudential literature as well as from case and statute law. He took great care to ensure his decisions were philosophically and intellectually sound, as well as relevant and specific to the case at hand. One of his most controversial decisions was *R. v. Martin* ([1947] 1 WWR 721) where he held that the defendant could not be convicted for shooting with the intent to commit bodily harm if he was so drunk as to lack the power to form an intent to shoot. Instead, Ford found him guilty of common assault, and fined him $100 plus costs. Later, as an appeal court judge, he was known for applying rules with great common sense.

Ford's judgment in *Mortimer v. British American Oil Company Ltd.* ([1949] 2 WWR 107) asserted *Rylands v. Fletcher* in finding the defendant company liable for gas leakage into a residential neighbourhood. Ford dismissed an appeal for a conviction under the *Canadian Wheat Board Act*, affirming the constitutional authority of Parliament to regulate grain trade in the province for business operating for the general advantage of Canada. Ford dissented in the appeal of *Turta v. Canadian Pacific Railway and Imperial Oil* ([1953] 8 WWR NS 609), insisting that, in dealing with the immense land title and registry questions involved, the focus should be more on the interpretation of the *Land Titles Act* than on the interpretation of case law.

Ford, Frank

Supreme Court of Alberta, Trial
    Division, Edmonton, May 3, 1926 -
    November 3, 1936
Supreme Court of Alberta, Appellate
    Division, Edmonton, November 3,
    1936 - October 13, 1954

The Honourable Frank Ford was
born in Toronto, Ontario, on March 4,
1873. He received his B.A. from Trinity University in Toronto, and his LL.B.
from Osgoode Hall. Ford articled with
Read, Read and McKnight of Toronto
and was called to the Ontario bar in
1895. He acted as D'Alton McCarthy's
private secretary, 1893-1997, and
served as Secretary and Solicitor to
the Premier, AG, and Treasurer of
Ontario from 1898 to 1903. He was a
partner with McCarthy, Osler, Hoskin
and Harcourt before moving west in
1904, where he was admitted to the
North-West Territories bar on October 24, 1904 and to the Saskatchewan
and Alberta bars on September 21,
1907. In 1906, Ford was appointed
Deputy AG for Saskatchewan. He remained in that office until 1910, when
he came to Edmonton to practice with
the firm of Emery, Newell, Ford, Bol-
ton and Mount. He practiced with this
firm until he was appointed to the
bench at Edmonton in 1926. Ford has
the distinction of being named KC in
three provinces: Saskatchewan in 1907,
Ontario in 1910, and Alberta in 1913.
He served as Chancellor of the Edmonton Diocese of the Anglican
Church of Canada from 1913 to 1943,
and Chancellor of the University of
Alberta from 1941 to 1946. He received
honorary LL.D.s from the University
of Alberta in 1946 and from Laval

University. Ford retired on October 13, 1954 and died on March 21,
1965.

Ford was a meticulous and exacting judge. As a trial judge, he found
against a defendant who struck a
seven-year-old girl in *Marano and
Marano v. Lett* ([1929] 1 ALR 1st 34).
Ford held that although the driver
claimed he was driving carefully and
did not see the girl cross the street, it
was his responsibility to avoid the
child. In *Knight Sugar Company Limited v. Alberta Railway and Irrigation
Company* ([1935] 3 ALR 1st 86), Ford
had to rule separately on the ownership of mines and minerals, and on
petroleum and natural gas rights.
Appealed in both cases, the latter to
the JCPC, Ford's judgments were upheld. Ford sat for eighteen years on
the AD. Some of his written judgments were dissenting views, as in *R.
v. Rivet* ([1944] 2 ALR 1st 132). His
dedication to learning and careful
administration of justice were hallmarks of his career, and he encour-
aged the participation of the popular
press, often sharing his judicial
notebooks with journalists in order to
have the law reported to the public as
carefully as it had been made.

Forsyth, Gregory Rife

Supreme Court of Alberta, Trial
    Division, Calgary, March 26, 1979 -
    June 30, 1979
Court of Queen's Bench of Alberta,
    Calgary, June 30, 1979 -
Supernumerary Justice, Calgary, July
    25, 1991 -

The Honourable Justice Gregory
Rife Forsyth was born in Calgary, Al-

berta, on June 15, 1928. He attended the University of Alberta, receiving his B.A. in 1950 and his LL.B. in 1951. He was admitted to the Alberta bar on June 3, 1952, and started a career with the Legal Department of the Canadian Pacific Railway. He was admitted to the Ontario bar in 1955 and he was appointed QC on December 22, 1971. Forsyth was practicing with the Calgary firm of Howard, Dixon, Mackie and Forsyth when he was appointed to the bench in 1979. He was particularly active in writing judgments on corporate civil cases, and presided over the civil action surrounding Amoco's takeover of Dome Petroleum in 1988.

Forsyth heard a wide range of reported cases, including sales of goods, mortgages, builders liens, trustees and bankruptcy, corporate law, oil and gas law, criminal negligence, fish and game, and matrimonial causes. In *Gaschnitz v. Westhill Resources Ltd.* ([1980] 13 ALR 2d 248), the surface rights owner had a crop loss attributed to the work of the resource company, and applied for compensation additional to the province's program. Forsyth denied the application on the grounds that he had enough. Creating a complex formula for determining the landowner's compensation, the judge covered a wide range of statutory and regulatory law. *Petrasuk v. Petrasuk* ([1982] 19 ALR 2d 260) was a petition for divorce filed by the wife in Red Deer, the husband in Calgary with property assets of three million and a bankruptcy proceeding. Requesting a *decree absolut*, the wife was not granted one, but was awarded an inquiry into the matter. Forsyth used an impressive array of cases, statutes,

and rules of court in penning his judgment. In *Walker v. Canadian Newspapers Company Limited and the Lethbridge Herald* ([1985] 37 ALR 2d 179), the plaintiff manager formed a staff association to discuss policy changes, and was asked by the new publisher to either quit the association or resign. The plaintiff refused, was fired, and sued for damages. Forsyth held that the plaintiff had a choice, and was offered other employment, and thus rejected the claim. Using primarily oral testimony, Forsyth reported this case with a story line that read in large parts like a narrative.

Foster, Nina Leone

Court of Queen's Bench of Alberta, Edmonton, April 18, 1984 -

The Honourable Justice Nina Leone Foster was born on August 5, 1944. She was admitted to the Alberta bar on June 14, 1968, and began to practice law with the Edmonton firm of Wood, Moir, Hyde and Ross. Foster was a partner in the firm of Foster, Chatwin and Belzil when she was appointed to the Bench in 1984.

Fraser, Catherine Anne

Court of Queen's Bench of Alberta, Edmonton, March 7, 1989 - March 1, 1991
Court of Appeal of Alberta, Edmonton, March 1, 1991 -
Chief Justice of Alberta, March 12, 1992 -

Born in Campbellton, New Brunswick on August 4, 1947, the Honourable Justice Catherine Anne Fraser moved to Edmonton in 1959. She graduated from the University of Alberta with a B.A. in 1969 and an LL.B. in 1970 for which she received the George Bligh O'Connor Silver Medal in Law. Fraser then attended the London School of Economics and Political Science, where she completed her LL.M in 1972. She was admitted to the Alberta bar on June 21, 1971. Fraser practiced commercial and corporate law with the Edmonton firm of Lucas, Bishop and Fraser before being appointed to the Bench in 1989, and was named QC on December 30, 1983. She served as Chairman of the Public Service Employee Relations Committee from 1983 to 1989, and is currently a Director of the Canadian Institute on the Administration of Justice. Fraser has conducted courses on women and the law at the University of Alberta, Faculty of Law and, in 1987, she was the recipient of the YWCA Tribute to Women Award in the category of Business, Industry, and Profession.

Fraser is the first woman to be appointed Chief Justice of Alberta. Sitting on the QB for just three years before being appointed to the CA, most of Fraser's decisions were made as an Appeal Court justice. Many of these decisions were in the area of company law, and several were concerned with impaired driving charges under the criminal law. In *R. v. Oester* ([1989] 69 ALR 2d 65, 285), Fraser denied an application for the right to legal counsel on the grounds that the accused chose his boss for his solicitor knowing his lack of legal knowledge. In *R. v. Sendypoint* ([1991] 114 ALR 2d 326), the accused made application for a stay of proceedings on the grounds of abuse of process and infringement of his right to a duty trial. Fraser held that the safety of the community was more important. Finally, in *Dalhousie Station Ltd. et al. v. Calgary* ([1991] 123 AR 203), a case that had prominent media coverage the developer was awarded under municipal law zoning rights for the shopping centre complex after strong opposition by community groups. Fraser handled many complex cases in commercial and company law and her judgments are marked by a careful interpretation of both statute and case law.

Fraser, Harry Blackwood

District Court of Northern Alberta, Edmonton, December 19, 1944 - August 28, 1963

His Honour Harry Blackwood Fraser was born in Bradford, Ontario on March 28, 1889. He received his LL.B. from the University of Alberta in 1919 and was admitted to the Alberta bar on December 18, 1919. He practiced in Westlock prior to his appointment to the DC in 1944. Fraser retired on August 28, 1963, and died on October 29, 1964.

Gallant, Tellex William

Court of Queen's Bench of Alberta, Edmonton, June 21, 1984 -

The Honourable Justice Tellex W. Gallant was born on May 27, 1932. He graduated from the University of Alberta with a B.A. in 1956 and an LL.B. in 1958. After being admitted to the Alberta bar on May 19, 1959, he joined the Edmonton firm of Ogilvie and O'Byrne. Gallant was a senior partner of the successor firm of Ogilvie and Company when he was appointed to the bench in 1984.

Gardiner, Duncan McIntyre

District Court of Northern Alberta, Stettler, November 20, 1961 - March 10, 1969

His Honour Duncan McIntyre Gardiner was born on February 28, 1893. He articled under Lawrence E. Ormond in Hanna, Alberta and was admitted to the Alberta bar on December 14, 1926. He was named QC on December 31, 1959. Gardiner was practicing law in Stettler, Alberta, when he was appointed to the DC in 1961. During his career, Gardiner was active in civic affairs in Stettler, serving on the Town Council and as Mayor from 1949-1950. He retired on March 10, 1969, and died on February 6, 1985.

Gariepy, Charles Edouard

District Court of Northern Alberta, Edmonton, September 13, 1949 - March 19, 1963

His Honour Charles Edouard Gariepy was born in Montreal, Quebec, on March 19, 1888 and moved to Edmonton in 1893. He received his early education at St. Lawrence College in Montreal. He became a student-at-law in 1910 and attended Osgoode Hall in Toronto beginning in 1912. Gariepy served overseas with the 22nd Battalion of the Canadian Expeditionary Force, was wounded, and returned to Edmonton in 1918.

He was admitted to the Alberta bar on January 20, 1920 and began his practice with the firm of Knott and Gariepy in Edmonton. Appointed KC on December 30, 1943, Gariepy was with the Edmonton firm of Gariepy and Hart when he was appointed to the DC in 1949. He was an Alderman on Edmonton City Council from 1940 to 1949, and was a elected a Trustee of the Edmonton Separate School Board for fourteen years. Gariepy retired on March 19, 1963, and died in Edmonton on September 3, 1976.

Girgulis, William James

Court of Queen's Bench of Alberta, Edmonton, June 18, 1981 -

The Honourable Justice William James Girgulis was born in Saskatoon, Saskatchewan on July 2, 1933. He graduated from the University of Saskatchewan with a B.A. in 1954 and an LL.B. in 1956. While at University, Girgulis was active in many organizations and played for the University of Saskatchewan basketball team for five years before coming to Alberta. Girgulis settled in Edmonton in 1956 and articled with S.W. Field, QC before being admitted to the Alberta bar on June 5, 1957. He continued to practice with the firm of Field and Field until his appointment to the bench in 1981. From 1968 on, his practice was devoted almost exclusively to civil litigation. Girgulis was named QC on January 18, 1980.

Girgulis had only a few reported decisions, making his work on the bench difficult to ascertain from the law reports. Three of his major decisions reflect a penchant for collecting

Gordon Hollis Allen *(CA)*

Alexander Andrekson *(LASA)*

Arthur Beaumont *(CLA)*

Nicholas Du Bois Dominic Beck *(LASA)*

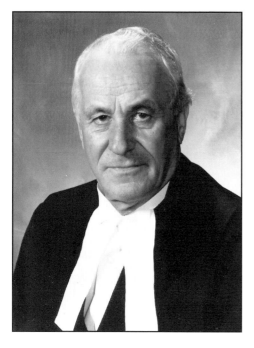

Roger Hector Belzil *(CA)*

Ronald Leon Berger *(LASA)*

Myra Beth Bielby *(LASA)*

Donald Haines Bowen *(AJ)*

John Robert Boyle *(LASA)*

John David Bracco *(LASA)*

William Robert Brennan *(AJ)*

Nelles Victor Buchanan *(QB)*

James Mitchell Cairns *(CA)*

Laurence Yeomans Cairns

Arthur Allan Carpenter *(GAI)*

James Creighton Cavanagh *(AJ)*

Robert Alan Cawsey *(AJ)*　　　　Paul Stephen Chrumka

Alfred Henry Clarke *(LASA)*　　　　Carlton William Clement *(CA)*

Carole Mildred Conrad   *(CA)*

John Spiers Cormack   *(AJ)*

Jean Edouard Leon Côté   *(CA)*

John Lyndon Crawford   *(PAA)*

Thomas Lynde Cross *(PAA)*

Arthur William Crossley *(AJ)*

Alan Joseph Cullen *(CLA)*

John Berchmans Dea *(LASA)*

André Miville Dechene *(AJ)*

Roy Victor Deyell *(LASA)*

Russell Armitage Dixon *(AJ)*

Lucien Dubuc *(PAA)*

Roy Manning Edmanson *(LASA)*

Manley Justin Edwards *(QB)*

William Gordon Egbert *(LASA)*

William Gordon Neil Egbert (QB)

Albert Freeman Ewing *(CA)*

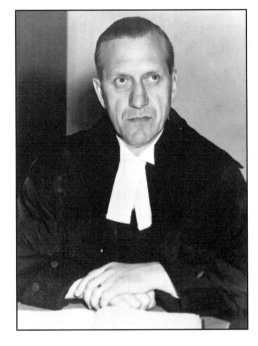

Lynden Eldon Fairbairn *(LASA)*

Hugh Cragg Farthing *(GAI)*

Joseph Bernard Feehan *(AJ)*

Elmor Best Feir *(QB)*

René Paul Foisy *(CA)*

Clinton James Ford *(CA)*

Frank Ford *(CA)*

Gregory Rife Forsyth *(AJ)*

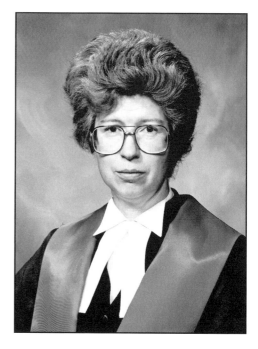

Nina Leone Foster *(LASA)*

Catherine Anne Fraser *(CA)*

Harry Blackwood Fraser *(QB)*

Tellex William Gallant

Duncan McIntyre Gardiner *(QB)*

Charles Edouard Gariepy *(QB)*

William James Girgulis *(LASA)*

Peter Greschuk *(AJ)*

William Joseph Haddad *(LASA)*

Asa Milton Harradence *(CA)*

Horace Harvey *(LASA)*

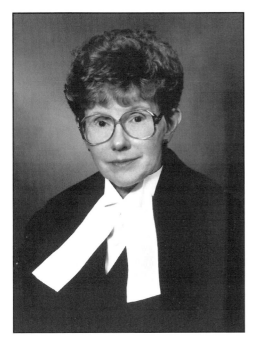

Mary Margaret McCormick
Hetherington
(CA)

Jack Kenneth Holmes
(LASA)

John McIntosh Hope
(AJ)

William Robinson Howson
(LASA)

Ernest Arthur Hutchinson *(AJ)*

James Duncan Hyndman *(CA)*

Howard Lawrence Irving *(CA)*

William Carlos Ives *(LASA)*

cases and statutes, presenting them with copious quotation, and covering the case reported along the way. For example, in *Marshall v. R.* ([1982] 18 ALR 2d 297), he quashed a committal order where the accused was not given an opportunity to make a submission to the presiding judge. In *Kresic et al. v. Alberta Securities Commission et al.* ([1985] 37 ALR 2d 342), he allowed the plaintiff's action in negligence alleging a breach of duties imposed by the *Securities Act* in vetting and approving a common stock prospectus. And in *Dreco Ltd. et al. v. Director of Employment Standards of Alberta* ([1985] 38 ALR 2d 163), the applicant's company was placed in receivership, and the receiver gave employees term notices without pay, ordering the company to pay them. The D.E.S. held that there should be no pay, and the plaintiff filed a *certiorari* to quash his decision. Girgulis held that the D.E.S. decision was "patently unreasonable", giving, however, little explanation apart from his conclusion.

Greene, George Wellington

District Court of Medicine Hat, Medicine Hat, December 18, 1915 - August 3, 1935
District Court of Southern Alberta, Medicine Hat, August 3, 1935 - July 14, 1936

His Honour George Wellington Greene was born in Athens, Ontario, on June 5, 1862. He studied law at Osgoode Hall in Toronto, receiving an LL.B. in 1887, and was admitted to the Ontario bar that same year. Following his legal education, Greene returned to his home town of Athens

where he practiced law for four years. He was elected to the Town Council in 1890 and was President of the Athens Board of Trade. In 1891, he moved to Red Deer, North-West Territories and became influential in the fledgling community's land and financing ventures. He was an agent for the Saskatchewan Land and Homesteading Company and opened Red Deer's first private bank. Greene was admitted as an advocate of the North-West Territories on September 24, 1894. He went into partnership with W. Ernest Payne in 1902 and was with Greene and Payne when he was appointed to the DC at Medicine Hat in 1915. While in Medicine Hat, he was the victim of an assassination attempt, but survived. Greene died on vacation in Athabasca, Alberta, on July 14, 1936.

Greschuk, Peter

District Court of Northern Alberta, Edmonton, October 14, 1953 - January 17, 1957
Supreme Court of Alberta, Trial Division, Edmonton, January 17, 1957 - June 30, 1979
Court of Queen's Bench of Alberta, Edmonton, June 30, 1979 - November 14, 1983
Supernumerary Justice, January 1, 1983 - November 14, 1983

The Honourable Justice Peter Greschuk was born in Edmonton, Alberta, on November 15, 1908. Educated at McCauley School and Victoria High School, he attended the University of Alberta where he received his B.A. in 1931 and his LL.B. in 1933. Greschuk articled with Harvie, Bury and Vanda in Edmonton before being admitted to the Alberta bar on January 19, 1935. From 1935 to 1942, he was with the Edmonton firm of Tighe and Wilson and, from 1942 until his appointment to the bench in 1953, Greschuk was a sole practitioner in Edmonton, where he specialized in civil and criminal law. In addition to sitting on the Alberta bench, Greschuk was a Deputy Judge of the Federal Court of Canada in Ottawa, 1975-1983, and a Judge of the SCNT, 1977-1983. After over thirty years on the bench, he retired on November 15, 1983 and was appointed QC on December 31, 1983. He was Chairman of the Task Force on the *Fatality Inquiries Act* in 1984. He also served as a member of the Misericordia Hospital Advisory Board for ten years, and was an executive member of the Edmonton Symphony. Greschuk died in Edmonton on April 24, 1996.

Greschuk was an industrious judge. While commercial law comprised the majority of his published judgments, there were several criminal cases and procedural matters which brought him some notoriety. He sat for the first trial of *R. v. Robert Raymond Cook* ([1960] 31 WWR 148) in Red Deer in 1959, in which the accused was sentenced to hang for the murder of his family. Cook was the last person to receive the death penalty in Alberta. He also heard the case of *R. v. Lefebvre* ([1982] 5 WWR 481), where it was held that the accused was not entitled to have his trial conducted in French in the Provincial Court of Alberta. This decision was also upheld on appeal. His major contribution to the development of commercial law was in simplifying the language of contracts and upholding the rights of purchasers to be fully informed of terms and conditions. Thus, in *Capital City Oil Well Servicing Co. Ltd. v. Non Marine Underwriters Member of Lloyd's, London, England* ([1958] 27 WWR 241), he awarded compensation for the plaintiff in an insurance contract because the language was confusing and the plaintiff thought his coverage was complete. In *Crown Lumber Co. Ltd. v. McTaggart Motors Ltd.* ([1961] 34 WWR 370), he did not allow a lien applied against property to give the lien holder standing as a secured creditor because there was no prior written agreement for payment. In *Hughes v. Gedosh, et al.* ([1971] 1 WWR 641), a right of entry order made by the Surface Rights Board to give an oil company access to drill was binding on future owners even without a caveat on the property title.

Haddad, William Joseph

District Court of Northern Alberta, Edmonton, August 18, 1965 - November 29, 1974

Supreme Court of Alberta, Appellate Division, Edmonton, November 29, 1974 - June 30, 1979

Court of Appeal of Alberta, Edmonton, June 30, 1979 - November 26, 1990

Supernumerary Justice, Edmonton, December 1, 1980 - November 26, 1990

The Honourable William Joseph Haddad was born in Meyronne, Saskatchewan, on November 26, 1915. In 1936, his family moved to Edmonton. He received his B.A. and his LL.B. from the University of Alberta in 1941.

After serving under articles with Nelles V. Buchanan, KC, he was admitted to the Alberta bar on November 5, 1942. In 1942, Haddad enlisted in the Canadian Navy. From 1943 to 1946, he served as a legal officer on the staff of the Commanding Officer of the Pacific Coast before being discharged from the Navy in 1946 with the rank of Lieutenant. After the war, Haddad joined A.L. Marks in partnership in the firm of Marks and Haddad, and in 1952 he joined the firm of Wood, Haddad, Moir, Hyde and Ross. In 1961, he began practicing with the Edmonton firm of Simpson, Haddad, Cavanagh, Henning, Buchanan and Kerr, where he remained until his first judicial appointment in 1965. He was appointed QC on December 31, 1957. Haddad served as Secretary-Treasurer of the Edmonton Liberal Association from 1962 to 1963 and was Chairman of the Edmonton Board of Police Commissioners from 1966 to 1971. From 1966 to 1974, Haddad was a member of the Alberta Securities Commission, and from 1974 to 1978 he was the Commission's Vice Chairman. Haddad was Director, Vice-President, and member of the Management Committee of the Edmonton Eskimos Football Club from 1958 to 1963. In addition to serving on the Alberta bench, Haddad was Justice of the CANT, 1974-1990. He retired on November 26, 1990.

Haddad presided over a number of professional misconduct cases, including most notably *Hay v. Institute of Chartered Accountants* ([1989] 63 ALR 2d 217), and *Nair v. The College of Physicians and Surgeons* ([1988] 61 ALR 2d 420). These particular decisions reflect the Court's willingness to enter into the regulation of professional misconduct on appeal. Haddad's opinions demonstrate his thoughtful reconsiderations in both allowing appeals and overturning decisions of the trial courts.

Harradence, Asa Milton

Supreme Court of Alberta, Appellate Division, Calgary, March 26, 1979 - June 30, 1979
Court of Appeal of Alberta, Calgary, June 30, 1979 - April 23, 1997
Supernumerary Justice, Calgary, April 25, 1994 - April 23, 1997

The Honourable Asa Milton Harradence was born in Blaine Lake, Saskatchewan, on April 23, 1922. He served as a Flight-Sergeant Pilot with the Royal Canadian Air Force in World War II, transferring to the Canadian Infantry in 1944. He attended the University of Saskatchewan from 1945 to 1950, where he received his LL.B. in 1949, and his B.A. in 1950. He came to Alberta in 1950 and articled with the Calgary firm of Nolan Chambers before being admitted to the Alberta bar on August 10, 1951. He was primarily a criminal lawyer and in 1975 was named one of the top ten criminal defence lawyers in Canada by *Canadian Magazine*. Harradence was senior partner in the firm of Harradence and Company when he was appointed to the bench in 1979. During his career, Harradence was elected Alderman on Calgary City Council, 1957-1959, and in 1962 he became leader of the Progressive Conservative Party of Alberta. However, when he was unable to win a seat in the 1963 Provincial Election, he resigned the Party leadership in 1964. He was named QC on December 31, 1969. On February 9, 1993, Harradence was appointed Honorary Colonel of the 416 Tactical Fighter Squadron in Cold Lake, Alberta. As a result of his background in the criminal law, Harradence was the only private individual in Alberta permitted to carry a concealed, restricted firearm. In addition to his appointments to the Alberta bench, Harradence was Justice of the CANT, 1979-1997.

While Harradence gave judgements on a wide variety of cases as an appeal judge, his written judgements stand out in criminal law cases. He appears on the bench as a judicial advocate for the private individual, and he never hesitated to point out the heavy hand of government or its officials, or the failure of police or officials to follow the letter of the law. He showed no tolerance for the stalling tactics of bureaucracies, the obfuscation of details, or threats to individual rights. For example, in *R. v. Sieben* ([1989] 70 ALR 2d 336), which concerned the arrest of individuals believed on reasonable and probable grounds to be driving while impaired, Harradence dissented, holding that the certificate of analysis regarding the breathalyzer should have been excluded as evidence. In *R. v. Bun Ly Pang* ([1994] 26 ALR 3d 317), where the accused was denied stay of proceedings at both the PC and QB when Crown counsel failed to make full disclosure of witness statements, Harradence upheld the appeal by ruling that the accused's right to make full answer and defense under the *Canadian Charter of Rights and Freedoms* had been breached.

Harvey, Horace

Supreme Court of the North-West Territories, Fort Macleod, Calgary, June 27, 1904 - September 16, 1907
Supreme Court of Alberta, Edmonton, September 16, 1907 - October 12, 1910
Chief Justice of Alberta, Edmonton, October 12, 1910 - September 15, 1921
Supreme Court of Alberta, Trial Division, Chief Justice, Edmonton, September 15, 1921 - August 27, 1924
Supreme Court of Alberta, Appellate Division, Edmonton, August 27, 1924 - September 9, 1949
Chief Justice of Alberta, Edmonton, August 27, 1924 - September 9, 1949

The Honourable Horace Harvey was born in Elgin County, Ontario, in 1863, the son of William Harvey, Liberal Member of Parliament for Elgin East, 1872-1874. He attended the University of Toronto, graduating with a B.A. in 1886, and an LL.B. in 1888. Harvey was called to the Ontario bar in 1889 and practiced in Toronto until 1893, when he moved west to Calgary, enrolled as an advocate of the Law Society of the North-West Territories on May 22, 1893, and began practice with Peter McCarthy. He was appointed Registrar of Land Titles for Southern Alberta in 1896 and, in 1900, he became Deputy AG of the North-West Territories and moved to Regina. He was appointed to the SCNWT in 1904 resident in Fort Macleod. When the province of Alberta was formed in 1905, he moved to Calgary and, finally, to Edmonton in 1907. Harvey served as Chairman of the Board of Governors of the University of Alberta from 1917 to 1940, and was Chairman of the Mobilization Board for National Services in 1940. Harvey was the longest serving member of the Alberta bench. A Quaker, he died in Edmonton on September 9, 1949.

By virtue of his judicial position, the breadth of the cases he heard, and his longevity, Harvey stands as a giant in the legal history of Alberta. He spans the entire formative period of western Canadian case law. In general, Harvey took a rather strict view of both common and statute law: he was not one to overthrow precedent, accepting the decisions of higher courts without question even if they contradicted his own judicial opinions. He felt that courts should not interpret statutes strictly nor set them aside, nor seek to enter the minds of their makers. The exception to this general view was somewhat revolutionary: in *R. v. Cyr* ([1917] 12 ALR 1st 320), Harvey, in opposition to Justice Scott, agreed with the judgment that women could sit as magistrates, very consciously departing from the English common law. This decision set in motion a momentous series of legal actions leading to the famous "Persons Case" in the 1920s. Regarding judicial procedure and rules of court, he insisted on strict compliance. Harvey himself wrote the *Alberta Rules of Court* in 1914 and they were not revised substantially until 1944. Again, one obvious exception was spectacular: in *McPherson v. McPherson* ([1933] 1 WWR 321), Harvey held, in a famous wife-swapping scandal involving a government minister, that a library was an open court and that the

decree nisi in the divorce was therefore valid. This unusual decision was overturned by the JCPC. When larger issues arose involving the welfare of society, or the role of conflicting interests, he believed that legislatures and not judges should resolve them. A dominant figure on the CA, contemporary lawyers often felt that he intimidated his fellow judges on the bench. Harvey's extensive dealings with criminal law focused especially in the technical development of rules for the admissability of evidence. Often he spoke out against improper police methods, and was also cautious in his application of due process of law. He tolerated neither prisoner mistreatment nor an accused's abuse of the law, and insisted that guilt be proved. He also stood for severe sentences. A great defender in the jurisdiction and effectiveness of the court, in *Hatfield v. Healy* ([1911] 3 ALR 1st 327), he held a newspaper in contempt of court for publishing opinions on the guilt of a party in a civil action, consciously seeking to prohibit American-style "trial by newspaper."

In the area of constitutional law, Harvey had to deal with a flurry of controversial legislation between 1935 and 1943 in which the Social Credit government attempted to control debt, creditor's rights, and banking in the province. Taking a strict stand on case law on the *British North America Act*, he held them unconsitutional and *ultra vires* of the Provincial Government. Some of the more notable cases were *Credit Foncier Franco-Canadian v. Ross* ([1937] 2 WWR 353) and *I.O.F v. Leth. North. Irrig. Dist* ([1938] 2 WWR 194). In the area of divorce law, he held that adultery must be proved beyond a reasonable doubt, dissenting with the Court in *Molnar v. Molnar* ([1948] 2 WWR 1165). Harvey also departed from the English courts by allowing divorce to proceed even though the plaintiff failed to disclose her adultery in *Sherman v. King's Proctor* ([1936] 2 WWR 152). Many of Harvey's most notable judgments in real property involved interpretations of the *Dower Act* of 1917, which allowed a wife to nullify a sale of property by her husband if she did not consent, as in *Spooner v. Leyton* ([1939] 2WWR 237). In the law of torts, especially in liability and negligence, he contributed to many important case decisions. He kept a very tight view of the doctrine in *Rylands v. Fletcher*, holding that it did not apply in many cases, as in *Northwestern Utilities Ltd. v. London Guarantee and Accident Company* ([1935] 3 WWR 446). His judgments in negligence, however, demonstrated some of Harvey's willingness to shape the rules to fit the practicalities of the case and circumstance, as in *Edmonds v. Armstrong Funeral Home Ltd.* ([1930] 25 ALR 1st 173).

Perhaps the greatest challenges in Harvey's career developed out of the unique circumstances of a country at war. In April 1918, with Canada at war with the Central Powers in Europe, the government issued an Order in Council under the *War Measures Act* to remove exemptions from the *Military Service Act* of 1917. In *Re. Lewis* ([1918] 13 ALR 1st 411), the Court held, with Harvey dissenting, that there was no such power under the *War Measures Act*, and ordered the release of the farmer who had been seized by the local military

authority. The Dominion Cabinet then directed that the orders be implemented without regard to any Court decisions. Shortly afterwards, a conscript named Norton applied for his discharge from military custody in an application for a writ of *habeas corpus*, which the commanding officer at Sarcee Barracks, Lieutenant-Colonel Moore, refused to honour. The Cabinet ordered Moore to evade the writ, and his troops set up machine guns in front of his headquarters to ward off the sheriff. In *Re. Norton* ([1918] 2 WWR 865), the Court held that the writ must be served, and Harvey proclaimed that "the military authorities and the executive government have set at defiance the highest court in this province." The incident caused much dissention in Calgary, but in Harvey's mind, expediency was no substitute for rule of law. The issue was resolved the following week when, in *Re. Gray* ([1918] 57 SCR 150), the SCC held the Orders in Council valid. He also delivered judgments on the law of sedition during wartime. In *R. v. Felton* ([1915] 9 ALR 1st 238), he held that the Crown did not have to prove seditious intent on the part of a German native whose remarks demonstrated his loyalty to the enemy, but that it could be inferred from words and circumstances.

Harvey became embroiled in controversy when the SCA was organized into Appellate and Trial divisions in 1921. Named Chief Justice of the TD, he challenged the designation of his colleague on the AD, David Lynch Scott, as Chief Justice of Alberta. The question was resolved by the JCPC in 1924, in favour of Justice Scott. However, when Justice Scott died a few months later,

Harvey was appointed to replace him as Chief Justice of Alberta on the AD.

During his long term on the Alberta bench, Harvey served on a number of major provincial commissions, including: the Commission on the Alberta and Great Waterways Company (1910); the Royal Commission to Investigate an Agreement between the City of Calgary and the Calgary Natural Gas Company Ltd. (1919); an Inquiry into the McGillivray Creek Coal and Coke Company Ltd. explosion, Coleman, November 23, 1926 (1927); and the Commission regarding the Administration of Justice (1934).

Hetherington, Mary Margaret McCormick

District Court of Alberta, Calgary,
    December 21, 1978 - June 30, 1979
Court of Queen's Bench of Alberta,
    Calgary, June 30, 1979 - October 4,
    1985
Court of Appeal of Alberta, Calgary,
    October 4, 1985 -

The Honourable Justice Mary Margaret McCormick Hetherington was born on September 7, 1933, in Lacombe, Alberta, the daughter of local lawyer James Stewart McCormick. She graduated from Dalhousie University in 1963 and was admitted to the Alberta bar on September 10, 1964. She established her own criminal and family law practice in Calgary. In 1978, Hetherington became Calgary's first female judge when she was appointed to the DC. She was the first woman to be appointed to the CA of Alberta in 1985, and was also appointed Justice of the CANT in 1985.

Hetherington's opinions and judicial rationale are often contained within the body of the court's decisions. In decisions which she did write, she often holds to a formal interpretation of the statute, rules and admissibility of evidence. In *Ford Motor Company of Canada v. Davis* ([1981] 15 ALR 2d 327), for example, Hetherington held that, under the *Alberta Rules of Court*, the plaintiff was allowed to set up a right of property against the trustee in bankruptcy, and thus was entitled to possession. In *R. v. Adams and Lambretta* ([1987] 52 ALR 2d 369), she upheld an appeal of an accused charged with first-degree murder on the grounds that the admission into evidence of his statement regarding his involvement deprived him of a fair hearing. Hetherington held that the admission of incriminating evidence without legal counsel would bring the administration of justice into disrepute.

Holmes, Jack Kenneth

District Court of Alberta, Red Deer,
    April 8, 1976 - June 30, 1979
Court of Queen's Bench of Alberta,
    Calgary, Red Deer, June 30, 1979 -

The Honourable Justice Jack Kenneth Holmes was born in Ponoka, Alberta on January 2, 1928. He graduated from the University of Alberta with a B.A. and an LL.B. in 1951. He was admitted to the Alberta bar on June 23, 1952, and practiced in Red Deer with the firm of Holmes, Crowe, Power, and Johnston. He was named QC on December 31, 1975. Appointed to the District Court at Red Deer in 1976, Holmes was moved to Calgary in 1979 when he was appointed to the QB. He returned to the QB at Red Deer in 1984.

Holmes has had few published opinions in the case reports, and most of those have been in the area of oil and gas where he exhibited a knowledge and understanding of the case law. In *Bramalea Ltd. v. Amoco Canada Petroleum Co.* ([1987] 88 ALR 2d 317), the tenant's lease expired and during negotiations the rent was paid weekly. The landlord claimed a yearly tenancy, but Holmes ruled that the tenant continued in possession as a tenant at will. And, in *Huhn v. Dome Petroleum Ltd.* ([1988] 87 ALR 2d 45), Holmes went on record objecting to the procedure of the province's Surface Rights Board in allowing the defendant company access to the well site on the plaintiff's land.

Hope, John McIntosh

Supreme Court of Alberta, Trial Division, Edmonton, December 23, 1976 - June 30, 1979
Court of Queen's Bench of Alberta, Edmonton, June 30, 1979 - February 26, 1992
Supernumerary Justice, Edmonton, September 16, 1991 - February 26, 1992

The Honourable John McIntosh Hope was born in Edmonton, Alberta on July 25, 1921. Educated in Edmonton, he attended the University of Alberta where he received his B.A. in 1950, and his LL.B. in 1951. He was admitted to the Alberta bar on May 30, 1951. Hope was named QC on December 29, 1967. Practicing with the Edmonton firm of Milner and Steer, he was appointed to the bench at Edmonton in 1976. Hope retired in 1992.

Hope wrote several judgments in the areas of contract, damages, and the criminal law. In *Re. Berry* ([1983] 46 ALR 2d 137), a purchaser of property in Australia gave the vendor title deeds of properties in Alberta to sell and apply the proceeds to the new property just purchased. The sale fell through, the purchaser became bankrupt, and the trustee in bankruptcy claimed that the deposit of the title deeds was fraudulent. Hope dismissed the action, holding that the trustee no longer had any right to them. In *Dessureault v. Alberta Racing Commission et al.* ([1984] 49 ALR 2d 238), a harness racer and trainer's licence was revoked for alleged conduct prejudicial to horse racing. Hope allowed the plaintiff an injunction for an application of reinstatement on the grounds that he had been denied due process. In *Bergen v. Sturgeon General Hospital District* ([1984] 52 ALR 2d 161), a healthy, 25-year old woman was diagnosed with a pelvic inflammatory disease when she had acute appendicitis. She was transferred to another hospital for an emergency operation she did not survive. Hope gave judgment for damages against three doctors, two nurses, and the defendant hospital for negligence. In these and other cases, Hope prepared learned judgments which made a careful analysis of the evidence of each person and the case law.

Howson, William Robinson

Supreme Court of Alberta, Trial Division, Edmonton, March 2, 1936 - May 6, 1942

Supreme Court of Alberta, Appellate
Division, Edmonton, May 6, 1942 -
October 20, 1944
Supreme Court of Alberta, Trial
Division, Chief Justice, Edmonton,
October 20, 1944 - June 25, 1952

The Honourable William Robinson
Howson was born on a farm in
Norwood, Ontario, on March 6, 1883.
Educated in Norwood, Howson
taught high school at Mathers Cor-
ners near Peterborough, Ontario,
before becoming a bank clerk in 1906.
He was the youngest manager in
Canada working for the Sovereign
Bank of Stirling. Transferred to the
Bank of Montreal when it absorbed
Sovereign in 1908, Howson found
advancement slow there and moved
to Alberta in 1910. He worked as a bill
collector for an implement firm in
Segewick before moving to Calgary to
become a real estate agent. He then
went to Edmonton to enroll in the
University of Alberta, receiving his
B.A. in 1915 and his LL.B. in 1916. An
excellent scholar, he was elected to
almost every student organization in
his undergraduate career, and was
awarded the Gold Medal upon graduation. Howson articled with A.G.
MacKay before being admitted to the
Alberta bar on January 11, 1916. Enlisting in the Canadian Army in World
War I, he served as a Sergeant with the
Tank Corps in France for two years.
After the war, he became a member of
the firm of Parlee, Freeman and
Howson in Edmonton. Howson was
named KC on January 3, 1935. He was
with the Edmonton firm of Parlee and
Company when he was appointed to
the bench in 1936. Active in politics
since 1921, he became leader of the

Liberal Party in 1932. Howson favoured
a balanced budget, calling for an investigation into the province's tax system,
and spoke out against the U.F.A.'s
plans for nationalization. The U.F.A.
were defeated in 1935 and he was
elected an Edmonton MLA in 1935, but
his party lost badly to the Social Credit
Party. He resigned the following year
when called to the SCA. During World
War II, Howson presided at German
prisoner-of-war trials in Medicine
Hat. Afterwards, in 1948, he sat on the
Alberta Royal Commission inquiry
into the Child Welfare Department.
Throughout his life, he practiced
farming and horse-breeding on his
farm near Fort Saskatchewan. Ill for
some time in the 1940s, he died on June
25, 1952.

Howson judged a variety of cases,
but displayed a particular interest in
estate law and wills. While most of his
decisions reflect an adherence to a
strict interpretation of the law, he
always paid special attention to the
intentions and well-being of the parties. Thus, in *Lazaruk v. Exilian* ([1936]
1 WWR 667), he put aside some
Alberta savings certificates from an
estate because he found the intention
of their issue to be the creation of a
joint tenancy. In *S. v. S.* ([1941] 1 WWR
205), he gave the custody of a young
girl to her grandparents because he
found them more suitable than her
mother; and in *Sterling Shoes Ltd. v.
City of Calgary* ([1941] 1 WWR 72), he
found the city liable for damage to the
plaintiff's shoe stocks because of water seepage through a crack in the
sidewalk outside. Perhaps his most
celebrated case was *Borys v. Canadian
Pacific Railway Company* ([1951] 2 WWR
147), which turned on the right of the

CPR to enter and extract petroleum from a quarter section owned by the plaintiff. Finding for the plaintiff, he held that possessing "rights and minerals" did not mean that the Crown has the right to lease the surface of the land, and thus the CPR could not use the land without Borys' consent.

Hutchinson, Ernest Arthur

Court of Queen's Bench of Alberta, Calgary, September 30, 1985 -

The Honourable Justice Ernest Arthur Hutchinson was born in Calgary, Alberta, on April 12, 1929. He attended the University of Alberta, receiving his B.A. in 1951 and his LL.B. in 1952. He articled to Gordon Allen with the firm of Porter, Allen and MacKimmie before being admitted to the Alberta bar on June 19, 1953. Hutchinson practiced with Mac-Kimmie Matthews in Calgary from 1953-1985, where he conducted an extensive general practice covering commercial, corporate, banking, real estate and land development, wills, estates and trusts, and oil and gas law. He was named QC on December 19, 1974. Hutchinson was Chairman of the Special Advisory Committee on Bar Admissions in 1977, and a member of the University of Calgary's Faculty of Law Council, 1975-1980 and Development Committee, 1979-1981. He has been an occasional lecturer on ethics and professional development and responsibility at the University of Calgary Faculty of Law. Hutchinson was President of the Law Society of Alberta, 1984-1985, and Director, 1983-1985, and Vice-President, 1985, of the Federation of Law Societies of Canada.

Hyndman, James Duncan

Supreme Court of Alberta, Edmonton, July 11, 1914 - September 15, 1921
Supreme Court of Alberta, Appellate Division, Edmonton, September 15, 1921 - January 15, 1931

The Honourable James Duncan Hyndman was born in Charlottetown, Prince Edward Island, on July 28, 1874. He was educated at Prince of Wales College and articled with Angus McLean, who was member of Parliament for Queen's in Prince Edward Island. He was called to the Prince Edward Island bar in 1899. In the same year, Hyndman moved to western Canada, settling in Portage La Prairie, Manitoba, where he practiced for four years with his uncle in the firm of McDonald and Hyndman. Married in 1902, his wife Ethel's father, Sir Louis Davies, was a Premier and later Chief Justice of Prince Edward Island. He came to Alberta in 1903. After being admitted to the North-West Territories bar on June 30, 1903, he became a partner in the Edmonton firm of Kennedy and Hyndman. Hyndman ran as a Conservative for a federal seat in the election of 1906, and a provincial seat in the election of 1913, losing both times. He was, however, elected Alderman on Edmonton City Council from 1910 to 1911. Hyndman was the youngest judge appointed to the SC in 1914. After his retirement on January 15, 1931, he became President of the Pension Appeal Court in Ottawa, Ontario until 1940. From 1940 to 1942, he served as the Federal Rent

Controller and from 1951 to 1954, he served as Deputy Judge of the Exchequer Court of Canada, as well as Chairman of the War Claims Commission. In the 1950s, Justice Hyndman was the Chairman of the *Great Lakes Security Act*. From 1961 to 1962, he was an advisor to the Finance Minister on retribution to Japanese Canadian citizens who were interned during World War II. In addition, Hyndman remained active in the financial world, becoming Vice-President of the Northwest Mortgage Corporation, and Director of the Edmonton Mortgage Company and the Dawson Coal Company. A Presbyterian, he was also a member of the Masonic Lodge, and participated in the Edmonton, Ranchmen's, and Canadian Clubs. In Ottawa, he was Reeve of Rockcliff and active in official and social circles. Hyndman was made a Commander of the Order of the British Empire in 1948. He died in Ottawa on October 11, 1971.

Hyndman, sitting largely on appeals, gave many decisions in the areas of criminal law, contracts, and mortgages. Sitting on appeal for the murder verdict in the famous case of *R. v. Picariello and Lassandro* ([1923] 1 WWR 644, 1489), he showed himself a staunch advocate of the death penalty for the murder of police officers. In *R. v. Rose* ([1918] 3 WWR 950), one of the major test cases for prohibition legislation, he upheld the *Liquor Act* but delivered, with comic eloquence, a speech on the folly of attempts to regulate social morality. His most important decisions were on the development of mortgage law in the province, where he penned a number of precedent cases.

In *Royal Trust Company v. Fraser et al.* ([1917] 12 ALR 1st 109), a volunteer died in May 1915 before the *Volunteers and Reservists Relief Act* came into force, leaving the mortgage on his estate without protection. Master in Chambers C.F. Clarry allowed the extension, but Hyndman denied it on appeal, ruling on the technicalities of the Act. *Crump et al. v. McNeill et al.* ([1918] 14 ALR 1st 206) was a complicated case involving a purchaser, subpurchaser, and vendor of a mortgaged property that contained significant coal reserves leased from the CPR. Hyndman prepared a judgment rich in English and Canadian legal sources to hold that the purchasers' agreement for the sale was good; since the vendor could not give title to the coal under the surface of the land, the purchasers were entitled to compensation.

Irving, Howard Lawrence

Court of Appeal of Alberta,
    Edmonton, February 15, 1985 -
Supernumerary Justice, Edmonton,
    April 28, 1995 -

The Honourable Justice Howard Lawrence Irving was born in Edmonton, Alberta, on December 28, 1924. He was educated at the University of Alberta, where he received his B.A. in 1948, and his LL.B. in 1951. He was admitted to the Alberta bar on May 27, 1952. Irving was practicing as a senior partner with the firm of Parlee Irving when he was appointed to the bench in 1985. He was named QC on December 30, 1965. His thirty-three years at the bar involved him in many important cases, and he often appeared before Courts, Tribunals, or Royal Commissions on behalf of the Government of Alberta. Irving has also served as Justice of the CANT since 1988.

Serving exclusively on the CA, Irving authored a number of reported decisions on cases ranging from constitutional and criminal law to contracts. Most of these decisions were delivered alongside those of his colleagues on the bench. In one of his first written judgments, *R. v. Plato* ([1985] 40 ALR 2d 200), he quashed a conviction for second degree murder where a juror was discharged with consent of counsel before the charge was given to the jury. Irving held that the Court had no jurisdiction to vary the number of jurors before a trial began, and ordered a new trial. In *Foundation Company of Canada Ltd. v. R. in Right of Alberta and Minister of Public Works* ([1986] 45 ALR 2d 77), a contractor claimed an equitable adjustment for extra costs due to delays caused by soil conditions different from those given in a soils report. The amount of additional costs given was adjusted partially according to the terms of equity. In *Winterhaven Stables Ltd. v. Attorney General of Canada* ([1988] 62 ALR 2d 266), the plaintiff sought a declaration that the various federal tax, education, and health acts were a system of direct taxation for provincial purposes and thus *ultra vires*. The appeal was dismissed, Irving holding that the plaintiff lacked standing to bring such an action. Irving's judgments were clearly written and succinct, and he did not hesitate to dissent when he disagreed.

Ives, William Carlos

Supreme Court of Alberta, Calgary, July 11, 1914 - September 15, 1921
Supreme Court of Alberta, Trial Division, Calgary, September 15, 1921 - August 16, 1944
Supreme Court of Alberta, Trial Division, Chief Justice, Calgary, September 25, 1942 - August 16, 1944

The Honourable William Carlos Ives was born in Compton, Quebec on October 29, 1873. Known as the "cowboy judge", he came to western Canada with his parents to a ranch near Pincher Creek in 1881. His father George was an original member of the NWMP in 1879. Ives left the family ranch at age fourteen to work as a cowhand. By age seventeen he was working the Cochrane Ranch, running over 1500 head of cattle. Saving his wages, he left Cochrane in 1894 on a train load shipment of cattle to Quebec. He stayed in Quebec to attend Coaticook College, and spent his summer vacations in Alberta. Ives earned his LL.B. at McGill University in 1899. After articling for the Montreal firm of Foster, Martin and Girouard, he was called to the Quebec bar in 1900 and practiced in Montreal for two years. He returned to the west and was admitted to the bar of the North-West Territories on March 14, 1901. Until 1906, he was a member of the firm of Conybeare and Ives in Lethbridge, Alberta. He then practiced on his own until his appointment to the bench in 1914. A prominent Conservative, he was defeated at Lethbridge in the federal elections of 1905 and 1909. After his retirement from the bench on August

16, 1944, Ives served as Chairman of the Salaries Control Advisory Committee, and the Royal Commission on Taxation of Annuities and Family Corporations in Ottawa. He also served on several labour-management arbitration boards. Ives created a family dynasty that intermingled with some of Calgary's most prominent and historical families. He and his wife Millicent May Troull had two children, Bill and Elizabeth. Their daughter married the son of Senator Pat Burns, Alberta's "Cattle King", and his sister married E.P. McNeill, a Macleod lawyer who joined Ives on the bench. An Anglican and Freemason, Ives died in Calgary during the annual Calgary Stampede on July 10, 1950. His ashes were scattered at the roundup camp on Spring Hill at the Cochrane Ranch.

Appointed to the TD at Calgary in 1921, Ives was well known on the bench for his placid demeanour. His colleagues referred to his sphinx-like "poker face." He never interrupted counsel, and rarely uttered a word during a trial except for the occasional injection of dry humour. He listened so carefully to the arguments that counsel seldom knew how he would rule on a case. When he made a judgment, however, it would be strong and decisive. Ives' written judgments were short and to the point. He rarely reserved cases, and considered that if a lawyer brought more than two law books into court his case must be weak. Noted for his impartialality, he was criticized at times for assisting young, inexperienced lawyers in the courtroom. In the end, his strength as a judge was his ability to assess human nature and the char-

acter of the parties and the witnesses. Ives adjudicated a number of celebrated cases, including *MacMillan v. Brownlee* ([1934] 2 WWR 511) in which Ives took the unprecedented step of reversing the jury's decision awarding a judgment of $15,000 against former Alberta Premier John E. Brownlee, who was accused of seducing Vivian MacMillan, a young women who worked in the government offices. While the jury found MacMillan's story convincing, Ives overturned their verdict on the grounds that she suffered no injuries - a requirement for a tort based on seduction. His decision to overturn a jury verdict was controversial, and the jury findings were eventually restored by the SCC. While some contemporaries believed that MacMillan was "set up" by the Liberals as a conspiracy to disgrace the Premier, Ives gave a conscientious decision based on the admissible evidence.

Another infamous case was *Powlett and Powlett v. The University of Alberta* ([1934] 3 WWR 322), in which a University of Alberta student suffered a breakdown after a brutal hazing ritual. Ives, who lost his own son in a suicide during the trial, awarded judgment for the Powlett family and damages of $40,000. Finally, *R. v. Solloway* and *R. v. Mills* ([1930] 1 WWR 486, 779) was one of the most debated trials in the province's history. The defendants were Ontario brokers who ran stock broker "bucket shops" across the country. They went short on shares of stock which they sold to customers for purchases which were not made and were convicted on four counts of conspiracy, fined $275,000, and sentenced to four months hard labour.

Jackson, John Ainslie

District Court of Lethbridge,
    Lethbridge, March 19, 1913 -
    August 3, 1935
District Court of Southern Alberta,
    Lethbridge, August 3, 1935 -
    October 2, 1945

His Honour John Ainslie Jackson was born in Seaforth, Ontario, on March 25, 1875. He received his B.A. from the University of Toronto in 1897 and his LL.B. at Osgoode Hall in 1900. He practiced in Blyth, Ontario until 1903 before moving to Ponoka, Alberta. He was admitted to the NWT bar on July 30, 1903 and practiced in Ponoka for ten years before his appointment to the DC at Lethbridge in 1913. A well-known sports enthusiast and former President of the Amateur Athletic Union, Jackson attended the Olympic Games in Paris, Los Angeles and Berlin. Following the Berlin Games in 1936, where he saw Hitler, Jackson returned to Canada convinced the Nazis were preparing for war and said so bluntly in many of his addresses. A prominent and popular figure in the Lethbridge legal community, Jackson retired on October 2, 1945, after thirty-two years on the bench. He died in Lethbridge on October 1, 1951.

Jennison, John Leslie

District Court of Calgary, Calgary,
    November 19, 1915 - December 1,
    1919

His Honour John Leslie Jennison was born in 1851 in Walton, Hants County, Nova Scotia, and was edu-cated at Dalhousie University. After being admitted to the Nova Scotia bar in 1883, Jennison practised in New Glasgow, where he remained for twenty-eight years. He served as Chairman of the School Board for three years and was elected Mayor of the town in 1892. He was named KC in 1907. Jennison came to Alberta in 1911, was admitted to the Alberta bar on February 2, and settled in Calgary where he formed a partnership with K.G. Craig. He remained with Craig until his appointment to the DC at Calgary in 1915. Jennison served one term as an Alderman on Calgary City Council, 1914-1915. In 1912, he became a member of the Archaeological Institute of America in Washington, D.C. He died in Calgary on December 1, 1919.

Johnson, Horace Gilchrist

Supreme Court of Alberta,
    Appellate Division, Edmonton,
    December 16, 1954 - December
    20, 1973

The Honourable Horace Gilchrist Johnson was born in Medonte Township, Simcoe County, Ontario, on January 1, 1899. Attending public and high school in Orillia, Ontario, he received his LL.B. from the University of Alberta in 1929. He was admitted to the Alberta bar on March 15, 1929. Johnson practiced law in Edmonton with the firm of Short and Cross until his appointment to the bench in 1954. He was named QC on December 30, 1949. Johnson also worked as a part-time Lecturer in law and commerce at the University of Alberta Faculty of Law. A devout member of the United

Church, he was a Freemason, and served on the Edmonton Library Board. In addition to serving on the Alberta bench, Johnson was a Justice of the CANT, 1967-1973. He retired on December 20, 1973, and died in Honolulu on March 13, 1982.

Johnson was one of the intellectuals of the court. His judgments dealt with a wide range of topics and were often accepted by the majority of the court. However, he also wrote some long and detailed dissenting opinions. One of the hallmarks of his judicial career was that he usually wrote his own opinion regardless of the opinion of the Court. Johnson's most extensive judgments involved commerce, administrative law, and wills and estates. He was primarily concerned in these judgments to establish and develop precedents. For example, in *R. v. Horban* ([1960] 31 WWR 139), Johnson established that the mere presence of the accused at the scene of a crime while failing to protest or leave the scene was not in itself evidence from which aiding and abetting could be inferred. Perhaps his most famous case, however, was his involvement in *R. v. Drybones* ([1967] 61 WWR 370), which involved a native man, Joseph Drybones, who was convicted of being intoxicated off of a reserve contrary to the *Indian Act*. Territorial Judge William Morrow overturned the decision, ruling that the Act was discriminatory according to the newly-passed *Canadian Bill of Rights*. The Crown appealed, sending the case to the CANT, where Johnson upheld Morrow's ruling, opining that the section of the Act was invalid. The Crown then took the case to the SCC, where Johnson's decision was upheld.

A quiet man, he went about his work with little fanfare and left a reputation as one of the most analytic and thoughtful judges of his era.

Johnstone, Thomas Cooke

Supreme Court of the North-West
     Territories, District of Western
     Assiniboia, Regina, October 8,
     1906 - September 16, 1907

The Honourable Justice Thomas Cooke Johnstone was born and educated in Ontario. He was called to the Ontario Bar in 1876 and he practiced in Toronto before going west to Regina where he was admitted as on one of the first advocates of the NWT bar on January 11, 1886. Prior to his appointment to the bench in 1906, Johnstone practiced in Regina for many years, serving as City Solicitor and Crown Prosecutor. As DC judge for Western Assiniboia, NWT, his jurisdiction covered the extreme southeastern section of what is now Alberta. When the SCNWT was divided between Alberta and Saskatchewan in 1902, Johnstone became Justice of the Supreme Court of Saskatchewan. He retired on November 29, 1913 and died on May 20, 1917.

Kane, Edward William Scott

Supreme Court of Canada, Appellate
     Division, Edmonton, March 1,
     1961 - April 29, 1974

The Honourable Edward William Scott Kane was born in Belfast, Northern Ireland on April 28, 1899, and came to Canada as an infant. He attended the University of Alberta, receiving his B.A. in 1920, and his LL.B. in 1921. Admitted to the Alberta bar on June 24, 1922, Kane began a long and successful practice in Edmonton. He was with the firm of Kane, Hurlburt and Kane when he was appointed to the SCC in 1961. Kane was named KC on December 10, 1943. He was a specialist in commercial law, particularly the commercial statutes unique to Alberta. He served as Secretary-Treasurer of the Law Society of Alberta from 1938 to 1952. Kane was appointed to the CANT, 1971-1973. Kane retired on April 29, 1974, and died on November 1, 1992.

Few of Kane's decisions were published in the law reports. He outlined the evidence presented in a case, summarized it, and gave his decision on the facts without citing case law, statutes, or extraneous matters. Most of his reported cases also concerned motor vehicle accidents. For example, in *R. v. Devlyn Corporation Limited* ([1969] 70 WWR 691), in a stated case he restored the original conviction based simply on an analysis of the evidence presented. In a different matter, however, *Re. Connor Estate* ([1970] 72 WWR 388), he dissented from Justice Sinclair's decision on the gift of an estate. The testatrix left the residue of her estate to be divided among her close friends as the trustee would determine at the time. While Sinclair allowed this, Kane held that the words were not sufficiently clear to allow such a disposition.

Kerans, Roger Philip

District Court of Northern Alberta, Edmonton, February 12, 1970 - October 1, 1975

District Court of Alberta, Edmonton, October 1, 1975 - June 30, 1979
District Court of Alberta, Associate Chief Judge, Edmonton, December 19, 1975 - June 30, 1979
Court of Queen's Bench of Alberta, Edmonton, June 30, 1979 - October 23, 1980
Court of Appeal of Alberta, Calgary, October 23, 1980 -

The Honourable Justice Roger Philip Kerans was born in Lashburn, Saskatchewan, on January 6, 1934. Although his early education was interrupted for one year by an attack of poliomyelitis, he went on to attend the University of Alberta with an academic scholarship from the City of Edmonton, and earned a B.A. in 1954 and an LL.B. in 1957. He was admitted to the Alberta bar on June 27, 1957, and the Yukon Territory bar in 1960. Prior to his appointment to the DC at Edmonton in 1970, Kerans practiced in Edmonton with Dantzer, Trofimuk, Kerans and Cristall. Active in community affairs, Kerans served as a Director of the Edmonton Symphony Society, the Catholic Indian and Metis Service, and the Edmonton Native Friendship Centre. At the age of thirty-six, Kerans was the youngest member to be appointed to the DC in Alberta. Kerans was also appointed Deputy Judge of the SCYT in 1975 and to the CANT in 1980.

Kerans' judicial decisions, especially as an Appeal Court judge, have had a profound influence on social, economic, and legal aspects of society in Alberta. In criminal matters, he has articulated a certain tolerance of police activities which, when deemed justifiable and admissible, enable the ends of justice to be met. In other instances, he has required the strictest application of the rule of law when measuring the weight of evidence. Frequently he speaks on the behalf of the Appeal Court. But while he is a judicial activist, his approach is formalistic. His *ratio decidendi* is supported by numerous precedents which he uses actively to mold the law into further precedents. In the end, some of his precedents have gained currency second only to the SCC.

In *McCulloch et al. v. Gazelle* ([1980] 14 ALR 2d 193), the plaintiffs were allowed to recover when the defendant wrongfully repudiated the contract, forcing them to resell and liquidate at a lower price. In *Black v. Law Society of Alberta* ([1986] 22 ALR 2d 1), Kerans applied the *Charter of Rights* to legal practice in Alberta. He held that the rules of the Law Society of Alberta prohibiting Ontario lawyers from becoming non-resident lawyers in Alberta and entering into partnership with plaintiffs who were resident Alberta members denied them mobility rights; the Society's rules were declared invalid. In *R. v. Horseman* ([1993] 8 ALR 3d 354), Kerans cited on behalf of the Court the "merger and consolidation theory" concerning Aboriginal treaty rights holding that First Nations do not have an unrestricted right to hunt and fish for food on private lands, upholding a conviction at the lower court for breaching the Alberta *Wildlife Act*. Lastly, in *R. v. Ryan Jason Love* ([1995] 36 ALR 3d 153), two undercover officers posed as criminals to befriend and entrap the defendant into having a hair sample pulled for a DNA analysis for blood found in a mur-

der victim's vehicle. Kerans, ruling with Conrad and Harradence, dismissed the appeal of the defendant who claimed unlawful search and seizure. Kerans argued that the exclusion of such evidence with a consequent acquittal would bring the criminal justice system into disrepute.

Kerr, Stanley Chandos Staveley

District Court of Northern Alberta, Edmonton, February 5, 1947 - May 19, 1953

District Court of Northern Alberta, Chief Judge, September 13, 1949 - May 19, 1953

His Honour Justice Stanley Chandos Staveley Kerr was born in Toronto, Ontario, on April 6, 1889. Educated at Upper Canada College, the University of Toronto, and Osgoode Hall in Toronto, he received his B.A. in 1911 and his LL.B. in 1916. He articled with his father before being called to the Ontario bar in 1914. Kerr came to Alberta in 1919, and was admitted to the Alberta bar on February 24, 1920. From 1920 to 1924, he practiced with the Edmonton firm of Short and Cross, and from 1924 to 1933 he was a member of the firm of Tighe and Kerr. In 1933, Kerr established the firm of Kerr, Dyde and Becker where he remained until his appointment to the DC at Edmonton in 1947. Kerr had a long and distinguished military career, and was particularly active in organizations promoting the welfare of war veterans. He had an interest in politics, and from 1929 until 1935 he served as Secretary of the Edmonton West Liberal Association. He was named KC on June 23, 1936. Kerr died in Edmonton on May 19, 1953.

Kidd, James George

District Court of Southern Alberta, Calgary, October 31, 1968 - October 1, 1975

District Court of Alberta, Calgary, October 1, 1975 - June 30, 1979

Court of Queen's Bench of Alberta, Calgary, June 30, 1979 - April 4, 1985

Supernumerary Justice, Calgary, November 1, 1983 - April 4, 1985

The Honourable James George Kidd was born on June 26, 1914. He was admitted to the Alberta bar on July 12, 1939. After serving with the Canadian forces in World War II, Kidd returned to Canada in 1945, and began a law practice in Medicine Hat. He often served as Crown prosecutor in criminal cases there and was named QC on December 31, 1955. Kidd maintained his practice at Medicine Hat until his appointment to the DC at Calgary in 1968. Appointed to the QB in 1979, he took a particular interest in criminal cases. Kidd died on April 4, 1985.

Kirby, William John Cameron

Supreme Court of Alberta, Trial Division, Calgary, October 18, 1960 - June 30, 1979

Court of Queen's Bench of Alberta, Calgary, June 30, 1979 - January 12, 1984

The Honourable William John Cameron Kirby was born in Calgary, Alberta, on January 9, 1909. His father was Postmaster at Rocky Mountain House, and Kirby was educated there and at Hanna. He attended the University of British Columbia, where he received a B.A. in 1930, and the University of Alberta, where he obtained a Teaching Certificate in 1932. He taught school at Hussar and Okotoks, Alberta, for six years before returning to the University of British Columbia to receive his LL.B. in 1941. After articling with Dugald Donaghy in Vancouver, he was admitted to the British Columbia bar in 1943. He then left to serve in World War II with the Canadian Army and by war's end he was a legal officer at the Pacific Command Headquarters, Victoria. Moving to Alberta, he was admitted to the bar on December 18, 1945. Kirby settled in Red Deer where he practiced for the next fifteen years. An active Conservative, he won the 1954 provincial by-election in Red Deer, but was defeated in the election of 1958. He was elected leader of the provincial Conservative Party that year but resigned in 1959. Kirby was with the firm of Kirby, Murphy, Armstrong and Beames prior to his appointment to the bench at Calgary in 1960. He was named QC on December 30, 1983, and retired on January 12, 1984.

As a judge, Kirby wrote many judgments in the civil law area, and particularly a number of damage awards for negligence. In *Lyster v. Fortress Mountain Resorts Ltd.* ([1979] 13 ALR 2d 162), Kirby awarded damages against the defendant company for improper maintenance of a ski lift when a cable broke causing an injury to a skier on the T-Bar. In *Macdonald v. Zetaulk* ([1979] 13 ALR 2d 321), he upheld a generous settlement against a driver who caused an accident by his excessive speed; and in *Kinnon's Estate v. Traynor and Pole* ([1983] 46 ALR 2d 75), he found the defendant guilty of negligence causing the death of a fifteen-year old girl, and awarded her family damages for the loss of her life expectancy. In these, and other decisions, Kirby displayed a genuine compassion for the victims of negligent acts, and did not hesitate to award generous settlements against those at fault. One of the highlights of his judicial career was the provincial commission he headed in 1976 to complete a review of the Provincial Courts of Alberta. His report served as background for the eventual amalgamation of the DC and SCA in 1979.

Kryczka, Joseph Julius

Court of Queen's Bench of Alberta, Calgary, July 3, 1980 - January 11, 1991

The Honourable Joseph Julius Kryczka was born in Coleman, Alberta, on June 4, 1935. He attended the University of Alberta, earning a B.A. in 1957 and an LL.B. in 1958. He articled in Calgary under David Clifton Prowse before being admitted to the Alberta bar on June 4, 1959. Kryczka practiced with Mason and Company in Calgary prior to his appointment to the bench in 1980. He was named QC on January 26, 1976. Kryczka was Chairman and Chief Negotiating Officer of the Canadian-Soviet Hockey Series in 1972. In 1990, he was inducted into the Alberta and Canadian Sports Halls of Fame for his active role in promoting the 1988 Winter Olympics. Kryczka died on January 11, 1991.

Kryczka contributed several published decisions in the QB, most of which were concerned with business law, insurance, mortgages, and taxes. In *Schmidt and Schmidt v. Aetna Casualty Company of Canada and Edelson Leipsic Insurance Ltd.* ([1982] 20 ALR 2d 307), the plaintiff homeowners appealed to recover under a fire insurance policy that had been ruled invalid. Kryczka held that since they failed to disclose that the primary purpose of their dwelling was to have a commercial taxidermy operation in the garage, they were guilty of misrepresentation. In *Aydelotte et al. v. Security Pacific National Bank et al.* ([1987] 55 ALR 2d 248), he limited the liability of the general partner selling assets to a purchaser to make a similar offer to the limited partners. In many cases such as these, Kryczka used primarily older authorities to continue the received view of case doctrine on such matters.

Laycraft, James Herbert

Supreme Court of Alberta, Calgary, Trial Division, July 31, 1975 - March 26, 1979

Supreme Court, Appellate Division, Calgary, March 26, 1979 - June 30, 1979

Court of Appeal of Alberta, Calgary, June 30, 1979 - December 31, 1991

Chief Justice of Alberta, Calgary, February 20, 1985 - December 31, 1991

The Honourable James Herbert Laycraft was born in Veteran, Alberta, on January 5, 1924, and was raised and educated in High River. He worked for the *High River Times* while in high school, and joined the Canadian Army in 1941 at the age of seventeen. Spending one year at Queen's University on a radar course, he served abroad with the Royal Canadian Artillery in Australia in World War II. Returning from the war, Laycraft attended the University of Alberta, where he received his B.A. in 1950 and his LL.B. in 1951. He articled with E.J. Chambers, and was admitted to the Alberta bar on June 4, 1952. Laycraft became a member of the Calgary firm of Nolan, Chambers, Might, Saucier and Peacock. A talented litigator, he was involved in the last Canadian appeal to the JCPC in Great Britain in 1959. He worked with Harry Nolan, QC on two landmark land registration and mineral rights cases: *Borys v. Canadian Pacific Railway Company* ([1951] 2 WWR 147) and *Turta v. Canadian Pacific Railway Company* ([1953] 5 WWR 529). Laycraft was appointed QC on December 30, 1963, and was practicing in Calgary with the firm of Jones, Black and Company when he was appointed to the bench in 1975. Laycraft was also appointed to the CANT, 1979-1991. He became Chief Justice of Alberta in 1985 and retired on December 31, 1991.

Laycraft stands out as a formidable and prolific judicial mind, thorough and analytical in his judgments. His judgments cover the areas of real estate law, contracts, torts, criminal law, administrative law, and later, constitutional law. Many of his TD cases are reported, including *Price v. Materials Testing Laboratories, Ltd.* ([1976] 5 WWR 280), in which he upheld *Jellett v. Wilkie* as a valid rule in Alberta land registration, and *Re: Civil Service Assn. and Alberta Human Rights Commission*

([1975] 62 DLR (3d) 531), where he dismissed a *mandamus* application regarding investigative procedures of the Alberta Human Rights Commission. He chaired an Alberta Commission of Inquiry in Edmonton into activities of the midway and carnival operator Royal American Shows, Inc. in 1977, along the way ruling that wire tap evidence collected by the police was admissible.

On the CA, Laycraft wrote for many of the court's decisions. In an early appeal decision in 1980, Laycraft delivered an important ruling on affirmative action, deciding in *Athabasca Tribal Council v. Amoco Canadian Petroleum Ltd.* ([1980] 5 WWR 165) that the province's *Individual's Rights Protection Act* did not bar such employment policies. In *R. v. Guthrie* ([1982] 21 ALR 2d 1), Laycraft contributed to refining the precedent set in the SCC on the right of the accused to remain silent. He helped the SCA to reverse a conviction for the obstruction of justice in exploring the grounds on which the accused may remain silent. In *R. v. Big M Drug Mart* ([1984] 1 WWR 625), Laycraft held *ultra vires* the *Lord's Day Act* prohibiting commerce on Sundays and the judgment was upheld by the SCC. In *Smale v. Wintemute* ([1986] 1 WWR 268), he upheld the constitutionality of the College of Physicians and Surgeons' power to assess and restrict extra billing by doctors.

Lees, William Andrew Dickson

District Court of Wetaskiwin, Wetaskiwin, July 6, 1909 - August 27, 1934

His Honour William Andrew Dickson Lees was born in Ottawa, Ontario, on August 27, 1859. Educated at the Ottawa Collegiate Institute, Lees attended the University of Toronto and Osgoode Hall Law School, where he received his LL.B. in 1883. He articled with his father's firm of Lees and Gimmet in Ottawa before being called to the Ontario bar in 1893. Lees practiced in Ottawa with Lees, Kehoe and Hall until coming to Alberta in 1904. He was admitted to the North-West Territories bar on February 5, 1904. He practiced law at Fort Saskatchewan alone and in association with W.M. Corbett until his appointment to the DC in 1909 at Fort Saskatchewan. Justice Lees' interest in agricultural issues and his position as a successful farmer made him particularly fitted to preside over courts in farming communities. He resigned on August 27, 1934, and died in Wetaskiwin on November 10, 1941.

Legg, Sidney Vincent

District Court of Northern Alberta, Edmonton, December 22, 1965 - October 1, 1975
District Court of Alberta, Edmonton, October 1, 1975 - June 30, 1979
Court of Queen's Bench of Alberta, Edmonton, June 30, 1979 - September 22, 1992
Supernumerary Justice, Edmonton, August 1, 1983 - September 22, 1992

The Honourable Sidney Vincent Legg was born in Calgary on July 23, 1918. He attended the University of Alberta, where he received his B.A. in 1941, and his LL.B. in 1942. Legg en-listed in the Canadian Army during World War II and attained the rank of Captain before being discharged in 1945. Legg was admitted to the Alberta bar on June 23, 1947, and he practiced in Stettler, with the firm of Legg & Sloan until 1959. In 1959, he was appointed Magistrate of the RCMP Police Court in Edmonton, where he remained until 1962. From 1962 to 1965, he was a Police Magistrate for the City of Edmonton. Legg was involved in many community service groups and activities. He also served as Chairman of the Law Enforcement Review Board. Legg died in Edmonton on September 22, 1992.

Legg's decisions were widely regarded as exceptionally fair. Most of his reported judgments involved both criminal and civil law, some precedent-setting. Two of his more notable criminal cases dealt with interpretations of obscene material. In *R. v. Pipeline News Alta.* ([1972] 1 WWR 241), Legg ruled that public opinion surveys had no weight in judging obscenity and according to his view of public tolerance the materials seized by the Crown were obscene. Later, in *R. v. Coles Book Stores Ltd.* ([1974] 6 WWR 404), he found *The Joy of Sex* not to be obscene. In a number of civil cases, Legg used English precedents to interpret the rules of contract law. In *Fayad and Fayad v. Pacula and Pacula* ([1974] 2 WWR 446), he held that contracts are unenforceable if any of the terms are uncertain.

Lieberman, Samuel Sereth

District Court of Northern Alberta, Edmonton, November 1, 1966 - February 12, 1970

Supreme Court of Alberta, Trial
    Division, Edmonton, February 12,
    1970 - December 23, 1976
Supreme Court of Alberta, Appellate
    Division, Edmonton, December 23,
    1976 - June 30, 1979
Court of Appeal of Alberta,
    Edmonton, June 30, 1979 -
Supernumerary Justice, Edmonton,
    April 15, 1987 -

The Honourable Justice Samuel
Sereth Lieberman was born in Edmonton, Alberta, on April 14, 1922.
He enrolled at the University of Alberta in 1939, but he left a year later at
the outbreak of World War II and
enlisted in the Royal Canadian Air
Force. Lieberman completed two tours
of duty as a pilot in the Royal Air
Force Coastal Command in England,
the Mediterranean, and the Middle
East. He attained the rank of Squadron Leader at the age of twenty-two.
Returning to the University of Alberta, Lieberman received his B.A. in
1947 and his LL.B. in 1948. After
articling with his father M.I. Lieberman
in Edmonton, he was admitted to the
Alberta bar on August 10, 1949. He
was named QC on December 31, 1961.
When he was appointed to the DC in
1966, Lieberman was a partner in the
Edmonton firm of Friedman,
Lieberman and Newson, where he
specialized in negligence insurance
law. Lieberman was the first Chairman of both the Legal Aid Society of
Alberta and the Alberta Board of
Review. As a Supreme Court justice,
Lieberman was Chairman of the
Alberta Boundaries Commission in
1970. In addition to serving on the
Alberta bench, Lieberman was also
appointed to the CANT in 1976. He

received an honorary LL.D. from the
University of Alberta in 1990.

Lieberman presided over many
criminal jury cases in the 1970s and
1980s ranging from murder to rape
and buggery. He also delivered
many critical decisions and precedents
on civil cases, especially regarding the
legal profession. In *Fraser v. Sykes*
({1971] 1 WWR 246), Liberman held
that the defendant, the Mayor of
Calgary, had publicly defamed the
plaintiff, a prominent Calgary lawyer
in a city development dispute. In *Con-
tinental Insurance Company v. Law Society of Alberta* ([1984] 56 ALR 2d 98), an
underwriter issued a bond making it
liable for claims against the Law
Society's insurance fund. The QB upheld the liability limited to each lawyer's claim, and the Court of Appeal concurred. Lieberman's judgment involved a cogent discussion of
case law and jurisprudence to support the Court's decision. *Royal Trust
et al. v. Law Society of Alberta* ([1985] 66
ALR 2d 76) concerned the legality of
the Law Society amending the Rules
of Professional Conduct to prohibit
members and their clients from
depositing more than $60,000 in trust
to individual trust companies or
using other financial companies. In a
suit brought by four trust and
mortgage companies, the QB held the
amendments *ultra vires*, and the Law
Society's appeal was dismissed.
Lieberman, writing for the Court of
Appeal, held that the Benchers had no
such authority to restrict the financial arrangements of their
members. As in his judgments,
Lieberman adhered rigorously to the
letter of the law and massed his sources
to give incontrovertible decisions.

Lomas, Melvin Earl

Court of Queen's Bench of Alberta,
    Calgary, April 28, 1981 -
Supernumerary Justice, Calgary, June
    20, 1996 -

The Honourable Justice Melvin Earl
Lomas was born on April 27, 1930. He
was admitted to the Alberta bar on
June 7, 1954, and was named QC on
December 19, 1973. Prior to his appointment to the bench in 1981, Lomas
practiced with the Calgary firm of
Macleod Dixon. In addition to the
Alberta bench, Lomas was also appointed Deputy Judge of the SCYT in
1982 and Deputy Judge of the SCNT
in 1989.

Few of Lomas' decisions were published in the law reports, and most of
those involved contracts. For example, in *Condev Project Planning Ltd. v.
Kramer Auto Sales Ltd.* ([1982] 18 ALR
2d 107), the defendant tenant was in
arrears for three years in monthly payments of electric power bills. Holding
for the builder-developer, Lomas explored a large number of leases in
English and Canadian case law to rule
for the plaintiff. In *First National Bank
of Oregon v. A.H. Watson Ranching Ltd.,
Thompson and Lyons* ([1985] 34 ALR 2d
110), an exchange rate from U.S. to
Canadian funds for converting a debt
owed in a promissory note for buying
cattle in California was at issue. Lomas
wrote a long judgment based on U.S.
and Canadian precedents for resolv-
ing exchange rate conflicts, including
treatises and legal texts on bills of
exchange. He also described the whole
story of the transaction. Lomas used a
similar method in his judgment for
McCaghren v. Lindsay ([1982] 17 ALR

2d 323). This was a petition to dismiss
an elected Cochrane Councillor for allegedly using his influence with the
Municipal Planning Commission for
one of his company's buildings. Lomas
searched the case law across the country for similar petitions, and rejected
this one because the original contract
was obtained before the defendant's
election.

Lunney, Henry William

Supreme Court of Alberta, Appellate
    Division, Calgary, May 23, 1928 -
    October 6, 1944

Born in Saint John's, New Brunswick in 1885, the Honourable Henry
William Lunney was educated at the
University of New Brunswick. He
graduated with a B.A. in 1906. In 1909,
he graduated from King's College with
a degree in Civil Law and was admitted to the bar of New Brunswick in
1910. He was a newspaper reporter in
St. John's and became a member of
the editorial staff of *The Montreal Star.*
Lunney came to Calgary in 1911 and
joined the staff of *The Calgary News
Telegram*. He was admitted to the Alberta bar on June 22, 1912 and began
to practice law with the firm of Reilly
and Lunney. He later formed the partnership of Lunney and Lannan where
he remained until his appointment to
the bench in 1928. He was named KC
on June 23, 1921. At the age of forty-
three, Lunney was the youngest judge
to be appointed to the AD. He retired
on October 6, 1944, and died on December 23, 1944.

Lunney was a quintessential indi-
vidualist on the bench. He often took
his own unique view of a case, and

was often in dissent. Even when he would agree with an associate, he would write a report stating his own reasoning. In *Cairns v. Cairns* ([1931] 3 WWR 335), Lunney joined with Justice McGillivray in holding that time extensions for an appeal are not usually granted, and there is a heavy burden of evidence to prove why such an extension should be granted. And in the *London Guarantee and Accident Company Limited et al. v. Northwestern Utilities Limited* ([1934] 3 WWR 641), the lower court had dismissed an action for damages resulting from the escape of gas from a gas line which caused a fire. While the court held for the appellant, Lunney dissented on the grounds that the act was caused by a third party, and his report was cited in nine subsequent cases on negligence. The hallmark of his career was the penchant to write as he saw it regardless of the views of his colleagues or the prevailing interpretation of law.

Lutz, Arthur Morton

Court of Queen's Bench of Alberta, Calgary, November 4, 1982 -

The Honourable Justice Arthur Morton Lutz was born in Grafton, Nova Scotia, on February 3, 1937. He received his B.A. from Acadia University in 1954, his B.Comm. from Mount Allison University in 1957, and his LL.B. from Dalhousie University in 1960. He moved to Alberta and was called to the Alberta bar on June 23, 1961. Lutz began his career as a general litigator in Edmonton in 1961 with the firm of Lindsay, Emery, Jamieson, Chipman, Sinclair, Lambert, and

Agrios. He practiced law in Calgary with German and Dinkel, later German and Company, from 1962 to 1966 before establishing his own firm of Lutz, Westerberg and O'Leary. He was practicing law with Lutz and Company when he was appointed to the bench in 1982. In addition to serving on the Alberta bench, Lutz was also appointed Deputy Judge of the SCNT on May 29, 1986, and Deputy Judge of the SCYT on February 10, 1987.

Lutz was the presiding judge in several well-known criminal cases, including *R. v. Steven Kessler* in 1987, *R. v. Keegstra* in 1992, and *R. v. Scott Olson* in 1983.

MacCallum, Edward Patrick

Court of Queen's Bench of Alberta, Edmonton, December 22, 1983 -

The Honourable Justice Edward Patrick MacCallum was born on January 20, 1936. He attended the University of Alberta where he received his B.A. in 1961, and his LL.B. in 1964. MacCallum was admitted to the Alberta bar on June 7, 1965. Prior to his appointment to the bench at Edmonton in 1983, he practiced in Barrhead with the firm of MacCallum and Ritter.

MacCallum wrote reported decisions in a number of civil cases. These were concerned with torts, commercial and administrative law, natural resources, and civil rights. One of his most important decisions was *Moysa v. Labour Relations Board Alberta* ([1986] 71 AR 70) dealing with discrimination in a workplace. In *Alta. v. Alta.* (Public Service Employee Relations Board)

([1990] 71 ALR 2d 45), MacCallum quashed a decision by the Board to award damages to the Union for employees' exclusion from a bargaining unit. He allowed an appeal reversing an order for a speculative and expansive valuation of shares in a company in a shareholders liquidation dispute in *Westfair Foods v. Watt* ([1992] 4 ALR 3d 268). He also presided over much of the litigation surrounding a major fire at the Suncor tar sands extraction plant in Fort McMurray in 1992. In addition to serving on the Alberta bench, MacCallum was also appointed to the SCYT in 1991 and to the SCNT in 1992.

MacDonald, Angus Marcellus

District Court of Macleod, Fort Macleod, September 15, 1921 - August 3, 1935
District Court of Southern Alberta, Lethbridge, August 3, 1935 - October 2, 1945

His Honour Angus Marcellus MacDonald was born in Souris, Prince Edward Island, in 1870. He was educated at St. Dunstan's College and Prince of Wales College in Prince Edward Island, and received a B.A. from Laval University in 1893. MacDonald moved to Regina in 1900 and to Lacombe in 1901. He was admitted to the North-West Territories bar on October 13, 1906. He practiced law in Lacombe until his appointment to the DC at Fort Macleod in 1921. He moved to the DC at Lethbridge in 1935. Upon his retirement on October 2, 1945, MacDonald settled in Calgary and died on October 14, 1960.

MacDonald, Hugh John

Supreme Court of Alberta, Trial Division, Edmonton, October 20, 1944 - January 17, 1957
Supreme Court of Alberta, Appellate Division, Edmonton, January 17, 1957 - March 2, 1965

The Honourable Hugh John MacDonald was born in South Hanson, Massachussetts, on November 10, 1898, moving to Edmonton with his parents in 1912. He was educated at Victoria High School, Saint Mary's College at Oakland, California, and the University of Alberta. During World War I, he trained with the United States Air Force. Returning to Edmonton, he obtained his B.A. in 1921, and his LL.B. in 1923. He was called to the Alberta bar on April 12, 1925. MacDonald had a long and successful practice in Edmonton with Wood, Buchanan & MacDonald from 1928 until he was called to the bench in 1944. He was named KC on February 14, 1940. He was also a keen student of politics, elected Alderman on Edmonton City Council, 1934-1940, and was a Liberal MLA, 1940-1944. MacDonald served for thirteen years as a trial judge before being appointed to the AD in 1957. In 1955, he chaired a Royal Commission to investigate administrative problems in the provincial government, but soon had to step down due to illness. While he continued to hold his appointment, his workload declined significantly. He died while on the bench in Edmonton on March 2, 1965.

MacDonald enjoyed a great reputation for care, courtesy, patience, and fairness. He was especially helpful rather than censorious towards younger lawyers when they made mistakes in court. He heard a wide variety of cases both civil and criminal, and his judgments have been reported in many areas. He ruled against banks, for example, when they did not conduct their business strictly according to detail, as in *Keyes v. Royal Bank of Canada* ([1946] 1 WWR 65); and narrowly defined options for making payments to maintain oil and gas leases in *Chipp v. Hunt and Hunt* ([1955] 16 WWR 209). He also delivered judgments on a number of cases involving the *Landlord Tenant Act*, and regarding personal injuries due to automobile accidents. MacDonald's judgment for the Appeal Court in *R. v. Hodges; R. v. Dream Home Contests (Edmonton) Ltd.* ([1959] 30 WWR 130), suggests that, despite his illness, he was able to appear on occasion to write a thoughtful deliberation on a case with complex legal questions and principles.

MacDonald, Hugh John

Supreme Court of Alberta, Trial Division, Calgary, March 25, 1968 - June 30, 1979
Court of Queen's Bench of Alberta, Calgary, June 30, 1979 - April 11, 1986
Supernumerary Justice, Calgary, April 11, 1982 - April 11, 1986

The Honourable Hugh John MacDonald was born in Strathmore, Alberta, on April 11, 1911. He attended Calgary's Mount Royal College and the Calgary Normal School, qualifying as a teacher. He taught school in Calgary from 1930 to 1934 before attending the University of Alberta, where he graduated with an LL.B. in 1938. MacDonald articled with J. Fred Scott of the Calgary firm of Scott and Milvain, and was admitted to the Alberta bar on September 21, 1939. After enlisting in the Royal Canadian Navy during World War II, he returned to Calgary, and became a partner in the firm of Shouldice, Milvain and MacDonald. He served as an Alberta MLA from 1948 to 1959. MacDonald was appointed QC on December 31, 1957. He was practicing as a senior partner with the firm of MacDonald, Cheesman, Moore, McMahon, and Tingle when he was appointed to the bench at Calgary in 1968. MacDonald retired on April 11, 1986.

MacDonald, William Alexander

District Court of Calgary, Calgary, March 13, 1926 - August 3, 1935
District Court of Southern Alberta, Calgary, August 3, 1935 - May 6, 1942
Supreme Court of Alberta, Trial Division, Calgary, May 6, 1942 - October 20, 1944
Supreme Court of Alberta, Appellate Division, Calgary, October 20, 1944 - January 17, 1957

The Honourable William Alexander MacDonald was born in 1879 in Port Hood, Inverness County, Nova Scotia. He was the brother of Angus Lewis MacDonald, a former Nova Scotia Premier. MacDonald received his B.A. at St. Francis Xavier University in Antigonish, and his LL.B. from Dalhousie University in 1910. After practicing law in Halifax for two years with W.F. O'Connor, MacDonald moved to Alberta, settling in Calgary. He was admitted to the Alberta bar on December 3, 1912. MacDonald entered into partnership with H.S. Patterson, KC, in Calgary in 1914, and continued in this partnership until his appointment to the DC in 1926. He was a longtime member of the Knights of Columbus and the Catholic Church. MacDonald retired on January 17, 1957 due to poor health, and died on June 25, 1958.

MacDonald was regarded as a patient and unassuming judge who used sound reasoning. In his early years on the bench he did not write many judgments, often agreeing with either Ford or Parlee. Later, he wrote more frequently but seldom dissented from his brethren. These judgments ranged from issues of constitutional law to judicature, natural resources, mechanics liens, and estates. Two judgments which received particular mention as precedents were in the area of estates. In *Re. Waines Estate* ([1944] 2 WWR 32), seven different parties squabbled over their shares of an inheritance. MacDonald took the matter into his own hands and decided each portion on his own view of the will. And in *Re. Marshall Estate* ([1948] 1 WWR 134), he provided the direction in the interpretation of a will involving heirs who predeceased the testator. In these and other cases, MacDonald exhibited a fine sense of distinction with which to apportion conflicting interests.

MacKenzie, John Horace

Court of Queen's Bench of Alberta,
    Red Deer, December 22, 1983 -

The Honourable Justice John Horace MacKenzie was born in Wainwright, Alberta, on May 10, 1932. He was educated at the University of Alberta where he received his B.A. in 1954 and his LL.B. in 1957. He articled in Edmonton and was admitted to the Alberta bar on May 24, 1958. MacKenzie practiced privately in Wainwright until 1963, when he joined the AG's department in Edmonton as a Solicitor. In 1964, he became a Crown Prosecutor in Red Deer and in 1966 was appointed Police Magistrate for the City of Red Deer. After magistrates were made PC judges in 1971, MacKenzie was appointed Assistant Chief Judge of the PC at Red Deer in 1977 before his appointment to the QB in 1983.

MacLean, Lawrence David

Supreme Court of Alberta, Trial
    Division, Lethbridge, December 21,
    1978 - June 30, 1979
Court of Queen's Bench of Alberta,
    Lethbridge, June 30, 1979 -

The Honourable Justice Lawrence David MacLean was born in Pincher Creek on June 30, 1927. He attended the University of Alberta, graduating in 1949 with a B.A. in Philosophy and Psychology, and in 1952 with an LL.B. MacLean articled with Gilbert C. Paterson in Lethbridge, and was admitted to the Alberta bar on June 8, 1953. He was named QC on December 31, 1969. MacLean practiced in Lethbridge with Rice and Company prior to his appointment to the bench there in 1978. One of his important decisions was given in *Lomond Grazing Association v. PanCanadian Petro-*

leum ([1985] 63 ALR 2d 120), where the plaintiff claimed a recalculation of the compensation owing from well rights of the defendant's production, and MacLean held for the plaintiff. Other cases include local disputes in the areas of contract, tort, and negligence.

MacLeod, Donald Ingraham

Court of Queen's Bench of Alberta, Calgary, March 14, 1990 -

The Honourable Justice Donald Ingraham MacLeod was born on December 13, 1936. He graduated in 1958 from the University of Alberta with a B.Sc. in Metallurgical Engineering, and received his LL.B. from the University of British Columbia in 1961. MacLeod was admitted to the Alberta bar on June 29, 1962. He was a senior partner with the Calgary firm of MacLeod, Lyle, Smith, McManus prior to his appointment to the bench at Calgary in 1990. He was appointed QC in 1978. MacLeod has appeared as a panelist in programs sponsored by the Legal Education Society of Alberta, and was a Sessional Lecturer at the University of Calgary Faculty of Law from 1982 to 1985. He is also a past Chairman of the Calgary Branch of the Engineering Institute of Canada. Until his appointment to the bench, MacLeod was a member of the Federation of Insurance and Corporate Counsel.

Macleod, James Farquharson

Stipendiary Magistrate of the North-West Territories, District of Bow River, Fort Macleod, January 1, 1876 - January 1, 1883

Stipendiary Magistrate of the North - West Territories, District of Alberta, Fort Macleod, January 1, 1883 - February 18, 1887

Supreme Court of the North-West Territories, District of Southern Alberta, Fort Macleod, February 18, 1887 - September 5, 1894

The Honourable James Farquharson Macleod was born on the Island of Skye, Scotland, in 1836, the son of Martin Donald Macleod and Jane Fry. The family immigrated to Upper Canada in 1845. Macleod attended Upper Canada College and entered Queen's University at age 15, receiving his B.A. in 1854 with honours in classics and philosophy. He failed the entrance exams twice at Osgoode Hall before being admitted in 1856. Articling with Alexander Campbell of Kingston, Ontario, he was admitted to the Upper Canada bar in 1860. Macleod practised law for ten years at Bowmanville, Ontario. His interest in the law, however, was surpassed by his enthusiasm for the military. In 1856 he joined the Volunteer Militia Field Battery of Kingston as a Lieutenant, transferring to the Voluntary Militia Rifle Company in 1862 and was promoted to Captain in 1863 and Major in 1866. Later, he served with the Canadian militia under Colonel Wolseley during the Red River troubles, 1869-1870, being promoted to Brigade Major in 1870 and Lieutenant Colonel in 1871. Late the next year, however, he left Canada for Scotland. It was there that he received Prime Minister John A. MacDonald's offer of a commission as Superintendent of the newly-formed NWMP in 1873. Becoming Assistant Commissioner on June 1, 1874, he led the force to what is now southern Alberta with the mandate to curtail the American whiskey trade in the area. Macleod established Fort Macleod in 1874 and Fort Walsh and Fort Calgary in 1875. He was given judiciary powers as the first SM of the NWT in 1876 and in 1887, Macleod was named to the SCNWT, where he served until his death in Calgary on September 5, 1894.

When Macleod arrived in what is now southern Alberta in 1874, he acted quickly and decisively to establish law enforcement. Capturing some outlaws, he tried them and confiscated their contraband immediately. As the sole judicial authority in the area, his command was habitual and unquestioned. This caused numerous disputes with Commissioner French at Swan River, leading to the resignation of French on January 1, 1876. Six months later, MacDonald appointed Macleod Commissioner of the NWMP as well as SM. Macleod resigned that commission in 1880, receiving a new one as full-time SM with an assize circuit for the southwest district of the NWT seated at Fort Macleod. In the meantime, he had earned good reports from both settlers and Aboriginals for his handling of civil and criminal disputes. Preferring swift and uncomplicated justice over cumbersome legal technicalities and rules of evidence, he controlled his court room with a deft hand and was seen to be stern, perceptive, and fair in this sparsely settled frontier outpost. Macleod negotiated with Chief Crowfoot of the Blackfoot Nation for the signing of Treaty No. 7 in 1877 and, with Major James Morrow Walsh, negotiated for the return of members

of the Dakota Nation under Sitting Bull to the United States in 1878.

As a judge, Macleod preferred to sit at trial proceedings rather than on appeal *en banc*. Riding Assize at Regina, Maple Creek, Dunmore, Medicine Hat, Lethbridge, Fort Macleod, Pincher Creek, and Calgary, he heard the full range of civil and criminal cases. He cleared the court dockets at Calgary perhaps more quickly than any other judge in the jurisdiction's history. He handled many famous western outlaws, including William Welsh, *alias* "Billy the Kid". In addition, he heard other non-judicial matters such as appeals from NWMP officers for pensions, from Metis for treaty script, and private disputes for arbitration. His relations with his brethren on the bench, however, were not cordial. This was due in part to the government's elevation in precedence of his junior justice, Hugh Richardson.

While Macleod sat on sixty-two appeal cases, he spoke on behalf of the Court only once. He concurred in the other cases without dissent. In a number of his own cases, moreover, his judgments were overturned. These included, for example, *R. v. Smith* ([1889] 1 TLR 189) on his jurisdiction, *McEwen v. Coal and Nav. Co.* ([1889] 1 TLR 203) on his award in a statement of claim, and *R. v. Walker* ([1893] 1 TLR 482) on his interpretation of the law of seduction. The cases suggest that his knowledge of technical aspects of the law was weak, that his judgments were perhaps arbitrary, and that his brethren regarded him as an historical artefact. Dispensing, however, a solid understanding of common-sense justice, his handling of the criminal calendar was usually exemplary. Maintaining an indefatigable schedule, he continued in his final years to travel the circuit by horse and buggy in spite of the onset of Bright's Disease. Added to this painful gall bladder disorder were mounting personal debts.

MacNaughton, Frederick Richards

Court of Queen's Bench of Alberta, Edmonton, December 19, 1980 - July 17, 1987

The Honourable Frederick Richards MacNaughton was born on April 17, 1923. He was admitted to the Alberta bar on July 8, 1952. He was named QC on December 20, 1967. Prior to his appointment to the Bench at Edmonton in 1980, he practiced with the firm of MacNaughton and Adilman in Wetaskiwin, Alberta. MacNaughton died on July 17, 1987.

MacNaughton was a trial judge, few of whose decisions were published in the law reports. His cases covered most areas of both civil and criminal law. His judgments were short, concise, and spartan in their language. One of his first major cases was *Higdon v. Smokey Lake General and Auxiliary Hospital* ([1982] 24 ALR 2d 97), which involved a municipal order for the expropriation of corporate property. MacNaughton held that a right to possession of land is not an interest in land, and therefore the application for the expropriation proceedings was null and void. *Bar-Don Holdings Ltd. v. Reed Stenhouse Limited and United States Fidelity and Guarantee Company* ([1983] 24 ALR 2d 248) concerned insurance for a mobile home in

transit between the U.S. and Canada. MacNaughton interpreted the policy to pertain only to mobile homes *in situ*, and dismissed the action against the insurance company and broker because the home was in transit. Judgments such as these reflected his close reading of the circumstances, and his tendency to not expand the words of contract or statute law. Finally, in *R. v. Favel* (1987), a murder case from his notebook that was not reported, he penned 89 pages of notes on the testimony of witnesses for the prosecution. This reflects the very serious manner in which he regarded all criminal trials for felonies.

MacPherson, Jack Leon

Court of Queen's Bench of Alberta, Calgary, March 15, 1985 - April 2, 1991

The Honourable Jack Leon MacPherson was born on August 16, 1922. He was admitted to the Alberta bar on August 27, 1952. Prior to his appointment to the bench at Calgary in 1985, MacPherson practiced law with the firm of MacPherson Kelly. He was named QC on December 19, 1973. MacPherson died on April 2, 1991.

MacPherson had an innate ability to work his way through the intricacies of transactions and relationships and reach decisions which would stand the test of time. Two of his most important judgments included *Brown v. Argali Holdings Inc. v. Shortreed (Estate) et al.* ([1987] 52 ALR 2d 86), involving the liability of lawyers who represented third parties. MacPherson held that a solicitor retained by the third party who incorporated the plaintiff company did not create a contractual relationship. And in *Card and Card v. Transalta Utilities Corporation* ([1987] 57 ALR 2d 155), he ruled that an unregistered easement for power poles on unsubdivided property cannot be enforced because the presence of such power poles did not constitute an exclusive occupation of land.

Mahaffy, James Jeffers

District Court of Red Deer, Red Deer,
    December 18, 1915 - August 3, 1935
District Court of Northern Alberta,
    Edmonton, August 3, 1935 -
    October 6, 1944

His Honour James Jeffers Mahaffy was born in Brampton, Ontario, of Irish immigrants on July 7, 1869. His father was a successful carriage maker and an Orangeman. Mahaffy was educated in the Toronto public schools, and attended Osgoode Hall Law School. He received his LL.B., and was called to the Ontario bar in 1895. He set up practice in Brampton, Ontario, with his brother-in-law and remained with him for the next twelve years, the firm moving to Scarborough in 1897. Mahaffy came to Alberta in 1907, settled in Medicine Hat, and was one of the last admitted to the North-West Territories bar on April 2, 1907. He was named City Solicitor for the town in 1908. Following in the political footsteps of his father, Mahaffy joined the Conservative Party. By the time he was appointed to the DC at Red Deer in 1915, Mahaffy had become a foremost barrister in the province. He held his position on the Court for thirty years. Few of his decisions appeared in the printed reports but nothing but bare outlines remain. He was regarded, however, as an independent judge, one who was informed on all the legal issues of the day, and who followed a less-traveled course. Mahaffy retired on October 6, 1944, and died on July 28, 1951 at the age of 82.

Manning, Marshall Edward

Supreme Court of Alberta, Trial
    Division, Edmonton, August 18,
    1959 - June 30, 1979
Court of Queen's Bench of Alberta,
    Edmonton, June 30, 1979 -
    December 28, 1979

The Honourable Marshall Edward Manning was born in Red Deer, Alberta, on December 2, 1905. He was educated in Camrose and taught school in Munson and Camrose. He attended the University of Alberta, graduating with a B.A. in 1932 and an LL.B. in 1933. While studying law at the University of Alberta, Manning was a lecturer in the Mathematics Department. After being admitted to the Alberta bar in 1935, he practiced law in Calgary. In 1944, Manning moved to Edmonton, where he practiced with the firm of Scott, Milvain and Manning until his appointment to the bench in 1959. Manning was appointed Chairman of the Royal Commission on the Great Slave Lake Railway Inquiry in 1958. He retired on December 28, 1979, and died in Victoria, British Columbia on March 29, 1989.

As a judge, Manning did not write many reported judgments, but he did set several precedents. One of the most notable was the practice of having counsel appear on behalf of children in domestic litigation. A strong advocate of trial by jury, in *R. v. Lyding* ([1965] 54 WWR 286, and 55 WWR 655, 704), Manning did not allow a hearing by judge alone, contending that jury trial should be the accepted practice, and that the judge has the discretionary power to overrule the accused's election to be tried by judge alone. After a second trial, however, Justice Milvain contended that this discretionary power was limited, and reheard the election.

Marshall, Ernest Arthur

Court of Queen's Bench of Alberta, Edmonton, June 16, 1986 -

The Honourable Justice Ernest Arthur Marshall was born in Elrose, Saskatchewan on January 13, 1937. He received his B.A. from the University of Alberta and his LL.B. from the University of Saskatchewan in 1964. Marshall was admitted to the Alberta bar on November 12, 1965, and was named QC on January 18, 1980. Prior to his appointment to the bench at Edmonton in 1986, Marshall practiced in Peace River with the firm of Marshall, Norheim and Reimer.

Mason, David Blair

Court of Queen's Bench of Alberta, Calgary, August 22, 1985 -

The Honourable Justice David Blair Mason was born in Montreal, Quebec, on October 18, 1933. He moved to Alberta in 1945 and attended the University of Alberta, earning his B.A.

and his LL.B. in 1956. Mason articled with MacDonald Millard, QC, and was admitted to the Alberta bar on June 5, 1957. He began his career in Calgary with the firm of Millard Johnson, and in 1958 he entered into partnership with Louis A. Justason, QC. At the time of his appointment to the bench at Calgary in 1985, Mason was a senior partner with the firm of Mason Macleod Lyle Smith where he specialized in general litigation, including civil litigation, administrative law, personal injury, insurance, and expropriation. He also focused on labour law, and was chairman of several rights and interest arbitration boards. Mason was named QC on January 18, 1974. Between 1958 and 1985, he was an Agent of the AG for Alberta. He has been a member of the International Commission of Jurists and the National Academy of Arbitrators. In 1977, he was the Vice-Chairman of the Alberta Board of Industrial Relations, and from 1977 to 1983, he was Chairman of the Public Service Employee Relations Board of Alberta.

Matheson, Douglas Randolph

Court of Queen's Bench of Alberta, Edmonton, March 15, 1985 -
Supernumerary Justice, Edmonton, April 27, 1995 -

The Honourable Justice Douglas Randolph Matheson was born on May 6, 1921. He enlisted in the Royal Canadian Air Force in World War II and was a prisoner of war in Germany from 1944-1945. He was admitted to the Alberta bar on May 29, 1952, the Yukon Territory bar in 1976, and the Northwest Territories bar in 1977. He

John Ainslie Jackson *(LASA)*

Horace Gilchrist Johnson (CA)

Thomas Cooke Johnstone (SAB)

Edward William Scott Kane (CA)

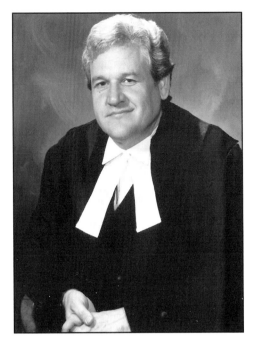

Roger Philip Kerans (CA)

Stanley Chandos Stavely Kerr (QB)

James George Kidd (AJ)

William John Cameron Kirby (AJ)

James Herbert Laycraft *(CA)*

Sidney Vincent Legg *(AJ)*

Samuel Sereth Lieberman *(CA)*

Henry William Lunney *(LASA)*

Arthur Morton Lutz *(LASA)*

Edward Patrick MacCallum *(AJ)*

Hugh John MacDonald *(LASA)*
(1944 - 1965)

William Alexander MacDonald *(CA)*

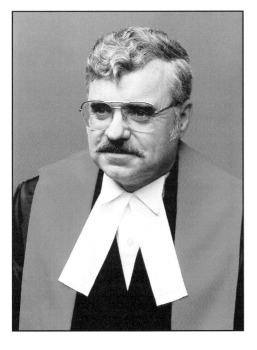

John Horace MacKenzie *(AJ)*

Lawrence David MacLean *(AJ)*

Donald Ingraham MacLeod *(LASA)*

James Farquharson Macleod *(LASA)*

Jack Leon MacPherson *(AJ)*

James Jeffers Mahaffy *(RDA)*

Marshall Edward Manning *(AJ)*

David Blair Mason *(LASA)*

Douglas Randolph Matheson

Joseph Duncan Matheson   *(QB)*

Ross Thomas George McBain   *(AJ)*

James Boyd McBride   *(LASA)*

Maitland Stewart McCarthy *(LASA)*

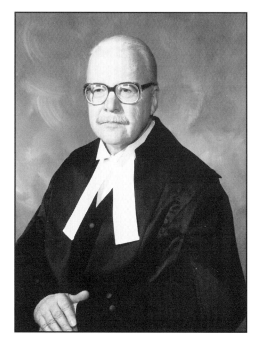

Neil Douglas McDermid *(CA)*

David Cargill McDonald *(AJ)*

John Cameron McDonald *(QB)*

John Walter McDonald *(LASA)*

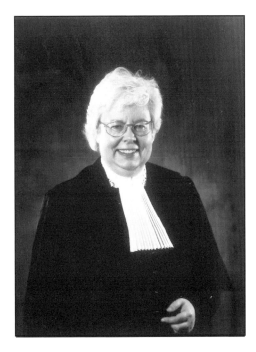

Elizabeth Ann McFadyen *(AJ)*

Alexander Andrew McGillivray *(CA)*

William Alexander McGillivray *(AJ)*

Joseph Patrick McIsaac *(QB)*

Colin Campbell McLaurin *(QB)*

Edward Peel McNeill *(QB)*

Donald Herbert Medhurst *(AJ)*

Tevie Harold Miller *(AJ)*

James Valentine Hogarth Milvain *(LASA)*

Charles Richmond Mitchell *(CA)*

Arnold Fraser Moir *(AJ)*

Robert Archibald Fraser Montgomery *(AJ)*

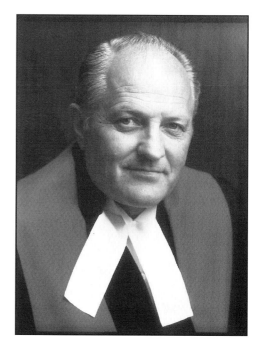

William Kenneth Moore *(AJ)*

William George Morrow *(CA)*

Virgil Peter Moshansky *(LASA)*

Alec Thirlwell Murray *(AJ)*

Henry William Newlands *(SAB)*

Michael Brien O'Byrne *(AJ)*

George Bligh O'Connor *(PAA)*

Willis Edward O'Leary *(LASA)*

Harold Hayward Parlee *(CA)*

Henry Stuart Patterson *(AJ)*

Delmar Walter Joseph Perras *(LASA)*

Marshall Menzies Porter *(LASA)*

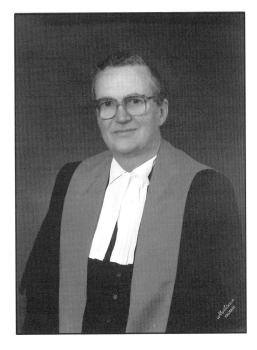

Peter Charles Garneau Power *(LASA)*

James Emile Pierre Prendergast *(GA)*

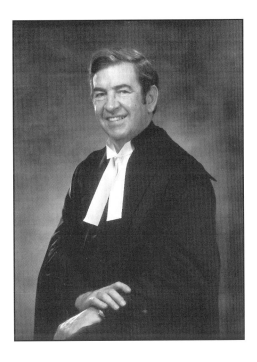

David Clifton Prowse *(AJ)*

Hubert Samuel Prowse *(LASA)*

Francis Hugh Quigley *(AJ)*

Hugh Richardson *(SAB)*

Harold William Riley *(GAI)*

was named QC on December 31, 1969. Prior to his appointment to the bench in 1985, Matheson practiced law with the Edmonton firm of Matheson and Company.

Matheson, Joseph Duncan

District Court of Peace River, Peace River, March 29, 1934 - August 3, 1935
District Court of Northern Alberta, Edmonton, August 3, 1935 - February 24, 1948

His Honour Joseph Duncan Matheson was born in Malagawatch, Inverness County, Nova Scotia, on February 28, 1873. He attended Dalhousie University, where he graduated with an LL.B. with Honours in 1899. After articling with Daniel McLennan in Port Hope, he was admitted to the Nova Scotia bar in 1899. He remained in Port Hope, practicing there for 13 years, before coming to Alberta in 1912. He was admitted to the Alberta bar on January 7, 1913. In 1916, Matheson moved to Fort Macleod, where he practiced for the next sixteen years. In 1922, he was Crown Prosecutor of the Fort Macleod Judicial District, and on June 4, 1928, he was named KC. Matheson practiced with D.H. Mc-Kinnon prior to his appointment to the DC at Peace River in 1934. He retired on February 24, 1948, and died on November 2, 1967.

McBain, Ross Thomas George

Court of Queen's Bench of Alberta, Calgary, December 22, 1983 -
Supernumerary Justice, Calgary, June 20, 1996 -

The Honourable Ross Thomas George McBain was born on May 31, 1926. He obtained his B.A. in 1948 and LL.B. in 1952 from the University of Alberta. He was admitted to the Alberta bar on July 10, 1958. He joined the Calgary firm of Barron and Barron where he specialized in labour law, and was a partner in Barron McBain when he was appointed to the bench in 1983. McBain was named QC on December 31, 1969. He was appointed Chairman of the Labour Relations Board in Edmonton in 1981.

McBride, James Boyd

District Court of Northern Alberta, Edmonton, December 19, 1944 - October 30, 1946
Supreme Court of Alberta, Trial Division, Edmonton, October 30, 1946 - January 17, 1957
Supreme Court of Alberta, Appellate Division, Edmonton, January 17, 1957 - January 2, 1960

The Honourable James Boyd McBride was born in Greenock, Scotland, in 1887. He was educated at Greenock Academy and the University of Glasgow before coming to Canada, where he completed his legal studies at the University of Alberta. He was admitted to the Alberta bar on December 30, 1912 and practiced law in a partnership with A.M. MacDonald in Lacombe. Moving to Edmonton, he was associated with the firm of Short, Cross, MacLean and McBride, later establishing his own law office. McBride was named KC in 1935. He was an active Liberal, serving as the Liberal Party of Alberta's Provincial Secretary in 1930 and General Secretary, 1932-1939, and as President of the Edmonton Liberal Association. McBride was interested in farming;he owned a 600-acre farm and routinely represented farmers before the Alberta Grain Commission. McBride was also active in the local business community: he was legislative counsel and President of the Edmonton Chamber of Commerce, 1934-1944, and was counsel and Director of several oil and gas companies. In addition, he was Director of the Alberta Motor Association and President of Edmonton's Burns Club, and the Edmonton Golf and Country Club. McBride died in Edmonton on January 2, 1960.

McBride heard a wide range of cases, include civil cases, divorce and matrimonial cases in chambers, and criminal cases. His judgments were learned, drawing on a vast array of case law, statutes, and treatises, and he was regarded as an impartial judge, earnest and determined to search for the truth in his decisions. In one of his early cases,*Woywedka v. Mokrey* ([1945] 2 WWR 405), he upheld a suit under the *War Measures Act* for the reimbursement of an "excess price" paid over ceiling for a 1940 Plymouth sedan. The same year, in *R. ex. rel. McClellan v. Clay* ([1945] 2 WWR 193), he scolded election officials of Vermilion River for improperly posting nomination and polling notices, improperly preparing voters lists, not swearing in the polling clerks, and not conducting a fully secret ballot. In *Begrie v. Whittaker* ([1952-53] 7 WWR 236), he invoked the "stop, look and listen" doctrine for drivers at railway crossings in assessing negligence for the driver of a car whose passenger was killed. Finally, in *Workmens Com-*

pensation Board v. U.S. Steel Corporation of the United States and Canada ([1956] 18 WWR 403), a complex estate case, McBride held that a conditional sales agreement does not pass title and ownership only to the purchaser. Perhaps his most significant case was *Huggard Assets Ltd. v. AG for Alberta* ([1949] 2 WWR 370), which disallowed provincial royalties on natural resources granted before 1930, but was eventually reversed by the JCPC. Whether the case was a matter large or small, McBride explored all the legal sources in coming to his decision and writing a judgment.

McCarthy, Maitland Stewart

Supreme Court of Alberta, Edmonton, July 11, 1914 - September 15, 1921
Supreme Court of Alberta, Trial Division, Edmonton, September 15, 1921 - May 3, 1926

The Honourable Maitland Stewart McCarthy was born in Orangeville, Ontario, in 1872. Son of an Ontario judge and nephew of the famous Ontario politician D'Alton McCarthy, KC, his early years were filled with law and politics. McCarthy was educated at Trinity College School in Port Hope and graduated with an LL.B from Trinity University, Toronto. He was admitted to the Ontario bar in 1897 and practiced in Laughton County. McCarthy moved west in 1903 and was admitted to the NWT bar on October 12, 1903. He settled in Calgary where he established the firm of Walsh and McCarthy. McCarthy was active in the Conservative Party from the day of his arrival in Calgary. He was elected MP in 1903, and re-elected in 1908. His move to Edmonton to practice with the firm of Eddinton, Hanne and Maitland precluded him from accepting leadership of the federal party in 1909. McCarthy was named KC on March 19, 1913. He left both Parliament and his legal practice when he was appointed to the bench at Edmonton in 1914. McCarthy was Anglican and a member of the Ranchmen's Club, the Rideau Club in Ottawa, and the Corporation of Trinity College School. He was also active in all outdoor sports. McCarthy retired on May 3, 1926 due to ill health, and died in Montreal while visiting there on May 27, 1930.

McCarthy was a generalist in the law, and offered judgments on a wide range of civil and criminal cases. One of his major judgments in criminal law was *R. v. Wilson* ([1919] 15 WWR 159), where the defendant had been convicted of wilful misconduct for hitting a cyclist who cut in front of him on a busy intersection. McCarthy overturned this verdict on grounds that cyclists had an equal duty to look out for motorists, and the defendant exercised his duty to the best of his ability. Two important railroad cases were *White and Walker v. Grand Trunk Pacific Company* ([1916] 11 ALR 1st 260), and *McLean v. C.P.R.* ([1917] 1 WWR 1466). In the former, he held the company negligent and liable for the death of cattle struck by a train at a crossing even though the animals had broken tether and walked onto the tracks. In the latter, he dissented from the majority who held the company liable for running over an inebriated man lying on the track, arguing that a reasonable person could not know a person was lying on the tracks in the dark. In *Denmore v. Trusts and Guarantee Company* ([1919] 1 ALR 1st 32), he ruled that, in contesting a will, the burden of proof always rests on the party contesting, especially if they are strangers. Throughout his career on the bench, McCarthy tended to rely more on common sense than legal technicalities in making his decisions at law.

McClung, John Wesley

District Court of Alberta, Edmonton, December 23, 1976 - December 21, 1977
Supreme Court of Alberta, Trial Division, Edmonton, December 22, 1977 - June 29, 1979
Court of Queen's Bench of Alberta, Edmonton, June 30, 1979 - December 19, 1980
Court of Appeal of Alberta, Edmonton, December 19, 1980 -

The Honourable John Wesley "Buzz" McClung was born in Edmonton, Alberta on July 15, 1935. His grandmother, the pioneer women's activist Nellie McClung, was one of five litigants who were successful in persuading the JCPC to declare that the *British North America Act* recognized women as persons in 1929. McClung attended the University of Alberta where he received his B.A. in 1957 and his LL.B. in 1959. He was admitted to the Alberta bar on June 17, 1959 and began practice with famed Edmonton litigator Neil D. Maclean, QC who instilled in him a love for criminal law. During his eighteen years of practice, McClung earned a reputation as a formidable criminal lawyer, and was once listed as one of Canada's top ten defense counsel. He was admitted to the Northwest Territories bar in 1959 and was named QC on December 19, 1973. He was a partner in the Edmonton firm of McClung Frohlich and Rand when appointed to the bench in 1976. McClung headed the course in criminal procedure for the Bar Admissions course for nearly eight years and had been Sessional Lecturer in advocacy and evidence at the University of Alberta Faculty of Law. McClung was also appointed Deputy Judge of the SCYT, 1978-1983, and has been a Justice of the CANT since 1980.

McClung has authored numerous reported decisions, many in the area of criminal law. He is known as an elegant and compelling writer, especially when delivering difficult and complex judgments. Selecting four cases alone from 1982 reflects the nature of his judgments. In *R. v. Casey* ([1982] 18 ALR 2d 272), he dissented from the Court's affirmation of sentences for assault causing bodily harm and possession of a weapon. He contended that the crime was too serious to allow a reduction in the sentence, and that a message should be sent for any repeat performances. *R. v. Robertson* ([1982] 39 AR 273) concerned the accused's conviction of kidnapping indecent assault, and being declared a dangerous sexual offender. McClung affirmed the declaration and conviction, but reduced the sentence on the grounds that the accused confessed voluntarily and had written a letter of apology to the parents of the victim. In *R. v. Jacobs* ([1982] 39 AR 391), the trial judge imposed a convic-

tion of two months imprisonment for a driver who caused the deaths of two persons. The Crown appealed the sentence, and McClung lengthened it by nine months because of the crime's severity. These judgments reflect McClung's vision of the administration of the criminal law as a deterrent to violent crime. A recent and controversial decision was *Vriend v. Alberta (Province)* ([1996] 161 AR 16; 184 AR 351). An earlier QB judgment held that the province's *Individual Rights Protection Act* did include sexual orientation protection for a gay man dismissed from his position in a Christian college. In overturning this ruling, McClung, writing for the majority decision, held that legislatures and political forums, not the courts, are the best venues for initiating and directing social change.

McDermid, Neil Douglas

Supreme Court of Alberta, Appellate Division, Calgary, August 14, 1963 - June 30, 1979
Court of Appeal of Alberta, Calgary, June 30, 1979 - June 5, 1986
Supernumerary Justice, Calgary, August 15, 1978 - June 5, 1986

The Honourable Neil Douglas McDermid was born in Calgary, Alberta on June 5, 1911, the son of N.I. McDermid, who had established one of the oldest pharmacy and drug businesses in western Canada. He attended the University of Alberta, where he graduated with a B.A. in 1932, and an LL.B. in 1935. He articled with Senator George Ross in Calgary. After being admitted to the Alberta bar on June 18, 1936, McDermid joined the Calgary firm of Brown, Moyer, Brown, where he specialized in corporate law. In the late 1930s, McDermid and his partner Robert Brown, one of the first investors in the Turner Valley oil fields, worked together to stimulate investment in the oil industry. McDermid became an expert in oil and gas law and when Brown became President of Home Oil Company, McDermid served as his solicitor. McDermid was also counsel for fellow lawyer Eric Harvie, whose firm, Western Leaseholds, profited greatly from oil and gas development after the Leduc discovery in 1947. In 1944, McDermid joined the firm of Macleod, Riley, McDermid and Dixon where he remained until his appointment to the bench in 1963. He was named QC on December 31, 1953. McDermid was one of the founders, with Eric Harvie, of the Glenbow Foundation and became the first Chairman of the GAI in 1966. He served as an Alderman on Calgary City Council, 1950-1951, and as Director of the Calgary Children's Hospital in the 1950s. In addition to his appointments to the Alberta bench, McDermid was Justice of the CANT, 1971-1986. McDermid retired to Victoria, B.C. on June 5, 1986 and died there on February 27, 1989.

McDermid was appointed directly to the AD and was a frequent author of judgments for the Court in cases involving criminal law, divorce, contracts, commercial law, and oil and gas law. In *R. v. Irwin* ([1967] 61 WWR 102), he ruled that in an exchange of illegal goods between the appellant accused and an undercover police officer, the attempted sale was in itself undeniable proof of guilt. And in *R. v. Dawood* ([1976] 1 WWR 262), when a shopper was convicted with theft for switching a price tag on an item she paid for, McDermid reversed the conviction on the precedent that once a sale is complete there can be no theft.

Since McDermid was a recognized expert in commercial and contract law, he wrote some leading precedents in these areas. In *Re. Paulette's Application to File a Caveat* ([1976] 2 WWR 193), McDermid reversed a SCNT decision recognizing a land claim by sixteen chiefs for Aboriginal title to unpatented crown land. He held that the Torrens system requires the initial registration of the state, and that Canada's land is held by no one but the Crown. In the area of family law, he helped set the tone of a more intolerant view of negligent fathers, and also held in *Husted v. Husted* ([1979] 11 ALR 2d 246) that ex-spouses could not claim property retrospectively under the *Matrimony Act*. In an important pre-*Charter* civil rights and constitutional case, McDermid ruled in *Canadian Pacific Ltd. v. AG of Alberta et al.* ([1980] that the provincial *Individual's Rights Protection Act* does not have jurisdiction for interprovincial companies. In later years, McDermid gave fewer judgments. A hard-working, open-minded judge, he was regarded by his colleagues as good-humoured, self-effacing, and a brilliant jurist to the end of his career.

McDonald, David Cargill

Supreme Court of Alberta, Trial Division, Edmonton, January 1, 1974 - June 30, 1979

Court of Queen's Bench of Alberta, Edmonton, June 30, 1979 - January 1, 1996

Court of Appeal of Alberta,
Edmonton, January 1, 1996 -
April 7, 1996

The Honourable David Cargill
McDonald was born in Prince Albert,
Saskatchewan, on May 23, 1932. His
family moved to Edmonton when he
was young, but he later attended Trinity College in Port Hope, Ontario.
McDonald returned to Edmonton and
graduated from the University of Alberta with a B.A. in 1953. He then
attended Oxford University in England as a Rhodes Scholar, and received
a B.A. (Juris) in 1955, and a B.C.L. in
1956. He was admitted to the English
bar prior to returning to Canada in
1958. After being admitted to the Alberta bar on May 27, 1958, McDonald
became a member of the Edmonton
firm of McCuaig, McCuaig, Des-
rochers, Beckingham and McDonald,
where he remained until his appointment to the bench in 1974. McDonald
served as Counsel to Justice William
G. Morrow on the 1967 Royal Commission on the Administration of
Justice in Hay River, Northwest Territories. He was a full-time Sessional
Lecturer at the University of Alberta
Faculty of Law, 1956-1957. Thereafter,
he continued to lecture on the law of
evidence for twenty years, on administrative law for four years, and on
professional responsibility for three
years. McDonald was awarded an
Honorary LL.D. from the University
of Alberta in 1985. He was also active
in his local community, serving as
Chairman on many committees, char-
ity boards and societies, including a
term as President of the Edmonton
Symphony. In addition to serving on
the Alberta bench, McDonald was

Deputy Judge of the SCNT, 1977-1985,
and Deputy Judge of the SCYT, 1982-
1996, Justice of the CANT in 1996, and
a member of the Court Martial Appeal
Court of Canada, 1990-1996. He died
in Edmonton on April 7, 1996.

During his twenty-three years as a
trial judge, McDonald displayed an
outstanding intellect and rigour with
a strong emphasis on legal and historical principles. He also continued
to publish, lecture, and serve on many
commissions and judicial bodies. From
1977 to 1981, he chaired the three-
person Royal Commission appointed
to investigate activities of the RCMP.
His recommendations led to the creation of the Canadian Security and
Intelligence Service in 1982. From 1974
to 1977, McDonald was the founding
President of the Canadian Institute
for the Administration of Justice, and
in 1984 he became President of the
Canadian Section of the International
Commission of Jurists. McDonald was
the author of *Legal Rights in the Canadian Charter of Rights and Freedoms*.
His judgment regarding challenges to
the Provincial Court in view of
government's attempt to set back the
salaries of its judges, *R. v. Campbell*
([1994] 160 AR 81; C.A. [1995] 169 AR
178), was an impressive treatise on the
independence of the judiciary in the
British parliamentary tradition.

McDonald, John Cameron

District Court of Northern Alberta,
Edmonton, March 18, 1944 -
September 15, 1951

His Honour John Cameron Mc-
Donald was born in Owen Sound,
Ontario, in 1882. After qualifying as a

teacher, he taught in Owen Sound for several years before attending the University of Toronto where he earned his B.A. in 1905. He received his LL.B. at Osgoode Hall, Toronto, in 1908. McDonald practiced in Owen Sound until 1915, when he moved to Alberta and was admitted to the Alberta bar on October 28 of that year. Settling in Edmonton, he formed a partnership with his uncle Alexander G. MacKay under the name of MacKay, McDonald and Company. McDonald continued his practice there until his appointment to the DC in 1944. He was named KC on January 3, 1935. McDonald died in Toronto on September 15, 1951.

McDonald, John Walter

District Court of Southern Alberta,
    Fort Macleod, May 24, 1940 -
    November 8, 1950
District Court of Southern Alberta,
    Chief Judge, Fort Macleod, March
    18, 1944 - November 8, 1950

His Honour John Walter McDonald was born near Toronto, Ontario, on May 21, 1879. He was educated at Richmond Hill High School, and the University of Toronto, graduating with an LL.B. in 1905. In that same year, he received a B.C.L. from Osgoode Hall Law, Toronto. McDonald practiced in Toronto with the firm of Denton, Dunn and Boultbee until 1907, when he moved to Alberta. He was admitted to the Alberta bar on 1907. Settling in Fort Macleod, he practiced with Malcolm McKenzie for three years before forming his own partnership in 1912 as McDonald, Martin and MacKenzie. McDonald

was appointed KC in 1919. He was also made Crown Prosecutor that year, and was widely recognized for the success he achieved in handling criminal cases. His two most famous murder trials were *R. v. Basoff* (1920) [unreported] and *R. v. Zitto* (1923) [unreported]. McDonald was elected Mayor of Fort Macleod in 1923, at which he served to 1930 and 1934-1938. A member of the Liberal Party, he lost in the provincial elections of 1926 and 1930, and was elected leader of the provincial party in 1930. He also served on the local school board, several community organizations, and was an honorary Chief of the Blood Indians. Appointed to the DC in 1940, Mc-Donald moved to Calgary. He died there on November 8, 1950.

Several of McDonald's judgments were published in the law reports. In *Re. Farm Creditor's Arrangement Act, 1934; re. Bryce* ([1942] 3 WWR 102), he allowed Mrs. Bryce to make a proposal for land that was transferred to her by her dead husband, against the objections of the mortgage company. And, in *Re. The Soldier's Relief Act; re. Bly* ([1944] 3 WWR 208), he gave a soldier's wife a special exemption from property taxes in Magrath because of her expenses in caring for and supporting their five children. McDonald acquired a reputation on the bench as a judge with a keen interest in how the law worked in practice.

McFadyen, Elizabeth Ann

District Court of Alberta, Edmonton,
    January 5, 1976 - June 30, 1979
Court of Queen's Bench of Alberta,
    Edmonton, June 30, 1979 -
    February 1, 1993

Court of Appeal of Alberta,
    Edmonton, February 1, 1993 -

The Honourable Justice Elizabeth Ann McFadyen was born in Saskatoon, Saskatchewan, on August 31, 1940. She won numerous awards and scholarships while studying law at the University of Saskatchewan, where she graduated with an LL.B. in 1965 and was called to the Saskatchewan bar in 1966. McFadyen worked with the Saskatchewan AG's Department before moving to Ottawa to join the Tax Litigation Section of the federal Justice Department in 1970. Transferred to Edmonton as Director of the Justice Department's Edmonton office in 1971, McFadyen was admitted to the Alberta bar on December 21, 1971. In 1976, McFadyen became the first woman appointed to the federal courts in Alberta. She has also been a Justice of the CANT since 1993.

As a judge, McFadyen was very active in writing judicial opinions for the QB in the 1980s. She heard numerous appeals of convictions for impaired driving, many suits for wrongful dismissal, and several applications for personal injury claims and breaches of contract. In one of her first written opinions on the QB, McFadyen held in *R. v. Chromiak* ([1979] 14 ALR 2d 232) that an accused whose right to retain and instruct counsel was denied could not have a conviction sustained against him. Thereafter, most of the criminal cases which she heard involved appeals against convictions for impaired driving based on technical objections. These included procedures for using the breathalyzer, the right to counsel before taking it, the amount of time that expired before samples were analyzed, their availability for further testing, the qualifications of technicians, and the credibility of witnesses. In most of these cases, McFadyen rejected the appeal and upheld the conviction, thereby establishing guidelines for the continued use and development of the breathalyzer as a lawful test. There were also many wrongful dismissal suits, where the decision rested upon the terms of the contract and the oral evidence and testimony concerning its fulfillment. With regard to suits for damages, McFadyen denied perhaps as many as she upheld, basing her decisions on a close reading of the particulars. Some of these cases, such as *Laidler v. Grumetza* ([1980] 18 ALR 2d 304), were complex involving a series of countersuits and counterclaims for damages. Finally, with respect to breach of contract, an early case was *Canadian Union College v. Canistell Ind.* ([1979] 17 ALR 2d 98), where a defendant kept a deposit for the sale of a building. McFadyen held that since the defendant's losses exceeded that of the deposit, the plaintiff's failure to execute the contract caused its breach. McFadyen's judgments followed a clear line of reasoning and held legal prescriptions to their objectives without allowing deviation for procedural and evidentiary technicalities.

McGillivray, Alexander Andrew

Supreme Court of Alberta, Appellate
    Division, Calgary, May 8, 1931 -
    December 12, 1940

The Honourable Alexander Andrew McGillivray was born in London, Ontario on February 11, 1884. He was educated at St. Francis College in Richmond, Quebec and attended Dalhousie University, where he received his LL.B in 1906. He came west in 1907 and was one of the last advocates admitted to the NWT bar on May 14, 1907. McGillivray practiced in Stettler until 1910, when he moved to Calgary to practice with the firm of Tweedie and McGillivray. He was named KC on February 4, 1919 and served as Crown Prosecutor in several prominent criminal cases including the famous Prohibition era murder trial, *R. v. Picariello and Lassandro* ([1922] 1 WWR 1989). In 1925, McGillivray was elected leader of the Conservative Party of Alberta, and, in 1926, he was elected Conservative MLA for Calgary. He resigned as leader of the Conservative Party in 1929. A resident of Elbow Park, he was an active member of both the Ranchmen's Club and the Calgary Golf & Country Club. As a lawyer, McGillivray was acknowledged as a distinguished litigator with a vast knowledge of legal lore. A skilful writer, he drew up the contracts which laid the foundations for the creation of the Alberta Wheat Pool. When he was appointed directly to the AD in 1931, at the age of forty-seven, he was one of the youngest Supreme Court justices of Appeal in Canada. The *Toronto Mail & Empire* hailed him as one of the most brilliant practising barristers in western Canada. McGillivray died in Edmonton on December 12, 1940.

McGillivray's appeal court decisions during his relatively brief tenure on the bench were important. He established the reputation of a judge whose vast knowledge of the law was tempered by sympathetic consideration of the circumstances. McGillivray wrote the majority judgment in *R. v. Stewart* ([1934] 1 WWR 423) which effectively overturned a previous jury decision to convict a man of being a member of unlawful assembly as part of the "hunger march" in Edmonton in 1932. In *Cairns v. Cairns* ([1931] 3 WWR 335), he assisted in writing the judgment that established the grounds for an appeal court's acceptance of extensions for further time to appeal cases. In 1938, McGillivray was a commissioner for the Royal Commission of Inquiry into the Alberta oil industry. The commission's report, known as the "McGillivray Report" of 1940, recommended instituting conservation measures to preserve the Turner Valley oil field. He studied the subject so thoroughly that in the end he was able to understand and describe the intricacies of petroleum engineering. McGillivray's death by a heart attack took the legal community by surprise. Aged fifty-six, he had seemed destined for a long and distinguished career as an interpreter and maker of Canadian law.

McGillivray, William Alexander

Supreme Court of Alberta, Appellate
    Division, Calgary, December 5,
    1974 - June 30, 1979
Court of Appeal of Alberta, Calgary,
    June 30, 1979 - December 16, 1984
Chief Justice of Alberta, Calgary,
    December 5, 1974 - December 16,
    1984

The Honourable William Alexander McGillivray was born in Calgary on October 14, 1918. He was the only son of the distinguished SCA Justice Alexander Andrew McGillivray. Educated at a Victoria boarding school and Calgary High School, he attended the University of Alberta where he graduated with a B.A. in 1938 and an LL.B. in 1941, graduating first in his class and receiving the Horace Harvey Gold Medal. He was admitted to the Alberta bar on June 23, 1942. McGillivray practiced law in Calgary between 1943 and 1974 and was a Bencher of the Law Society of Alberta, 1958-1969, before becoming President, 1969-1970. Named QC on December 31, 1957, he was also admitted to the Saskatchewan bar in 1965. McGillivray was with the firm of Fenerty, McGillivray, Robertson, Prowse, Brennan, Fraser and Bell when he was appointed to the SCA at Calgary in 1974. With this firm he handled a number of high profile cases concerned mainly with civil law. An active sportsman who, in his youth, was provincial champion in both tennis and table tennis, McGillivray was a member of Calgary's Ranchmen's and Glencoe Clubs. He died in Calgary on December 16, 1984.

McGillivray was appointed directly to the position of Chief Justice of Alberta and wrote many reported judgments, especially in criminal law. In *R. v. Budic* ([1979] 1 WWR 11), McGillivray held that the trial judge must instruct the jury to consider whether the accused knew that his act of murder was wrong; because this was not done, the conviction for first-degree murder was quashed and substituted with the verdict of not guilty on account of insanity. McGillivray also upheld the discretionary power of the court to determine whether a

convicted felon is a "dangerous offender" under the *Criminal Code* in *Carleton v. R.* ([1981] 6 WWR 148). In *R. v. Macdonald* ([1983] 42 ALR 2d 228), McGillivray quashed the appeal of a man convicted for trading in securities without a licence. In *R. v. Faid* ([1984] 52 ALR 2d 338), he dismissed an application for the reduction of eligibility for parole in a life sentence for second degree murder from thirteen years to ten. However, in *R. v. Pineau* ([1984] 50 ALR 2d 279), where the accused was convicted of causing death by criminal negligence, McGillivray reduced the sentence on appeal from $2000 and two years in jail to eighteen months because of mitigating circumstances. In *R. v. Elliott* ([1984] 56 ALR 2d 113), the issues of whether the accused stole the property, or stole it in Canada, were addressed upon appeal, with McGillivray holding in a split decision that the Crown had proved neither. On the civil side, he set precedent on the federal taxation of oil and gas exports at the U.S. border in *Castor v. CanDel Oil Ltd.* ([1979] 11 ALR 2d 282).

Throughout these cases, he was known for his adept handling of complex issues, and his persuasively written judgment. McGillivray sometimes figured in controversy, and some of his appeal court rulings were strongly opposed by women's groups. One of his most controversial decisions was on appeal in the year before his death in *R. v. Brown* ([1983] 26 ALR 2d 328). Explaining why the Court reduced a sentence of sexual assault from eight months to four, he contended that "when a lady accompanies a man home at 3 a.m. to drink beer and smoke marijuana, one might not be too surprised if something happened under those circumstances." An excellent judicial administrator beloved by both the bench and bar, McGillivray's death in 1984 was a great shock to the legal community in Alberta.

McGuire, Thomas Horace

Supreme Court of the North-West
    Territories, District of
    Saskatchewan, Prince Albert, April
    25, 1887 - August 16, 1897; October
    6, 1898 - February 18, 1902
Chief Justice of the North-West
    Territories, Calgary, February 18,
    1902 - January 3, 1903

The Honourable Thomas Horace McGuire was born in Kingston, Ontario, on April 21, 1849. His father James was a merchant and farmer of Fermanagh, Ireland before immigrating to Canada West. McGuire attended public school in Kingston, where he won a scholarship to the Collegiate Institute in 1864, and entered Queen's University in 1866, where he won the Mowat scholarship as the best matriculant. He went on to win scholarships and prizes in classics, rhetoric, mathematics, logic, botany, zoology, natural philosophy, metaphysics, and chemistry. When he graduated in 1870, with a B.A., he won the Prince of Wales Gold Medal for the top student of the undergraduate class. He received an honorary LL.D. at Queen's in 1909. McGuire was called to the Ontario bar in 1875, and was named QC in 1883. He was the Editor of the *Kingston Daily News* and *Canadian Freeman*, an Alderman on Kingston City Council, 1879-1884, a member of the Separate School Board, and a member

of the Conservative Association. He was also President of the St. Patrick's Society, the St. Vincent de Paul Society, the Kingston Mechanics Institute, and Vice-President of the Catholic Literacy Association. McGuire was a vigorous campaign speaker, and a graceful editorial writer. His widespread renown led to his appointment as one of the two Ontario barristers outside of the North-West Territories to its first Supreme Court in 1887. In 1897, at the height of the Klondike gold rush, McGuire was transferred to Dawson City to establish the Yukon Territorial Court, but returned to Prince Albert in September 1898. Named the first Chief Justice of the North-West Territories in 1902, he retired from the bench in 1903, but continued an active legal career in Saskatchewan. McGuire was appointed a Royal Commissioner to revise and consolidate the ordinances and statutes affecting the new province of Saskatchewan in 1906. In 1913 he was a lecturer for the first session of the Law Faculty of the University of Saskatchewan and served as Senator of the University of Saskatchewan and Chairman of the Educational Council of Saskatchewan. In 1916, he was appointed to a Royal Commission of Inquiry into the unauthorized disclosure of a provincial Cabinet report on the Mortgage Loan question. In 1919, and again in 1922, he was appointed a member of the Saskatchewan Educational Council, where he assisted in drafting the educational structure of the province and French language schools. He died in Prince Albert on July 13, 1923.

McGuire was known for his unparalleled knowledge of the common law, his fine command of the English language, and his sensitivity to frontier customs and practices. Revelling in legal intricacies and complexities, he was fully at home hearing appeals where the nuances, irregularities, and sophisticated legal questions could challenge his intellect and invite logical and philosophical analysis. A tall, handsome, and well-read man, McGuire's eloquent judgments are filled with allusions to classical figures in literature and philosophy. He came to specialize in the more complex issues of civil law actions. One of his first decisions written for the Court *en banc* was *Walters et al. v. Canadian Pacific Railway Company* ([1887] 1 TLR 88). His judgment in dismissing an appeal of the defendant company's warehousemen for alleged negligence in a fire that destroyed the goods of the plaintiff outlined fully the grounds on which such an appeal could, and could not, be found. Likewise, in *Davis et al. v. Patrick* ([1893] 2 TLR 9), his definition of whether certain kinds of information contained in statements of claim were injurious to other parties or merely statements of facts established parameters which became precedent. In *Emerson v. Bannerman*, ([1890] 1 TLR 224), he castigated by logic the argument of the plaintiff that the defendant's bill of sale was invalid because of its language. McGuire dealt with important jurisdictional issues in *Re. Claxton* ([1890] 1 TLR 282), in which he deferred to the Parliament of Canada, citing the supremacy of federal law over territorial. He upheld the federal *Homestead Act* in holding that the *Exemption Ordinance* of the Territorial Legislature was *ultra vires*, and affirmed the jurisdiction of his

Court to do so. The next year, in *R. v. McClung* ([1891] 1 TLR 379), he ruled that a trial judge's decision to poll a jury is discretionary, and that the liquor consumed by jurors did not warrant discharging the accused nor constitute grounds for a new trial after he was found guilty. McGuire's last case on the bench was at Calgary, *Corticetti Silk Co. v. Balfour & Co.* ([1902] 5 TLR 385). Here he held that a ledger of debts is not a chattel, but the property of the assignee, and therefore could not be seized by a sheriff. The logic in his argument was clear, articulate, and unequivocal.

The hardships of travel on circuit in a remote and harsh country took their toll on McGuire, and he was contemplating retirement already in 1890. However, he adapted and eventually thrived in the new frontier of the west and was particularly interested in the administration of local justice by Justices of the Peace, writing a manual outlining their responsibilities and procedures. In 1902, he accepted the appointment as the first Chief Justice of the SCNWT at Calgary. McGuire was clearly the junior judge to his colleague Justice Richardson, and his appointment caused friction between the two men. This probably resulted in McGuire's retirement from the bench on January 3, 1903.

McIsaac, Joseph Patrick

District Court of Northern Alberta, Grande Prairie, November 5, 1943 - August 20, 1963

His Honour Joseph Patrick McIsaac was born in Antigonish, Nova Scotia, on August 20, 1888. After graduating with an LL.B. from Dalhousie University he came to Alberta in 1912 and established a legal practice in Camrose. He was admitted to the Alberta bar on June 24, 1912. McIsaac enlisted in the Canadian Expeditionary Force during World War I and served in France with the 52nd Battalion. In 1919, he moved to Grande Prairie and became that city's first Crown Prosecutor. He was named KC on December 28, 1934. McIsaac died in Grande Prairie on August 20, 1963.

McLaurin, Colin Campbell

Supreme Court of Alberta, Trial
    Division, Calgary, September 23,
    1942 - September 1, 1968
Supreme Court of Alberta, Trial
    Division, Chief Justice, Calgary,
    June 27, 1952 - September 1, 1968

The Honourable Colin Campbell McLaurin was born in Sarnia, Ontario on September 1, 1893, and came to Calgary in 1907. His father was a Baptist missionary in Alberta. After graduating from the Calgary Normal School, McLaurin was a school principal in Medicine Hat from 1913 to 1918. He served for a brief period in the Royal Air Force at the end of World War I, and then attended the University of Alberta, receiving his LL.B. in 1922. He was admitted to the Alberta bar on June 2, 1922. For the following twenty years, McLaurin practiced in Calgary with the firm of Fenerty and McLaurin where he specialized in corporate and insurance law. He was named KC on August 21, 1935. McLaurin was active in politics as well as in community affairs. In 1930, he ran as a Liberal against R.B. Bennett, QC and lost in the federal election. He received an honorary LL.D. from the University of Alberta at Calgary in 1961, became the first Chancellor of the newly-autonomous University of Calgary in 1966, and held that post until 1970. McLaurin received the Centennial Medal in 1967 in honour of his service to the nation, and Alberta's 75th Silver Anniversary Medal. He retired on September 1, 1968. He was the first Chairman of the Alberta Press Council when it was formed in 1972, and held that position until 1975. Suffering a hearing impairment in his later years, he left the bulk of his estate to the Colin McLaurin Foundation to assist the hearing impaired. He died in Calgary on April 1, 1981.

McLaurin was famous for dealing with cases quickly, succinctly, and abruptly. For example, in *R. v. Barrett* (1960) [unreported], he heard it at 4:05 in the afternoon rather than holding it over to the next day, and concluded with judgment and sentence at 5:35 pm. The speed with which he worked, however, did not seem to interfere with either his logic or his research. His written judgments, while cogent and concise, were often terse. They did not seem to be intended either for discourse or for quotation. Some of his most important work was done on royal commissions and provincial inquiries. McLaurin was a member of the Royal Commission on Coal from 1944 to 1946, and served as a member of the Royal Commission on Diesels in 1957. He also sat on government inquiries into pre-arranged funerals, Banff Park leases, and investigations into improper professional conduct.

As a judge, McLaurin did not write many judicial opinions which were published in the law reports. He appeared on the bench in many cases, but usually concurred with the majority, or the dissenting, opinion. Most of the few cases he wrote opinions for were short ones involving standard questions of debt or criminal liability. Two of the more interesting cases in which he provided lengthy judgments included *Jennins v. Wolfe* ([1950] 1 WWR 935). The case involved the loss of the hide of a grizzly bear by a taxidermist. The hunter claimed not only the value of the hide, but also an additional value for its being a "prize" hide. McLaurin rehearsed case law from England through Canada to find equivalent circumstances, and gave an award for the value of the hide but not its value to the hunter. And in *R. v. Canadian Utilities Ltd.* ([1954] 13 WWR 705), a boy aged sixteen was electrocuted while sliding down a slag heap at an abandoned coal mine near East Coulee, Drumheller. He reached up and grabbed the line, which was near ground level, on his way down. Citing cases from England, and rulings by the JCPC, McLaurin found damages against the company for its negligence.

McNeill, Edward Peel

District Court of Macleod, Fort
    Macleod, March 19, 1913 -
    September 15, 1921
District Court of Calgary, Calgary,
    October 6, 1920 - August 3, 1935
District Court of Southern Alberta,
    Calgary, August 3, 1935 - May 24,
    1940

His Honour Edward Peel McNeill was born in Dublin, Ireland on December 23, 1863. He came to Canada with his parents in 1873, where they resided in Uxbridge, Ontario. He was educated at Uxbridge High School, received his B.A. from the University of Toronto, and his LL.B. from Osgoode Hall Law School. He served with the Queen's Own Rifles from 1885 to 1889, where he developed a keen interest in shooting. McNeill practiced in Toronto from 1896, and was a member of the firm of Ferguson and O'Brien 1889-1890, and Burton and McNeill 1890-1899, when he moved to the NWT. He was admitted to the bar of the NWT on November 24, 1899, and was in the Fort Macleod firm of Haultain, McKenzie and McNeill from 1899 to 1906. Practising alone from 1906-1909, he ran as a Conservative MLA for Fort Macleod in 1909, losing by only fifteen votes. He then formed the firm of McNeill and Martin in Calgary, where he worked until he was appointed to the SCA in 1916. McNeill was made one of the first Benchers of the Law Society of Alberta in 1907, and was named KC on March 12, 1913. Community activities included Chairman of the Macleod Horse Show Association, an active member of the Presbyterian Church, the Macleod Club, and the Calgary Golf and Country Club, and the Freemasons. His passion for rifle shooting led to his appointment as honorary Secretary-Treasurer of the Canadian Military Institute of Toronto. McNeill retired on May 24, 1940, and died on November 23, 1954.

McNeill was on the bench for nearly twenty-five years, but his reported cases were infrequent. The decisions were short, concise, and practical with few citations of case law and statutes.

O'Hanlon v. Cockx and Hughes ([1935] 3 WWR 481), for example, involved conditional sales agreements, which were used extensively in the Depression years to make sales. The case involved the sale and seizure of a truck and, since the word "truck" was never entered into the agreement, McNeill extrapolated the relationships from the documents to find for the plaintiff. In *Re. The Garagemen's Lien Act; re. Gollan and Edmonton Credit Company* ([1938] 1 WWR 670), the car owner Powell was in debt to Gollan for repair work. Powell, holding a conditional sales agreement, abandoned the car, and Gollan demanded that the defendant holder of the agreement pay his debt. McNeill held for the plaintiff because of the ramifications of such cases for the economy, giving a wide interpretation of the relevant statutes. His concern for the practical application of the law is also revealed in "Grants of Probate and Letters of Administration", an article he wrote in the first volume of the *Alberta Law Quarterly* in 1934. Written in an unusually lively style, he presented a detailed introduction to wills and their administration in Alberta with references to practices in other western Canadian provinces.

Medhurst, Donald Herbert

District Court of Southern Alberta, Medicine Hat, November 28, 1974 - October 1, 1975
District Court of Alberta, Medicine Hat, October 1, 1975 - June 30, 1979
Court of Queen's Bench of Alberta, Calgary, June 30, 1979 -
Supernumerary Justice, March 14, 1990 -

The Honourable Justice Donald Herbert Medhurst was born on December 17, 1924, in Foremost, Alberta, a community founded by his grandfather. He was educated in Foremost before attending the University of Alberta, where he graduated with an LL.B. in 1949. After being admitted to the Alberta bar on June 14, 1951, Medhurst established the firm of Pritchard, Medhurst, Lerner and Wilkins in Medicine Hat. He was practicing with this firm when he was appointed to the DC in 1974.

Medhurst heard a wide range of cases which were published in the law reports of his era. His decisions included matters concerning public utilities, municipal corporation by-laws, real estate agreements, mortgages, contracts, matrimonial property, fraud, negligence, misrepresentation, and professional organizations. For example, in *Town of Castor v. Candel Oil Co.* ([1980] 11 ALR 2d 282), a 1963 natural gas agreement had a "favoured nations clause" that allowed the defendant to increase prices to equate with other customers. When the price of gas rose significantly, the plaintiff paid but sued to test the validity of the clause. Medhurst ruled that the clause was valid, relating only a few direct precedents. In *Royal Trust Corporation of Canada et al. v. Law Society of Alberta* ([1985] 38 ALR 2d 343), The Benchers had amended the Society's rules to prohibit members from depositing over $60,000 in trust to individual trust companies, or to corporations other than trusts. The plaintiff claimed that this amendment was *ultra vires* the Benchers powers. Medhurst ruled that it was, and limited the actions of the Benchers in a short and pithy judgment, citing only the most relevant authorities. Finally, in *Olson v. Spring Instant Greenhouses Ltd. et al.* ([1986] 41 ALR 2d 325), the plaintiff accountant had his salary reduced by a third because he also worked for associated companies, and he sued for wrongful dismissal. Medhurst upheld his claim in a highly literate account of his work and of defendant's obligations.

Miller, Tevie Harold

District Court of Northern Alberta, Edmonton, December 20, 1974 - October 1, 1975
District Court of Alberta, Edmonton, October 1, 1975 - July 8, 1976
Supreme Court of Alberta, Trial Division, Edmonton, July 8, 1976 - June 30, 1979
Court of Queen's Bench of Alberta, Edmonton, June 30, 1979 - August 21, 1996
Court of Queen's Bench of Alberta, Associate Chief Justice, Edmonton, February 24, 1984 - January 6, 1996
Supernumerary Justice, Court of Queen's Bench of Alberta, January 6, 1993 - August 21, 1996

The Honourable Tevie Harold Miller was born in Edmonton, Alberta, on January 1, 1928. Educated in Edmonton, he attended the University of Alberta, receiving a B.A. in 1949 and an LL.B. in 1950. After being admitted to the Alberta bar on May 23, 1951, Miller joined the firm of his father Abe W. Miller, a noted criminal lawyer in Edmonton. He became a senior partner of Miller, Witten, Pekarsky and Vogel in 1964. Miller engaged primarily in general counsel work and litigation, appeared fre-

quently in all levels of courts in Alberta, and on four occasions appeared before the SCC. He was named QC in 1968 and admitted to the Northwest Territories bar in the same year. Miller had a lengthy background of community involvement. He served as President of many organizations, including the United Way, the Edmonton Symphony Society, the General Alumni Association, and the Edmonton Liberal Association. He was Chancellor of the University of Alberta 1986-1990. For several years, he was a member of the Board of Governors of the University of Alberta, and a Sessional Lecturer at the University of Alberta Faculty of Law. He was also the first person to be made an honorary life member of the Alberta Association of Registered Nurses. He died in Edmonton on August 21, 1996. In addition to serving on the Alberta bench, Miller was also Deputy Judge of the SCNT 1976-1993 and Deputy Judge of the SCYT 1978-1993.

Miller presided over many criminal cases involving juveniles, as well as civil custody cases. His judgments were widely regarded as compassionate, thoughtful, and humane. He was distinguished by the number of his decisions which were reported, and by the number of precedents which emanated from his judgments. These included judgments written on the law of negotiable instruments, matrimonial property, defamation, and discrimination. Perhaps one of his most important cases was *Re. Wong and Hughes Petroleum Ltd.* ([1983] 28 ALR 2d 155), where a board of inquiry asked him to determine three questions of law based on a case of sexual discrimination. He held that the dismissal of a woman because of her pregnancy was not discrimination on the basis of sex, and thus no damages were claimable. In *Jones v. Jaworski* ([1989] 18 RFL (3d) 385), Miller broke new ground in varying a custody agreement to grant a father custody of children from a previous marriage when the mother moved to another province. His careful and sympathetic appraisal focused steadily on the best interests of the children.

Milvain, James Valentine Hogarth

Supreme Court of Alberta, Trial
    Division, Calgary, August 18, 1959
    - September 26, 1968
Supreme Court of Alberta, Trial
    Division, Chief Justice, Calgary,
    September 26, 1968 - February 14,
    1979

The Honourable James Valentine Hogarth Milvain was born near Lundbreck in the Livingstone District of the Northwest Territories on St. Valentine's Day, 1904. The son of an English immigrant to Canada in 1888, his mother Winnifred Helen Mac-Kintosh was the niece of G.H. MacKintosh, Lieutenant Governor of the NWT. Raised on a ranch, Milvain was educated at Lee School near Pincher Creek, at high school in Pincher Creek, and attended the University of Alberta where he had hoped to graduate in electrical engineering. Lacking language credits, he entered the Arts program and became a leading debater. Entering the Faculty of Law, he graduated with an LL.B. in 1926. Milvain articled with the firm of Virtue and Paterson of Lethbridge,

and credited A.G. Virtue with shaping his work ethic and mastery of detail. He moved to Calgary in 1927, where he worked with Fred Scott, and his close associates, J.J. Saucier and Max Peacock. He was admitted to the Alberta bar on November 14, 1927. From 1930 to 1945, Milvain was a member of the Calgary firm of Scott and Milvain. Both he and his wife, Edwina Belle, whom he married in 1932, were active in politics. She ran for the Unity Party and he unsuccessfully sought a federal seat as a Conservative in Calgary in 1935. He was named KC on December 31, 1943. Milvain formed another firm with F.L. Shouldice and Hugh John MacDonald in 1946, which became Milvain, MacDonald, Cheeseman and Moore in 1954. He left these associates in 1956 for the firm of Nolan, Chamber, Might, Saucier, Peacock and Jones, which was later renamed Chambers, Might, Saucier, Milvain, Peacock, Jones and Black. In 1959, Milvain was among those who argued and won the last Canadian case heard before the JCPC, *Wakefield v. Oil City* ([1959] 29 WWR 638), and he served as President of the Law Society of Alberta, 1958-1959. Appointed to the bench in 1959, he was made Chief Justice of the TD in 1968, Alberta's first native born Chief Justice. After his retirement on September 14, 1979, he again practiced law as a consultant with the firm of Atkinson, McMahon, Tingle and Harrison, the firm he founded. He received an honorary LL.D. from the University of Alberta in 1979 and from the University of Lethbridge in 1989. The Chief Justice Milvain School was named for him in Calgary in 1983, and in 1987 he was appointed an Officer of the Order of Canada. An avid hunter and fisherman, Milvain died on October 22, 1993.

Milvain's decisions and written judgments over twenty years would fill several volumes. They were especially numerous on capital felonies, negligence, judicial procedure, corporate law, contracts, and family law. They were also, at times, textual analyses of the law reminiscent of legal tracts. For example, in *Roenich v. Alberta Veterinary Medical Association* ([1968] 62 WWR 689), the plaintiff sought to overturn a malpractice citation under the Association's administrative procedure. Drawing upon case law and Anglo-Canadian jurisprudence, Milvain demonstrated the extent to which malpractice did not occur, and the doctor was restored to the rolls. In *Royal Insurance Co. Ltd. v. Portage La Prairie Mutual Insurance Co. Ltd. v. Bischoff* ([1968] 62 WWR 503), the question was whether the plaintiff had the right to sue the defendant to recover insurance costs from an underinsured party. Milvain constructed a model out of the case law on the subject to make the determination. Many of his decisions also involved the validity of municipal and provincial laws. For example, in *Canadian Freightways Ltd. v. Calgary City and Att. Gen. for Alberta* ([1967] 58 WWR 601), he ruled that the city had no power to licence trucks, and held that its by-law was *ultra vires*. Finally, many procedural issues came before him, as in *R. v. Muirhead* ([1975] 1 WWR 680), in which he held that PC judges have the jurisdiction to quash arrest warrants after the accused have appeared in court. Milvain served as Chairman of the Federal Conciliation Board inquiring into the contract dispute between the Canadian railways and the labour unions in 1960, was involved in several other inquiries, and supervised the windup of the failed Principal Group and its subsidiaries in 1987.

Known in the profession as "Uncle Val", Milvain was a warm and personable individual who prided himself on being an approachable judge, one who was ready to hear what people had to say outside of the courtroom. A dispute which reflected this interest involved the Cree Indian Band and the Southern Alberta Irrigation District (*Saint John's Calgary Report*, Feb. 16, 1979). The Band, who blocked the Peigan irrigation canal and ignored a court order to vacate the area, were cited for contempt of court when they did not appear to answer the charges against them. Milvain issued a public invitation to their leader Chief Nelson Small Legs to discuss the matter in chambers "Chief to Chief". The matter was resolved in chambers. In another case, a young unmarried woman left her infant child with another couple to raise, and went to California where she married (*The Albertan*, Feb. 12, 1979). Returning to Calgary several years later to reclaim the child, the foster parents contested. Milvain held that while the foster parents were excellent, he had to turn the child over to her natural mother. The child was taken out of the courtroom shrieking and crying. "She screamed in my soul", Milvain said. Six months later, he received a call from the new husband, who put the child on the line to tell the judge that she was very happy. Stories such as these were reported in the press throughout his tenure on the bench.

Near the end of his life, Milvain expressed concern with the progress of society. He lamented on what he saw as a spreading lawless spirit in society, a large crime wave, and an age of ugliness, and argued for the return of the death penalty. He also felt that the use of Legal Aid needlessly prolonged court cases which should have been settled out of court, and that, with the *Charter of Rights and Freedoms*, courts would throw the work of legislation back to the legislatures rather than having to create law where the government had no policy.

Mitchell, Charles Richmond

District Court of Calgary, Calgary,
    November 21, 1907 - May 31, 1910
Supreme Court of Alberta, Appellate
    Division, Calgary, March 13, 1926 -
    November 3, 1936
Supreme Court of Alberta, Trial
    Division, Chief Justice, Calgary,
    November 3, 1936 - August 16,
    1942

The Honourable Charles Richmond Mitchell was born in Newcastle, New Brunswick, on November 19, 1872. He was a nephew of the Honourable Peter Mitchell, a founding father of Confederation. Educated at Harkin's Academy in Newcastle, he received his B.A. from the University of New Brunswick in 1894, and his LL.B. from King's College in Windsor, Nova Scotia in 1897. Mitchell articled with the Honourable A.G. Blair in Saint John's before being admitted to the New Brunswick bar. He then practiced for a short time with the Honourable L.T. Tweedie, who later became the Lieutenant-Governor of New Bruns-

wick. Mitchell moved west in 1898 and settled in Medicine Hat. He was admitted to the bar of the NWT on May 21, 1898 and practiced there as a Crown Prosecutor, a City Solicitor, and an agent for the AG of Canada until his appointment to the DC in 1907. He resigned as a DC Justice in 1910 to run for the provincial Liberals, and on June 29, 1910, he was elected MLA for Medicine Hat. He was defeated in 1913, then re-elected the same year for the riding of Bow Valley. Mitchell was named KC on May 4, 1912. An outstanding speaker in the House, he quickly took a leadership role in the government of his former judicial colleague A.L. Sifton. He helped draft both the *Equal Suffrage Act* and *Liquor Act* of 1916. From 1920 to 1921, Mitchell was the AG of Alberta as well as Minister of Health, and Minister of Public Works. In 1921, he lost his seat when the United Farmers of Alberta formed the government. He left provincial politics and returned to the bench at Calgary in 1926. He received an honorary LL.D. from the University of Alberta in 1939. Mitchell died in Edmonton on August 16, 1942.

Mitchell authored numerous decisions in the Depression years on debtor-creditor disputes, and in accident, insurance, and negligence claims. In *Wheatland v. Iron Creek* ([1929] 1 WWR 531), an indigent who lost his homestead through foreclosure was given relief from the municipality he moved to and petitioned to be reimbursed by the one he moved from. Mitchell used English Poor Laws, cases, and legal treatises to hold that the original municipality had no obligation to the other one. In *Wagner v. Pine Lake* ([1931] 2 WWR 481), a physician tried to hold a municipality liable for his services given to a resident indigent. Mitchell, using a similar range of judicial discourse, held that each visit must be approved by the corporation because the legislation does not contemplate future visits without express written orders for payment. In *Wolfe and Wolfe v. City of Edmonton* ([1932] 1 WWR 129, 855), he held the city liable for "gross negligence" in not keeping a pedestrian crosswalk on Jasper Avenue clear of snow. Mitchell also used his legislative experience in interpreting statutes. Thus, in *Bliss et al. v. Malmberg* ([1929] 3 WWR 641), he upheld the motorist's "duty to sound horn" as a reasonable test in vehicular accident cases. Mitchell's career on appeals was largely in the shadow of Justice Harvey, with whose judgments Mitchell often concurred. Harvey also paid him high tribute at his death.

Moir, Arnold Fraser

Supreme Court of Alberta, Appellate
    Division, Calgary, May 18, 1973 -
    June 30, 1979
Court of Appeal of Alberta, Calgary,
    June 30, 1979 - September 24, 1987

The Honourable Arnold Fraser Moir was born in Fort Macleod, Alberta, on November 23, 1918. He attended the University of Alberta, earning a B.A. in 1942. He received the Gold Medal for his class when he graduated from the University of Alberta with an LL.B. in 1946. He continued to study law at Harvard University where he received his LL.M. in 1948. Moir was admitted to the Alberta bar on May 30, 1947. He

developed an active practice as a litigation lawyer in Edmonton and was a member of the Edmonton firm of Wood, Moir, Hyde and Ross. He became one of the leading civil lawyers in Edmonton during his twenty-six years in practice, with appearances in some celebrated cases and Royal Commissions. Moir was appointed QC on December 31, 1959. Elevated in 1973 to both the bench at Calgary, and the CANT, Moir was appointed to the Alberta Court of Appeal in 1979. He was a Sessional Instructor at the University of Alberta's Faculty of Law for many years, and President of the Law Society of Alberta 1970-1971. As a Bencher of the Law Society of Alberta and President, 1970-1971, Moir was an advocate for progressive change in the administration of justice leading the way in instituting legal aid and negligence insurance in Alberta. He was also appointed to the CANT in 1973. He died on September 24, 1987.

Moir was one of the more prominent writers of judgments of the AD in the 1970s. His style was distinctive, based on cases and writings from around the common law world, and some of his judgments were small tracts within themselves, especially on the subject of the law of evidence. *R. v. Fraser* ([1981] 15 ALR 2d 25) involved a charge of murder with a conviction for manslaughter under self-defence. Tried before Moir alone on appeal, the defence was based on the deceased making a homosexual attack on the accused. Examining case law and legal writings in Great Britain and Australia, where more of these circumstances were prosecuted, and the amount of violence that was committed at the crime, Moir held that the trial judge had misdirected the jury and ordered a new trial. In *Duhamel v. R.* ([1982] 17 ALR 2d 127), the accused was charged with two armed robberies, acquitted on the first one because his culpable statements were not admissible, and convicted on the second when the judge allowed the statements to be entered. The defendant appealed, but Moir held that the Crown could relitigate that evidence and dismissed the appeal. Finally, in *Clarke & Gerbrandt et al.* ([1985] 34 ALR 289), Moir allowed a new trial because evidence of a witness that was disallowed should have been admitted. In these and other appeal cases, Moir helped define evidentiary law in the province.

Montgomery, Robert Archibald Fraser

Court of Queen's Bench of Alberta, Calgary, November 4, 1982 -

The Honourable Justice Robert Archibald Fraser Montgomery was born in Toronto, Ontario, on July 5, 1928. He attended the Royal Canadian Naval College in Royal Roads, British Columbia, 1945-1947, before entering Queen's University, Kingston, in 1948. He graduated from Queen's with a B.Comm. and a B.A. in 1951. Montgomery received his LL.B. from the University of Toronto in 1954. He was admitted to the bars of British Columbia in 1955, Ontario in 1956, and Alberta on November 13, 1958. Montgomery began his career at National Revenue Taxation, Ottawa, in 1955, before joining the law firm of Borden Elliot in 1957. He moved to Calgary in 1958, and practiced with

the Calgary firm of Macleod Dixon where he specialized in civil litigation until his appointment to the bench in 1982. Montgomery was named QC on December 29, 1977.

Montgomery had a number of decisions reported which concerned largely mortgages, contracts, and municipal affairs. *MacDonald v. MacDonald* ([1985] 36 ALR 2d 336) was a suit for alimony under provincial statutes. The applicant sought a reduction of payments because he was in arrears. His application, however, was rejected in chambers. Since the original sum was determined in Ontario, and divorce proceedings were in progress, Montgomery ordered a lump sum payment that amounted to approximately half of the sum owing. And in *Prete v. Governors of the University of Calgary et al.* ([1989] 65 ALR 2d 381), the University was sued by a cyclist who fell off her bike and suffered injuries as a result of hitting a new second speed bump in a parking lot. Montgomery dismissed the action, holding that the University could not foresee such an accident, and the rider must exercise due caution.

Moore, William Kenneth

Supreme Court of Alberta, Trial Division, Calgary, January 20, 1972 - June 30, 1979
Court of Queen's Bench of Alberta, Calgary, June 30, 1979 -
Court of Queen's Bench of Alberta, Associate Chief Justice, Calgary, April 28, 1981 - February 24, 1984
Court of Queen's Bench of Alberta, Chief Justice, Calgary, February 24, 1984 -

The Honourable Justice William Kenneth Moore was born in Calgary, Alberta on December 5, 1925. He enlisted in the Canadian Navy in 1944, serving as a Special Telegraph Operator in the North Atlantic. After being discharged in 1945, he attended the University of Alberta where he graduated with a B.A. in 1949 and an LL.B. in 1952. During his years as a student, Moore played professional football for the Calgary Stampeders in 1946 and 1951, and for the Edmonton Eskimos in 1949 and 1950. Moore was admitted to the Alberta bar on June 10, 1953 and established a legal practice in Calgary. He was named QC on December 29, 1967. Prior to his appointment to the bench, he practiced law with Moore, Lougheed, Atkinson, McMahon and Tingle in Calgary. He served as Vice-Chairman of the Canadian Judicial Council, 1988-1990.

As Chief Justice, Moore has skillfully steered the trial court through major administrative challenges of increased caseloads since 1984. Moore also authored a long string of reported decisions on a wide variety of cases. In one of his earlier trials, *R. v. Engen* ([1983] 45 AR 1), a driver who was stopped and given a breathalyzer test was allowed an appeal because he was not informed of his right to retain legal counsel. Many of his written judgments were delivered on civil cases. In *Re Sulpetro Limited Retirement Plan Fund* ([1988] 66 ALR 2nd 18), he examined U.S. and Canadian cases to rule on the distribution of funds to equal members of a pension fund. In the major case of *Medicine Hat v. A-G (Canada)* ([1983] 30 ALR 2d 218), the constitutional right of the federal government to tax a municipality that distributed its natural gas and electricity to its residents directly was challenged by the municipality. Moore held that the city was not an agent of the provincial Crown, and that the collection of taxes did not affect the city's management of its affairs. These decisions reflect careful analysis of the nature of rights in law and how their boundaries are determined.

Morrison, Frederic Augustus

District Court of Stettler, Stettler,
    October 7, 1916 - February 25, 1929

His Honour Frederic Augustus Morrison was born at Scotch Ridge, in the Parish of Saint James County in Charlotte, New Brunswick, on September 28, 1875. His grandfather had founded the settlement with other clansmen from Sutherlandshire. Morrison was educated in the public school of Scotch Ridge. He had a distinguished academic career at Dalhousie University, where he graduated from with a B.A. in 1897 and an LL.B. in 1901. In 1903, Morrison moved west and practiced law for two years in Winnipeg and Regina before settling in Vegreville, Alberta in 1905. He was admitted to the NWT bar on November 29, 1905 and practiced in Vegreville for nine years before his appointment to the DC at Stettler in 1916. He did not author, however, any written judgments which were reported in the law reports. Morrison was interested in politics and ran twice as a Conservative candidate for the federal Parliament, both times unsuccessfully. He served as Town Clerk and Legal Counsel to the Town Council in Vegreville. Active in the

Masonic and Elk Clubs, he was also a member of the Granite Curling Club, the Mayfair Country Club, the Burns Society, and the Presbyterian Church. He died in Edmonton on February 25, 1929.

Morrow, William George

Supreme Court of Alberta, Appellate
    Division, Calgary, May 28, 1976 -
    June 30, 1979
Court of Appeal of Alberta, Calgary,
    June 30, 1979 - August 13, 1980

The Honourable William George Morrow was born in Edmonton, Alberta on February 5, 1917. He received his B.A. from the University of Alberta in 1938, and his LL.B. from Dalhousie University in 1939. After articling with his father in Edmonton, he was admitted to the Alberta bar on June 19, 1940. He joined the Canadian Navy in 1942, where he did active duty on a minesweeper. Following the War, he returned to his father's firm. Admitted to the Northwest Territories bar in 1959, and the Yukon bar in 1960, Morrow practiced in Edmonton with the firm of Morrow, Reynolds, Stevenson and Kane from 1940 to his apppointment to the bench of the Northwest Territories. He was named QC on December 31, 1953. Morrow, along with J.H. Laycraft, R.A. MacKimmie, W.A. Stevenson, and J.V.H. Milvain, was counsel in *Wakefield v. Oil City* ([1959] 29 WWR 638), which became the last Canadian Appeal to the JCPC in July 1959. He litigated several major oil and gas cases in the 1940s and 1950s. In addition to his service on the SCA and the Territorial Court of the Northwest Territories,

Morrow was Justice of the SCNT, 1966-1976, Deputy Judge, SCNT, 1976-1980, Justice of the CANT, 1971-1980, and Justice of the CAYT, 1971-1980. He received an honorary LL.D. from both the University of Alberta in 1972, and the University of Calgary in 1974, as well as a D.U.C. from the University of Calgary in 1975. Morrow died in Edmonton on August 13, 1980.

Morrow's judicial career had a great impact on the administration of justice in Canada, especially as it relates to Aboriginals. A judicial reformer and visionary, he identified Aboriginal societies as a crucial component of the Canadian national identity. He replaced John Howard Sissons as resident Judge of the Territorial Court of the Northwest Territories in 1966 and served until 1976, when he was appointed to the AD. During his tenure in the north, Morrow was especially sensitive to Aboriginal rights and he sought to make Canadian law flexible enough to accommodate the traditions and values of First Nations. Morrow was involved in several landmark northern cases, involving the complexities of international wildlife legislation, native hunting rights and witchcraft. Most notably, he heard *R. v. Drybones* ([1967] 61 WWR 370) where a native charged with a drinking offence under the *Indian Act* was subject to a more severe penalty than a non-native person under the *Liquor Ordinance*. In *R. v. Bernhardt* ([1971] 4 WWR 693), the accused had been convicted of child neglect that stemmed from a drinking problem. Morrow reduced the sentence, altered the terms of probation, and conceived of a sanction that the accused could fulfil. In *R. v. Kupiyana* ([1972] 2 WWR 418), where an Inuit was charged with violating the *Migratory Birds Act*, he dropped the charge and questioned the sufficiency of the Act. Morrow also championed inclusion of more Aboriginals in jury trials. As an appeal court justice, he wrote a creative judgment in the area of land rights in *Seifeddine etc. v. Governor v. Tornado* ([1980] 11 ALR 2d 229). The appellant, who tried to remove caveats requiring single residence lots, was denied by the surrounding landowners, and appealed. Citing nineteenth-century English case law, Morrow held that the landowners' desire to retain their building scheme was in conformity with English property law.

In 1968, Morrow was Commissioner of an Inquiry into the Administration of Justice in Hay River, where he addressed the problem of rising criminality among the younger Aboriginal people. He sought remedies in their local customs and behaviourial norms. He also gave many lectures on these problems, wrote some influential articles for the *Alberta Law Review*, and contributed material to the *Trial Judges Journal* and the *Journal of Natural Resource Management and Interdisciplinary Studies*.

Moshansky, Virgil Peter

Supreme Court of Alberta, Trial
    Division, Calgary, May 27, 1976 -
    June 30, 1979
Court of Queen's Bench of Alberta,
    Calgary, June 30, 1979 -
Supernumerary Justice, Calgary,
    September 14, 1993 -

The Honourable Virgil Peter Moshansky was born in Lamont, Alberta, on September 14, 1928. Educated in Lamont, he attended the University of Alberta, graduating with a B.A. in Political Science in 1951, and an LL.B. in 1954. He articled with W.O. Parlee, QC, of Smith, Clement, Parlee and Whittaker in Edmonton before being admitted to the Alberta bar on May 31, 1955. He established a practice in Vegreville, where he remained for the next twenty-one years. When he was appointed to the bench in 1976, Moshansky was with the firm of Moshansky and Blonsky, where he specialized in civil and criminal litigation. He was appointed QC on January 26, 1976. Always very involved in the community, Moshansky served as Mayor of Vegreville, Alberta, from 1970 to 1976. From 1956 to 1976, he served as Agent and Special Counsel to the AG of Alberta. The first judge to be appointed to the SCA from outside the major cities in 1976, Moshansky is also the first lawyer of Ukrainian ethnic origin appointed directly to the SCA. Possessed of a keen interest in aviation, Justice Moshansky has his own plane, a Piper Arrow, which he uses to get around Alberta quickly while conducting his judicial duties. He presided over the six month trial in 1981-1982 arising from the PanArctic air crash at Edmonton International Airport. Moshansky served as Chair of PanArctic Oils Ltd., International Jet Air Ltd., and Menfred Manufacturing Co., and headed the Royal Commission of Inquiry into the Air Ontario crash at Dryden, Ontario, which killed twenty-four people. Moshansky was named as the recipient of an Aerospace Laurel Award for 1992 from *Aviation Week & Space Technology Magazine*, which is presented annually to honor individuals who make significant contributions in the field of aerospace.

Murray, Alec Thirlwell

Court of Queen's Bench of Alberta,
    Edmonton, October 30, 1987 -

The Honourable Justice Alec Thirlwell Murray was born in Medicine Hat, Alberta, on August 7, 1932. He attended the University of Alberta, obtaining a B.Comm. in 1954 and an LL.B. in 1961, and was admitted to the Alberta bar on June 13, 1961. Prior to his appointment to the bench at Edmonton, Murray practiced with the firm of Parlee, McLaws, Irving, Henning, Mustard and Rodney. He was appointed QC on January 30, 1978.

Newlands, Henry William

Supreme Court of the North-West
    Territories, District of Western
    Assiniboia, Regina, January 2, 1904
    - September 16, 1907

The Honourable Henry William Newlands was born in Dartmouth, Nova Scotia on March 19, 1862. Attending public school in Halifax, he articled there with the famous maritime firm of Thompson, Graham and Tupper and was called to the Nova Scotia bar in 1883. Newlands moved in that year to Winnipeg, Manitoba, where he practiced for several years as a partner in the firm of McDonald, Tupper, McCarther and Dexter. He then travelled to Prince Albert, NWT, and was admitted to the North-West Territories bar on April 8, 1886.

Newlands was appointed Inspector of the Land Titles Office in Regina in 1897 and served as a legal advisor to the Yukon Territory Council in 1901. He returned to the NWT in 1904 to replace Richardson on the bench at Regina. His work in the District of Western Assiniboia brought him into the area of what is now southwestern Alberta. Subsequently, he was appointed to the Supreme Court of Saskatchewan, 1907-1918, and to the Court of Appeal of Saskatchewan, 1918-1921. He also served on several royal commissions, including the commission to review the statutes and ordinances applicable to the new province of Saskatchewan in 1906, and for the revision and consolidation of the provincial statutes in 1918. Newlands was quite active in his local community of Regina. He was elected President of the Canadian Club in 1908, and of the Society for the Advancement of Art, Science and Literature in 1910. A devout Presbyterian, he supported the Liberal Party and became Lieutenant Governor of Saskatchewan. Newlands retired on February 17, 1921, and died in 1954.

Newlands was an expert on real estate law and his reported decisions and written judgments reflect that expertise at both the trial and appeal levels. He also delivered a number of written judgments on cases involving foreign companies in the Territories, ranging from banks and insurance companies to equipment manufacturers. However, in only one of those cases reported was he listed as a member of the bench in southern Alberta: *Daye v. H.W. McNeill Co.* ([1903] 6 TLR 23).

Noel, Joseph Camillien

District Court of Wetaskiwin,
    Wetaskiwin, November 21, 1907 -
    July 6, 1909
District Court of Athabasca,
    Edmonton, July 6, 1909 - March 16,
    1920

His Honour Joseph Camillien Noel was born in Lotmiere, Quebec on May 12, 1864. He was educated at Sherbrook College and Bishop's College in Lennoxville, Quebec. Reading law with Penneton and Mulvena in Sherbrooke, Noel was admitted to the Quebec bar in 1887. He practiced in Inverness, Quebec until 1901, when he joined the great gold rush to the Yukon Territory. He set up a practice in Dawson City with his brother August and D.M. McKinnon. John Cormack joined the firm called Noel, Noel and Cormack, and in 1906 the firm moved to Edmonton. Noel was appointed to the DC at Wetaskiwin in the next year. He was appointed to the newly established District of Athabasca in 1909, where he presided over the DC sitting in Edmonton until his death. A Catholic and a Liberal, his father had been a close personal friend of Sir Wilfrid Laurier. Noel followed in his father's footsteps, and visited Laurier whenever he was in Ottawa. Diagnosed with pernicious anemia in 1919, he left for Montreal, hoping to go to Baltimore for further treatment. However, his health never recovered for the journey, and he died in Montreal on March 16, 1920.

Noel had few of his judgments published in the law reports. In *Cangeme v. The Alberta Coal and Mining Co.* ([1912] 2 WWR 1059), Chief Justice Harvey set aside his judgment against a contractor who sought compensation under the *Workmen's Compensation Act* with harsh words because it was in error. And, in *Nikkiczuk v. McArthur* ([1916] 9 ALR 508), Noel's award under the same Act was appealed. In a 2-1 decision, the CA held that the accident of frostbite to the applicant's feet while constructing a railway at minus 60 celsius "arose" out of his employment, and thus the appeal was denied.

O'Byrne, Michael Brien

Supreme Court of Alberta, Trial
    Division, Edmonton, September 19,
    1967 - June 30, 1979
Court of Queen's Bench of Alberta,
    June 30, 1979 -
Supernumerary Justice, December 24,
    1990 -

The Honourable Justice Michael Brien O'Byrne was born in Seattle, Washington on September 9, 1925. During World War II he served with the Royal Canadian Navy. He attended the University of Alberta, graduating with a B.A. in 1950 and an LL.B. in 1951. After being called to the Alberta bar on May 23, 1952, O'Byrne set up practice in Edmonton. He was with the firm of Ogilvie, O'Byrne and Gallant in Edmonton when he was appointed to the bench in 1967.

During his judicial career, O'Byrne has lectured in law at the University of Alberta and the University of Victoria. He also instituted an educational leave program for judges. O'Byrne's judgment in *Ares v. Venner and Seton Hospital* ([1969] 70 WWR 96) established a modern exception to the hearsay rule of evidence by allowing the written perceptions of nurses to be admitted in a negligence action against a doctor. While the case was over-turned on appeal, the SCC restored O'Byrne's ruling in 1970. His appeal judgment in *Huggard Assets Ltd. v. Attorney General for Alberta and Minister of Lands and Mines in Alberta* ([1949] 2 WWR 370, [1950] 1 WWR 69) upheld the ground-breaking case on the ownership of natural resources.

O'Connor, George Bligh

Supreme Court of Alberta, Trial
    Division, Edmonton, January 13,
    1941 - October 30, 1946
Supreme Court of Alberta, Appellate
    Division, Edmonton, October 30,
    1946 - January 13, 1957
Chief Justice of Alberta, Edmonton,
    January 25, 1950 - January 13, 1957

The Honourable George Bligh O'Connor was born in Walkerton, Ontario, on March 15, 1883. In 1905, he graduated with an LL.B. from Osgoode Hall in Toronto, winning the Silver Medal and was called to the bar of Ontario that same year. O'Connor immediately moved to Edmonton and was admitted to the bar of the North-West Territories on November 6, 1905. He practiced with the firm of Gries-bach, O'Connor and Company and was appointed KC in 1913. He was with this firm when he was appointed to the bench in 1941.

O'Connor's reported judgments are brief and concise, dealing with mainly civil law. Two examples include: *Shandro v. Municipal District of Eagle No. 81* ([1946] 1 WWR 505), where O'Connor held for the plaintiff whose land had been up for tax sale, was leased by the municipality, but returned to the owner when taxes were paid, awarding him the lease payments; and *Roe v. MacLeod (Silver Glade Roller Bowl)* ([1946] 2 WWR 482), a negligence case. O'Connor considered various principles in tort law to establish that the company was negligent for the injury suffered by the plaintiff because of an improperly fitted roller skate, in spite of the risks involved and signs posted at the arena. He served on several important inquiries, including the 1943 Royal Commission on wages paid to coal miners. He died in Edmonton on January 13, 1957.

O'Leary, Willis Edward

Court of Queen's Bench of Alberta,
    December 22, 1983 - September 27,
    1994
Court of Appeal of Alberta,
    September 27, 1994 -

The Honourable Justice Willis Edward O'Leary was born in Vulcan, Alberta on September 6, 1931 but grew up in Calgary. He received a degree in Business Administration from the University of Denver, and obtained his LL.B. from the University of British Columbia in 1962 where he was the Gold Medallist in Law. He then attended Harvard Law School and received an LL.M. in 1963. After being admitted to the Alberta bar on July 2, 1964, O'Leary practiced with the Calgary firm of Fenerty and Company for two years before becoming a partner in the firm of Lutz, Westerberg, O'Leary and Stevenson in 1966. As a lawyer, O'Leary specialized in litigation and oil and gas law. He was with the successor firm of Westerberg, O'Leary, Fenerty and MacDonald when he was appointed to the bench in 1983. He was also appointed Justice of the CANT in 1994.

Parlee, Harold Hayward

Supreme Court of Alberta, Trial
  Division, Edmonton, December 19,
  1944 - April 9, 1945
Supreme Court of Alberta, Appellate
  Division, Edmonton, April 9, 1945
  - February 28, 1954

The Honourable Harold Hayward Parlee was born in Sussex, New Brunswick on March 22, 1877. He was educated at Mount Allison University, Sackville, and received his B.A. from Dalhousie University in 1899, and his LL.B. from Saint John's Law School in 1900. He was admitted to the New Brunswick bar in 1901. Practicing in New Brunswick for the following year, Parlee moved to Alberta in 1902. He was called to the NWT bar on September 24, 1906. Parlee established the firm of Parlee and Company in Edmonton and practised with them for the next thirty-eight years. He was named KC on March 19, 1913. Parlee was a lawyer for the Canadian Bank of Commerce, and he was named as one of the "Banker's Toadies" in a Social Credit Broadside in 1937 that resulted in the imprisonment of the Socred member of the Legislative Assembly, Josepf Unwin, on the charge of inciting to murder. Appointed to the SCA at Edmonton in 1944, he was elevated to the AD the next year. Parlee was President of the Law Society of Al-

berta, 1933-1935, and Chairman of the Board of Directors of the University of Alberta from 1940 to 1950, where he was influential in the dynamic growth of the University. He received honorary LL.D.s from the University of Alberta and from the University of Mount Allison in 1945. Parlee died in Edmonton on February 28, 1954.

An expert in oil and gas law, Parlee's major decisions were in those areas. He also wrote judgments on motor vehicle law and statutory interpretation. His judgments were regarded as strong and authoritative. Often he disagreed with his senior colleagues Harvey and Ford, if not in the decision, then in its reasoning. Parlee's judgments were short. He identified the facts succinctly, identified the questions of law, and then gave brief but thorough references to the leading authorities. Eschewing legal principles and doctrines in his writings, brevity and conciseness was his motto.

Parlee wrote judgments on negligence, oil and gas law, administrative law, and commercial law. His decisions were regarded as strong, authoritative, and brief. In *Charuk v. Harvey et al.* ([1945] 3 WWR 571), he rejected an appeal to override the ruling of a military tribunal to imprison a conscript for failing to report and was skeptical of the claim that the plaintiff was a Jehovah's Witness minister. In *Halwa and Halwa v. Olson and Ervin et al.* ([1948] 1 WWR 1049), Parlee allowed the plaintiffs to rectify a mistake made in a transfer document, and reserved for them the rights to mines and minerals in a property because it was never their intent to give them up. In a negligence case, Parlee overturned a trial judgment which denied negligence on the part of the operator of a truck which killed a mechanic in a garage in *Kirschman v. Nichols* ([1950] 2 WWR 420). Parlee found both parties equally negligent, considering that the driver did not check the gear before starting the engine.

Patterson, Henry Stuart

District Court of Southern Alberta, Calgary, April 7, 1960 - October 1, 1975

District Court of Alberta, Calgary, October 1, 1975 - June 30, 1979

Court of Queen's Bench of Alberta, Calgary, June 30, 1979 - November 3, 1988

Supernumerary Justice, Calgary, September 1, 1979 - November 3, 1988

The Honourable Henry Stuart Patterson was born in Calgary, Alberta, on October 9, 1913. He was educated at the University of Alberta, where he received his B.A. in 1936, and his LL.B. in 1937. After articling with H.S. Patterson, Sr. he was admitted to the Alberta bar on June 23, 1938. He was a partner in the Calgary firm of Patterson, Patterson and MacPherson prior to his appointment to the DC there in 1960, and eventually to the QB in 1979. Patterson was President of the Law Society of Alberta from 1948 to 1949, and he was named QC on December 30, 1963. He served as Chairman for the Provincial Committee on Adoption Procedures 1963-1964. Patterson retired on November 3, 1988, and died in Calgary on March 1, 1990.

Patterson has had a few reported judgments of significance, primarily on corporate and constitutional law. In *Royal Bank of Canada v. Cressler Hotels Ltd.* ([1980] 14 ALR 2d 279), a builder's lien was filed against the defendant when his company was struck from the corporate rolls. Patterson held that, as the company was doing business, the lien could be maintained as if the company had not been registered. In *R. v. Bienart* ([1985] 39 ALR 2d 198), a private religious school was not approved by the province. The pastor of the school would not cease classes, and was thus convicted. While the defendant held that God did not allow governments domain over the Church, the Court held that withholding the school from operation did not abrogate the *Education Act*, nor the *Charter of Rights and Freedoms* provisions for the free expression of religion, and the conviction was upheld. Patterson's judgments displayed a fine sense of the hierarchy of rights, and of interests under statute law, which were molded into a concept of the public good.

Perras, Delmar Walter Joseph

Court of Queen's Bench of Alberta, Edmonton, October 4, 1989 -

The Honourable Justice Delmar Walter Joseph Perras was born on October 20, 1934. He graduated from the University of Saskatchewan with a B.A. in 1961, and an LL.B. in 1962. He was admitted to the Saskatchewan bar in 1963 and the Alberta bar on September 5, 1984. From 1973 to 1976,

Perras was a Sessional Lecturer in the College of Law at the University of Saskatchewan. He was also Director of Public Prosecutions for the Province of Saskatchewan from 1976 to 1983. He joined the Department of the AG of Alberta in 1983 and was made Deputy AG in 1984. Perras is one of the founding members of the Western Canada Crown Seminar which is held annually in Banff, Alberta. He has also published several articles on criminal justice.

Picard, Ellen Irene

Court of Queen's Bench of Alberta,
    Edmonton, January 1, 1986 - April
    27, 1995
Court of Appeal of Alberta,
    Edmonton, April 27, 1995 -

The Honourable Justice Ellen Irene Picard was born in Blairmore, Alberta on February 2, 1941. She graduated from the University of Alberta with a B.Ed. in 1964, an LL.B. in 1967, and an LL.M. in 1980. Picard was admitted to the Alberta bar on August 29, 1968, and she practiced law in Edmonton with the firm of Matheson and Company until 1972. She was a Professor at the University of Alberta Faculty of Law from 1972 until 1986, where she was also Associate Dean of Law, 1974-1975 and 1980-1981. She became a Willis Cunningham Visitor at Queen's University in 1986, and a Visiting Professor at the University of Auckland in 1985. Picard is a founder of the Health Law Institute at the University of Alberta and she was its Director from 1977 to 1986. She was also a Professor in the Faculty of Medicine and taught law and medicine to stu-

dents and physicians for ten years. The Health Law Institute of the Faculty of Law at the University of Alberta hosts an annual lecture, the Picard Lecture, in her name. Picard has lectured and written extensively in the area of health law, and she is the author of the textbook *Legal Liability of Doctors and Hospitals in Canada* which is in its third edition and has been cited often by the Courts. Picard has been a Board and Executive Member of the Alberta Institute of Law Research and Reform, as well as a consultant to the Law Reform Commission of Canada on a number of projects. Picard received an honorary LL.D. from the University of Alberta in 1992. Appointed to the Alberta bench, Picard was also appointed Deputy Judge of the SCNT, 1992-1995, and is a Justice of the CANT since 1995.

Picard has written judgments for a number of cases relating to health and family law. In *McKale v. Lamont Auxiliary Hospital and Nursing Home District No. 23* ([1987] 3 WWR 748), an employee appealed a decision of the Alberta Human Rights Commission. Picard upheld the Board's decision that a nursing home's policy of replacing male employees for operational reasons was justified under the *Individual's Rights Protection Act.* She investigated fully the expert testimony as well as the facts and case law, concluding that discrimination is allowed in order to uphold the dignity and privacy of patients. In *McVey v. Petruk et al.* ([1991] 77 ALR 2d 88), she upheld the defendant's election of a jury trial in a medical negligence case, outling guidelines for ensuring that expert testimony can be made understandable and feasible for a jury.

D.G.S. v. S.L.S. ([1990] 74 ALR 2d 168) was a troubling child custody trial in which the father was awarded custody in view of the irrational and abusive actions of the mother. Picard did, however, provide for supervised access with the mother to allow the possibility of rehabilitiation and reform.

Porter, Marshall Menzies

Supreme Court of Alberta, Appellate
    Division, Calgary, September 1,
    1954 - October 12, 1969

The Honourable Marshall Menzies Porter was born in Sarnia, Ontario, on October 12, 1894, and he moved to Medicine Hat, Alberta, in 1913. After receiving his LL.B. from Dalhousie University in 1917, he remained in Halifax and joined the Canadian military. In 1919, he returned to Alberta where he was admitted to the Alberta bar on March 20, 1920. Prior to his appointment to the bench in 1954, he was a senior partner in the firm of Porter, Allen and MacKimmie. Porter's firm pioneered oil and gas law during the second oil boom after 1947. Porter was Vice-President of Home Oil Company, then the largest independent producer of crude oil in Canada, and he was President of the Alberta Salt Company until its sale in 1951. He also represented the Province of Alberta in the transfer of natural resources to the Provincial Government from the Federal Government in 1935. Porter was President of Western Printing and Lithographing Limited and the *Farm and Ranch* newspaper. He was a Director of the Bank of Nova Scotia and he served as Counsel for the Alberta Wheat Pool.

Porter was also a Director and Honorary Treasurer of the Calgary Exhibition and Stampede. Porter received honorary degrees from Dalhousie University, Indiana Technical College and Curry College in Boston. He retired on October 12, 1969, the first judge of the AD forced to leave by reason of the requirement for retirement at age 75. He died on July 29, 1985.

Porter was a very active justice and one who wrote a large number of decisions on constitutional, criminal, and natural resources law. He was a very independent mind on the bench. Writing minority opinions on numerous occasions, some of his most important judgments were in dissent. For example, in *Deputy Sheriff of Calgary v. Walter's Trucking Service* ([1965] 51 WWR 407), he contended that the right of the Crown with respect to debts owed it arose from the common law. As the Crown was divided in Canada, that division must be examined closely to determine the priority of claims in a case involving competing interests. Porter was also concerned with procedural grounds in many of his judgments. Thus, in *R. v. Parson* ([1957] 21 WWR 337), he held in a minority opinion that a local magistrate who had failed to fulfil all his duties to the defendant should be prohibited from continuing a preliminary inquiry. Porter was also interested in civil rights questions. In *R. v. Martin* ([1961] 35 WWR 385), the Court was faced with the validity of non-intrusive physical tests for impairment. Porter argued that such tests were of questionable legality; an accused must not only be protected from involuntary confessions, but also from involuntary acts such as walking a line to demonstrate guilt.

Tempered by mercy and an understanding of changing social attitudes, Porter's judgments also challenged received views. In *R. v. J.* ([1957] 21 WWR 248), an acquittal of the defendant on a charge of gross indecency was appealed. Porter upheld the decision of the Police Magistrate, finding that the act did not constitute gross indecency under the statute, and questioned whether the case should have been prosecuted at all. In *R. v. Belzberg* ([1961] 35 WWR 402), he ignored recommendations that the defendant's advanced age be considered in sentencing and, in upholding the conviction of attempted bribery of a public official, imposed a prison sentence of six months. Finally, he heard a number of cases involving natural resources, delivering several precedents and opening up legal questions in this area of the law. In *Duncan v. Joslin and Joslin* ([1965] 51 WWR 346), he ruled that the leasing of mineral rights by someone without the authority to do so did not equal an act of possession or ownership. In *Trans Mountain Oil Pipeline Company v. Jasper School District No. 3063* ([1956] 20 WWR 680), in supporting the majority decision he reserved consideration of the application of tax acts without examining taxing bodies other than the province. Throughout his career on the bench, Porter was a probing judge and one of the best legal minds of the mid-century.

Power, Peter Charles Garneau

Court of Queen's Bench of Alberta, Calgary, November 27, 1979 -

Supernumerary Justice, Calgary, April 27, 1995 -

The Honourable Justice Peter Charles Garneau Power was born in Montreal, Quebec on April 16, 1930. Educated in Montreal, he attended Dalhousie University where he graduated with a B.Comm. in 1953 and an LL.B. in 1956. After being admitted to the Alberta bar on July 4, 1957, Power joined the Edmonton firm of Milner, Steer, Dyde, Massie, Layton, Cregan and MacDonnell. He moved to Red Deer in 1960, and became a partner in the firm of Robinson, Holmes, Crowe, Paisley and Power. He was practicing with the successor firm of Crowe, Power, Johnston, Ming, Scammell and Manning when he was appointed to the bench at Calgary in 1979. He was named QC on December 19, 1973. Active in civic affairs, Power served as an Alderman on Red Deer City Council from 1961 to 1966, and as a Red Deer Public School Trustee from 1971 to 1979.

Power decided numerous cases which were reported in his era. They ranged widely from business and commercial matters such as banking agreements, builders contracts, mortgages and guarantors, workers compensation, and negligence, to matrimonial law, criminal law, and language rights. For example, *Hornburg et al. v. Toole, Peet & Co. Ltd., Canadian Home Assurance Company, Marhlinger and Smith* ([1980] 13 ALR 2d 363), the plaintiff had his country residence insured from the defendant company, and did not inquire whether the residence had to be permanent or temporary. Power dismissed the claim, presenting a line of precedents from English to Cana

Yaroslaw Roslak *(LASA)*

Charles Borromée Rouleau *(LASA)*

Henry Slater Rowbotham *(LASA)*

David Lynch Scott *(LASA)*

William Sellar *(QB)*

Melvin Earl Shannon *(AJ)*

Arthur Lewis Sifton *(GAI)*

William Charles Simmons *(LASA)*

William Robert Sinclair *(LASA)*

John Howard Sissons *(LASA)*

Sidney Bruce Smith *(LASA)*

Vernor Winfield MacBriare Smith *(AJ)*

Luke Hannon Stack (*LASA*)

William Alexander Stevenson (*CA*)

Joseph John Stratton (*LASA*)

Charles Allan Stuart (*LASA*)

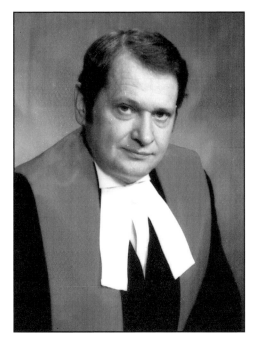

Allen Borislaw Zenoviy Sulatycky   *(LASA)*

Edward Rusling Tavender

Hedley Clarence Taylor   *(PAA)*

Marguerite Jean Trussler   *(LASA)*

Louis Sherman Turcotte   *(CLA)*

Thomas Mitchell March Tweedie   *(LASA)*

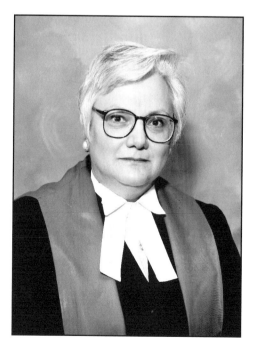

Joanne Barbara Veit   *(LASA)*

Charles Gladstone Virtue   *(LASA)*

Allan Harvey Joseph Wachowich *(LASA)*

John Hilary Waite *(AJ)*

William Legh Walsh *(LASA)*

Edward Ludlow Wetmore *(SAB)*

Bruce Cavanagh Whittaker *(AJ)*

Ernest Brown Wilson *(AJ)*

William Roland Winter *(LASA)*

Clarence George Yanosik *(LASA)*

dian case law. In *Carma Developers Ltd. et al. v. Groveridge Imperial Properties (Calgary) Ltd. and Lincoln Developments Ltd.* ([1985] 36 ALR 2d 355), a contract was allegedly breached in a sale of land, and the plaintiff claimed damages. Power, holding for the plaintiff, presented a plethora of cases and legal articles on the subject with extensive quotation, allowing the material to speak for itself. In *Hartley v. Giokas and Avery* ([1989] 64 ALR 2d 240), a plaintiff was injured when a power boat in which he was riding was struck by another boat owned by the defendant who was operating a boat at night and without lights. Power, holding for the plaintiff, followed the evidence closely with few citations, and told a good story in the process. Finally, in *Wills v. Saunders* ([1989] 64 ALR 2d 262), the defendant doctor at the Foothills Hospital was sued for negligence in causing eye damage through lacerated arteries while inserting a line for intravenous feeding. Power held that he was negligent and his procedure improper, citing a long list of injury cases caused by professionals. Power's judgment style varied depending upon the subject and the issue.

Prendergast, James Emile Pierre

Supreme Court of the North-West
  Territories, District of Northern
  Alberta, Calgary, February 18, 1902
  - September 16, 1907

The Honourable James Emile Pierre Prendergast was born in Quebec City on March 22, 1858. His early education was at the Commercial Academy and Quebec Seminary, after which he attended Laval University. He ob-

tained his B.A. in 1878, and his LL.B. in 1881. He practiced in Quebec before moving to Manitoba in 1882. Settling at Winnipeg, he practiced as a partner with Nicholas Beck from 1883 to 1888. Prendergast entered politics as a Conservative in the provincial election of 1886, when he won the La Verandrye seat with a majority of seventeen. He became the first Provincial Secretary in the Greenway cabinet of Manitoba in 1888 when he switched to the Liberal Party, but resigned one year later to become leader of the opposition. He left the government over its decision to abolish separate schools. Elected Mayor of St. Boniface in 1893 and 1896, he retained his seat in the Legislature until 1897, when he was appointed County Court Judge of the Eastern Judicial District on April 2, 1897. He went on to serve as a member of the Board of Education of Manitoba, 1884-1890.

Prendergast was appointed to the SCNWT, District of Northern Alberta, in 1902, succeeding Rouleau as the Catholic judge on the bench. He sat as a trial judge at Calgary until the creation of the provinces of Alberta and Saskatchewan in 1905, when he moved to the Supreme Court of Saskatchewan on September 16, 1907. Once a position became vacant in his home province, he was appointed to and served on the Court of King's Bench of Manitoba, 1910-1922, and on its Court of Appeal, 1922-1944. He became Chief Justice of Manitoba in 1944. Prendergast was a member of the Council of the University of Manitoba from 1895 to 1902, and a Senator of the University of Saskatchewan from 1908 to 1910. He also served on a number of government commissions, including a Provincial Commission appointed to consolidate the statutes of Saskatchewan in 1908, a Dominion Commission to investigate the sale of Manitoba School Lands, and a commission to investigate corruption of the police in Winnipeg in 1918. A devout Roman Catholic, he was President of the St. Jean Baptiste Society in St. Boniface in 1886 and 1910, just as he had been in Regina in 1906 and 1909. He was one of the first men to spread the gospel of Liberalism among French Canadians on the prairies. He also wrote verse and was a member of the Academy des Musée Santones in France. He retired on March 18, 1944, and died in St. Boniface on April 18, 1945.

Known as a courteous and skilful debater and a chivalrous opponent who fought without malice or bitterness, Prendergast displayed dignity, humility, and kindliness on the bench. Sitting as a trial judge, most of his reported decisions concerned commercial law, bankruptcy and insolvency, and indictable felonies. In criminal law, he believed in the sanctity of trial by jury, and rarely interfered with or tried to influence juries in their deliberations. In commercial cases, his judgments were brief and to the point. Sitting *en banc*, however, he seldom wrote the judgment of the Court until later in his career. Then, he often appears as dissenting. In the SCNWT at Calgary, 1902-1905, he sat on several cases *en banc*, only one of which was reported: *R. v. Lougheed* ([1903] 6 TLR 77). A guardian of the pluralist legalism of a mixed society, he may have found himself slightly out of touch with and overwhelmed by the strong common law personalities which he met on the territorial courts.

Primrose, Neil Phillip

Supreme Court of Alberta, Trial Division, September 1, 1954 - September 15, 1977

The Honourable Neil Phillip Primrose was born in Fort Macleod, Alberta, on July 30, 1905. Educated in Edmonton, he attended the University of Alberta and graduated with an LL.B. in 1926. He articled with the firm of Friedman and Lieberman of Edmonton before being admitted to the Alberta bar on November 3, 1927. He moved to Vegreville, Alberta in 1929, where he established a law practice. At the outbreak of World War II, Primrose enlisted with the Royal Canadian Air Force, attaining the rank of Wing Commander before being discharged. Following the war, he returned to Edmonton where he became a partner in the firm of Primrose, Weeks, Patterson and Lovekin. He practiced there until his appointment to the bench at Edmonton in 1954. He was named QC on December 31, 1951. Primrose served as President of the Alberta Union of Urban Municipalities and President of the Vegreville Chamber of Commerce. He resigned from the SCA on September 15, 1977. One month later, however, he was appointed Deputy Judge of the SCNT, and he maintained this position until his official retirement in 1985. Primrose died on March 16, 1991.

Prowse, David Clifton

Supreme Court of Alberta, Appellate Division, Calgary, September 1, 1972 - June 30, 1979

Court of Appeal of Alberta, Calgary,
    June 30, 1979 - July 26, 1988
Supernumerary Justice, Calgary,
    December 18, 1987 - July 26, 1988

The Honourable David Clifton Prowse was born in Taber, Alberta, on March 25, 1920 into a family of lawyers. Educated in Taber, Prowse attended the University of Alberta. At the outbreak of World War II, he left his studies to enlist in the Royal Canadian Air Force as part of a bomber squadron. He spent two years as a Prisoner of War after his plane was shot down over Germany. Returning to Canada following the war, Prowse resumed his studies at the University of Alberta, graduating with a B.Comm. in 1947, and an LL.B. in 1950 for which he received the Gold Medal. He was admitted to the Alberta bar on May 30, 1951. Joining the Fenerty firm in Calgary, Prowse became a prominent litigation lawyer before being appointed to the bench in 1972. He was also a Justice of the CANT, 1972-1988. He died in Bellingham, Washington, on July 26, 1988.

In 1982, Prowse wrote the first Appeal Court decision in Canada dealing with the *Canadian Charter of Rights and Freedoms* in *Southam Inc. v. Dir. of Investigations and Research of the Combines Investigative Branch, et al.* ([1982] 24 ALR 2d 307).

Prowse was one of the most active judges on the CA in writing judgments for the Court in the 1980s. His judgments ranged from labour law and industrial relations, public utilities, schools and municipalities, to land title, contracts, mortgages, negligence, and criminal law procedure. In *Murray et al. v. Council of*

Municipal District of Rockyview No. 44 et al. and Flintstone Fun Park Ltd. ([1980] 12 ALR 2d 342), the appellant appealed a decision of the Development Appeal Board to allow the defendant company's construction of the fun park near their land. Prowse wrote that since the plaintiff was not allowed to cross-examine the defendants at the hearing, that the Board acted improperly and the decision must be reversed. He presented a long list of cases, statutes, and treatises to substantiate the court's ruling. *Canadian National Transportation Limited and Canadian National Railway Company v. Alberta Provincial Court and Attorney General of Canada* ([1982] 18 ALR 2d 223) was a combines case on the constitutionality of federal legislation conferring jurisdiction on the AG of Canada to prosecute such cases. The applicants were accused of conspiring to lessen competition in the interprovincial transportation of goods and commodities. The Court held the federal legislation *ultra vires*, an infringement on the provincial power to administer criminal law. Prowse wrote a magisterial judgment, exploring cases, statutes, and treatises from U.S. and Canadian law, in limiting the federal power in this area to that of the provinces. Another example of his written judgments was *Medicine Hat v. Attorney General of Canada* ([1985] 37 ALR 2d 208), which concerned Parliament's amendment of the *Excise Tax Act* to impose federal taxes on the production and distribution of petroleum and natural gas. The City claimed that the amendment was *ultra vires* the federal government because the City was a Crown agent exempt under the *Constitutional Act*. The Court dismissed the appeal, rehearsing a wide range of legal authority in the common law world.

Prowse, Hubert Samuel

Court of Queen's Bench of Alberta, Calgary, November 27, 1979 -
Supernumerary Justice, Calgary, December 8, 1993 -

The Honourable Justice Hubert Samuel Prowse was born in Taber, Alberta on December 8, 1923 to a family of lawyers. Educated in Taber, he enlisted in the Canadian Army in 1941. Attached to RAF Bombing Squadrons, his plane was shot down in March 1944 and he was interned in Switzerland for the duration of the war. Following the war, Hubert Prowse attended the University of Alberta, graduating with a B.Comm. in 1948 and an LL.B. in 1951. He was admitted to the Alberta bar on June 10, 1952, and went on to become a successful lawyer in Lethbridge for many years. He was named QC on Decmber 29, 1967. Prowse moved to Calgary in 1972 where he joined the firm of Fenerty, McGillivray, Robertson, Prowse, Brennan, Fraser, Bell and Hatch, specializing in civil litigation. He was with the successor firm of Fenerty, Robertson, Prowse, Fraser, Bell and Hatch when he was appointed to the bench in 1979.

Prowse was an active member of the QB and wrote many published judgments. His reported cases were on the civil side, involving mechanics liens, employer-employee relations, contracts and guarantees, commercial law, insurance law, arbitration, and restraint of trade. In *Evans v. Holt* ([1982] 17 ALR 2d 365), a councillor voted on a question where he had a direct interest, and an application was made for his disqualification. Surveying the case law across the country, Prowse held that the application should be granted. *Norcen International Ltd. v. Suncor Inc.* ([1985] 36 ALR 2d 218) concerned the interpretation of a sublease where the defendant paid a royalty based on the selling price. The plaintiff sought recovery of the provincial government's compensation payments to the producer. Prowse related the facts and oral testimony, and applied case law from England and Canada to find for the defendant. And in *R. v. Alexson* ([1990] 72 ALR 2d 99) the accused, a Treaty Indian, was prosecuted for hunting elk on Crown land with a rifle. Acquitted at trial, Prowse on appeal allowed the prosecution, holding that Crown land was not "unoccupied Crown lands" under the *Wildlife Act*, and that the accused required permission from the Crown to hunt there.

Purvis, Stuart Somerville

Court of Queen's Bench of Alberta, Edmonton, July 3, 1980 -
September 25, 1986

The Honourable Stuart Somerville Purvis was born in Edmonton, Alberta on July 22, 1919. Educated in Edmonton, he received his B.A. from the University of British Columbia in 1938 and his LL.B. from the University of Alberta in 1943. He immediately enlisted in the Canadian Navy, serving in the North Atlantic until 1946. He was admitted to the Alberta bar on February 11, 1949, and became a partner in the Edmonton firm of Purvis, Johnston, Purvis, Allford and Finlay. He was named QC on December 30, 1963. Appointed to the QB at Edmonton in 1980, Purvis died on September 25, 1986.

Quigley, Francis Hugh

District Court of Southern Alberta,
    Calgary, February 12, 1970 -
    November 28, 1974
Supreme Court of Alberta, Trial
    Division, Calgary, November 28,
    1974 - June 30, 1979
Court of Queen's Bench of Alberta,
    Calgary, June 30, 1979 -
Supernumerary Justice, Calgary,
    November 25, 1988 -

The Honourable Justice Francis Hugh Quigley was born in Calgary, Alberta on November 23, 1926. He attended the University of Alberta, graduating with a B.Comm. in 1946 and an LL.B. in 1948. Quigley articled with Macleod, Riley, McDermid and Dixon before being admitted to the Alberta bar on June 10, 1949. Setting up practice in Calgary in 1951, he became a partner with G.W.H. Millican, QC, and in 1954, formed his own firm of Quigley and Russell. He became the youngest judge appointed as Magistrate in 1958. Quigley was named QC on December 31, 1959 and was appointed Chairman of the provincial Royal Commission on Juvenile Delinquency in 1966. Appointed Master in Chambers of the SCA at Calgary in 1968, he was moved to the DC in 1970.

Quigley's case load and published written judgments have increased with his experience on the bench and cover the whole ambit of the law. In *R.*

ex rel. Cochrane v. Schumaker ([1978] 5 ALR 2d 106), Quigley held that using the wrong mark on a ballot made it invalid no matter how clear the mark was made; the election, however, was ruled invalid because some of the voters were ineligible. In *CIBC v. Gardner Watson Limited and Belanger* ([1983] 25 ALR 2d 319), the bank held three cheques from Belanger which the brokerage company submitted for payment and were returned NSF. Quigley held that neither of the two firms had used due diligence to investigate their customer, and thus no award was given to anyone. *Groeneweg v. Groeneweg* ([1981] 40 AR 437) concerned a wife's application for matrimonial property. Since the date of valuation was not given in the document, Quigley used his discretion to make the nomination. In these, as in other cases, he drew broadly from English and Canadian case law, as well as from internal logic, to provide decisions which were consonant with the circumstances.

Rawlins, Bonnie Leigh

Court of Queen's Bench of Alberta,
    Calgary, March 8, 1989 -

The Honourable Justice Bonnie Leigh Rawlins was born in Leamington, Ontario on June 27, 1949. She received a B.A. from Wilfred Laurier University in 1969, a B.Ed. from the University of Toronto in 1970, a B.A. from York University in 1972, and an LL.B. from Osgoode Hall in Toronto in 1976. After being admitted to the Ontario bar in 1978, Rawlins moved to Calgary and was admitted to the Alberta bar on June 4, 1979. Rawlins became a partner with the Calgary firm of MacKimmie, Matthews where she specialized in corporate financing, estate and will administration, and liquidation. She has been a member of the International Commission of Jurists and she served as Vice-Chairman of the City of Calgary Taxi Commission from 1987 to 1989. Rawlins became Director of the Law Reform Federation in 1987. She has also lectured at programs sponsored by the Legal Education Society of Alberta at the University of Calgary and the Canadian Bar Association. In 1994, Rawlins studied mediation at Harvard University in Cambridge, Massachusetts.

Richardson, Hugh

Stipendiary Magistrate of the North West Territories, District of Saskatchewan, Fort Battleford, Regina, July 22, 1876 - February 18, 1887

Supreme Court of the North-West Territories, District of Western Assiniboia, Regina, February 18, 1887 - November 12, 1903

The Honourable Hugh Richardson was born in London, England on July 21, 1826, and came to Canada in 1831 when his father was appointed Manager of the Bank of Upper Canada in Toronto. He was admitted to the Upper Canada bar in 1847, and he practiced in Woodstock from 1852 to 1872, serving as a Crown Prosecutor from 1856 to 1862. Richardson enlisted as a Private in a company of volunteers in Oxford, Ontario, in 1860. He was quickly promoted to Captain, and helped to form the Oxford Rifles,

the first active Militia Battalion in Western Ontario. Promoted to Major, he led the Provisional Battalion against the Fenian raids at La Prairie in the winter of 1864-1865. Advanced to Lieutenant-Colonel in May 1866, he commanded against the Fenians at Sarnia and remained Commander of the Oxford Rifles until his retirement in 1875. Richardson joined the civil service in Ottawa in 1872, acting as Chief Clerk for the Department of Justice. He received the reports from the NWMP and acted at times as Deputy Minister. In 1876, he was appointed a SM of the NWT at Fort Battleford and a Justice of the SCNWT in 1887. Richardson retired from the bench in 1903 and returned to Ottawa in 1905, where he died on July 15, 1913.

As one of the first three Stipendiary Magistrates of the NWT, Richardson has been credited with drafting the 1875 *NWT Act*. Originally stationed at Fort Battleford, 1876-1882, he relocated to Regina when it was made Territorial capital in 1882. In the aftermath of the North-West Rebellion of May 1885, he presided at the trial of Louis Riel, seventy-two Cree allies, and the "white rebels" William Jackson and Thomas Scott (*R. v. Riel* No. 1 [1885] 1 TLR 20; No. 2 [1885] 1 TLR 23). Observers regarded him variously as biased against the Cree, erratic in his behaviour, and the great Preserver of Justice. However, his performance, especially the somewhat harsh sentences, was regarded a success in Ottawa, garnering an appointment to the first SCNWT in 1887 with precedence over the other judges.

Richardson was remembered more for his military career and the Riel trials than for his work on the bench, which has gone relatively unnoticed. Many of his subsequent trials involved liquor and horse stealing, property, and contracts with jurisdiction extended into what is now southeastern Alberta. While he did not write many reported judgments, most of the legal points on which he decided included the admissibility of evidence, jury verdicts, judicial procedure, statutory interpretation, and extradition. His legal knowledge was proven on several occasions, as in *Moore v. Martin* ([1890] 1 TLR 236), in which his procedural ruling was upheld by the Court *en banc* and the appeal quashed. Richardson was *ex-officio* member of the Territorial Council, 1877-1887, and then served as a legal expert to the advisory council of the Legislative Assembly. He drafted many of the *Ordinances of the NWT*, 1877-1888, and was given the task with A.E. Forget of revising and consolidating the *Ordinances* for publication in 1889. Richardson established the first *Rules of the Court*, and held a tight reign on local constables.

Richardson was regarded as a patient, punctual, and imperturbable man, held in high regard for his impartiality by settlers, Métis, and churchmen. His stern behaviour was exhibited when, after his daughter fell in love with a sub-constable and married him secretly, Richardson had the man held over to miss the wedding night, arrested him on four criminal charges, and tried to coerce a jury into delivering guilty verdicts. At Regina for the next twenty years, he was the presiding officer of the Court and handled its judicial administration. He retired when he was passed over as the Chief Justice of the NWT in 1902.

Riley, Harold William

Supreme Court of Canada, Trial
    Division, Calgary, January 17, 1957
    - January 1, 1973

The Honourable Harold William Riley was born in Calgary on September 15, 1910. The son of a Calgary pioneer and leading citizen, he was educated at Hillhurst Public School and Crescent Heights High School, where former Premier William Aberhart was principal. Riley attended the University of Alberta, paying his way by selling paint, and took prizes in chemistry, history, and law. An accomplished debater, he was captain of the track team. He graduated with an LL.B. in 1936 and was admitted to the Alberta bar on June 15, 1936. Articling with Marshall Porter, he remained with him for seven years. In 1944, Riley became a senior partner with the law firm of Macleod, Riley, McDermid, Dixon, and Burns, with whom he remained until his appointment to the bench at Calgary in 1957. He was named QC on December 30, 1949. An Anglican, he was a member of the Ranchmen's Club, the Calgary Petroleum Club, the Glencoe Club, and the Army, Navy and Air Force Veterans Association. Riley retired due to illness on January 1, 1973, and died in Calgary on November 6, 1979.

Riley was active on the bench, ruling on a wide variety of cases in the area of criminal law, torts, and court procedure. In *Baumann v. Springer Construction Ltd. et al.* ([1967] 58 WWR 592), Riley rejected defence assertions that changes to the *Vehicles and Highway Act* required an express consent for use of a vehicle at the time of the negligent act, basing his finding for the plaintiff on the facts and the remedial intent of the legislation. In *Salvino v. R.* ([1969] 72 WWR 292), Riley upheld the absolute discretion of the lower court to commit an accused for trial, rejecting an application for *certiorari*. His decisions were less frequent in his later years, due undoubtedly to illness. Riley was presiding judge at the second murder trial of Robert Raymond Cook, the last person to receive the death penalty in Alberta. While on the bench, Riley was an outspoken critic of Alberta's plan to implement a comprehensive government-funded legal aid program, and was a staunch advocate of individual ethical standards.

Roslak, Yaroslaw

Court of Queen's Bench of Alberta, Edmonton, December 31, 1987 - May 3, 1995

The Honourable Yaroslaw Roslak was born in Chortkin, Ukraine on August 18, 1927. He attended the University of Innsbruck in Austria before obtaining his B.A. in 1952 and his LL.B. in 1953 from the University of Alberta. He was admitted to the Alberta bar on July 23, 1954. From 1954 to 1959, Roslak was in private practice in Bonnyville, Alberta. He was with the AG's Department in Edmonton from 1959 to 1987, and served with its Criminal Division from 1965 where he was Director, 1975-1982. He was appointed QC on January 26, 1976. Roslak was President of the Alberta Crown Attorneys' Association, 1971-1973, and a member of the University of Alberta Senate, 1977-

1983. From 1984 to 1985, he was Chairman of the Criminal Law Section at the Uniform Law Conference of Canada, and from 1980 to 1987 he was the Law Conference's Commissioner. Roslak died on May 3, 1995.

Rouleau, Charles Borromée

Stipendiary Magistrate of the North West Territories, District of Saskatchewan, Fort Battleford, September 28, 1883 - February 18, 1887
Supreme Court of the North-West Territories, District of Northern Alberta, Calgary, February 18, 1887 - August 25, 1901

The Honourable Charles Borromée Rouleau was born at L'Isle-Verte in the County of Temiscouata, Quebec on December 13, 1840. Educated in Lower Canada he received his diplomas from the Ecole Normale Laval in 1859 and 1860, graduated from Laval University, and taught school at Aylmer. He was Inspector of Catholic Schools for the Ottawa District of Quebec from 1861 to 1873. During this period he also studied law, and was called to the Quebec bar on December 16, 1868. Rouleau ran as a Conservative for the Ottawa district in the federal election of 1875 and lost by a large margin. He was appointed Police Magistrate for the District from 1876 to 1883, wrote articles on legal and educational issues for Montreal newspapers, and authored *Notre systeme judiciaire*, a small booklet of suggested legal reforms for Quebec. He was appointed SM for the NWT, District of Saskatchewan in September 1983 stationed at Fort Battleford, and also served as an *ex-officio* member of the North-West Territorial Council, providing expert legal advice. In September 1884, Rouleau reported to the Dominion government that agitation among the Métis and Aboriginals in the NWT was real, and urged the government to settle their grievances quickly. When his family fled Fort Battleford for Calgary the following spring as the North-West Rebellion drew near, Rouleau watched from the other side of the river as Cree warriors burned his house to the ground.

Rouleau was appointed to the new SCNWT, Northern Alberta District, in 1887, resident at Calgary. He quickly became one of the city's most prominent residents, entertaining lavishly in his large house, and he became a founding member of the Ranchmen's Club. His brother, Dr. E.H. Rouleau, was head of the Holy Cross Hospital which he had helped to establish. His great ambition was to establish a francophone community in southern Alberta and toward this end, he planned and incorporated the town of Rouleauville in 1884, now the Mission district of Calgary. However, his efforts failed: many of the lots he owned went unsold and the predominant francophone character of the community had disappeared by the time it was annexed to Calgary in 1907. Rouleau lost virtually everything investing in gold mines after 1886 and, when he died in Calgary on August 25, 1901, his estate was heavily in debt.

Rouleau's first major trials arose out of the North-West Rebellion of 1885 (*R. v. Riel* ([1885] 1 TLR 20), *R. v. Riel* ([1885] 1 TLR 23). Not to be outdone by his colleague Richardson,

his average conviction at the trial for minor offenses such as theft was six years in the penitentiary, and those convicted for murder were executed by hanging. Known to dislike Aboriginals, and being a strong advocate of capital punishment, he believed that a few public hangings would give them pause for restraint. While Rouleau certainly passed stiff sentences, his reasons for judgment balanced equity with mercy, and he emphasized jurisprudence over common law precedents. Rouleau was one of the most scholarly members of the early bench. His extensive private library of legal works, including the British, Canadian, and American treatises, a complete set of colonial and provincial law reports, and all of the Canadian statutes, a rarity in the frontier West, was instrumental in the writing of his judgments. Rouleau was especially interested in criminal and constitutional law, and in court was a master of rhetorical questions. As a trial judge, he would write pithy and compact judgments. He did not hesitate to hold long trials, research the case after judgment had been reserved, and write a masterly opinion. Of approximately forty that were appealed, more than sixty percent were affirmed. On appeal, however, he could write very long opinions on the legal issues whether he was in the majority or minority. Of the decisions he authored for the SCNWT *en banc*, seven were appealed to the SCC, and four of those were affirmed.

Rouleau did not have the best of relations with his colleagues on the bench and quarrelled frequently with Justice McGuire. Rouleau's judgment in *Hull et al. v. Donohue* ([1893] 2 TLR

52), was reversed by the Court *en banc*. McGuire wrote a lengthy opinion on how the case should have been judged, and Wetmore concurred. Rouleau's dissenting opinion scorched his colleagues, concluding that the evidence he had found for was as clear as the "noonday light". He was vindicated when the decision was reversed by the SCC. In *R. v. Whiffin* ([1900] 3 TLR 3), he refused to throw out the judgment of a Police Magistrate who gave a sentence against statutory authority for several alcohol-related offenses. Rouleau also did not get along well with the ranching community. In a series of cattle-rustling cases, reported in the *Medicine Hat News* (Nov. 26, 1903), he ruled that branding was inadmissable as evidence of ownership and claimed that ranchers and stock associations branded cattle which were not their property. This concern for evidentiary rigour made him unique to his era in frontier communities.

Rowbotham, Henry Slater

District Court of Southern Alberta, Calgary, February 12, 1970 - October 1, 1975
District Court of Alberta, Calgary, October 1, 1975 - June 30, 1979
Court of Queen's Bench of Alberta, Calgary, June 30, 1979 -
Supernumerary Justice, Calgary, September 30, 1985 -

The Honourable Justice Henry (Harry) Slater Rowbotham was born in Rosetown, Saskatchewan on September 30, 1920. He attended the University of Saskatchewan, obtaining a B.A. before joining the Canadian Navy and the Royal Navy during World War II. Rowbotham served in the North Atlantic and European Theatres for more than five years. After the War, he returned to the University of Saskatchewan, graduating with an LL.B. in 1948. He was admitted to the Saskatchewan bar the following year, and practiced in Saskatoon for a brief period. Rowbotham was then employed in Ottawa in the Department of Defence Construction during the Korean War. In 1951, he settled in Calgary and was employed as Counsel for Western Leaseholds Limited and Gulf Oil Corporation Limited. He was called to the Alberta bar on August 7, 1956. With Melvin Shannon, Rowbotham formed the partnership of Shannon and Rowbotham and was with the successor firm of Cook Snowdon when he was appointed to the DC in February 1970.

Ryan, Matthew

Stipendiary Magistrate of the North West Territories, District of Qu'Appelle, Qu'Appelle Lakes, January 1, 1876 - July 1881

The Honourable Matthew Ryan was born in St. John's, Newfoundland in 1810. He was a journalist in St. John's until 1842, when he moved to Montreal. He worked as a journalist in Montreal before studying law. He was admitted to the Quebec bar on May 5, 1849. From 1849 to 1858, Ryan served in the Civil Service. In 1875, he left Montreal to enumerate the Manitoba native population. He continued in this position until he was appointed a SM in 1876. In 1880, at the behest of Commissioner W.M. Herchmer of the

NWMP, the Minister of Justice ordered an investigation into Ryan's conduct as a Magistrate. Although the findings of the investigation were never published, they led to his dismissal in July of 1881. Ryan always contended that he was unjustly treated by Herchmer and the government officials who believed his allegations. He died in Winnipeg in 1888.

Scott, David Lynch

Supreme Court of the North-West
    Territories, District of Northern
    Alberta, Calgary, September 28,
    1894 - September 16, 1907
Supreme Court of Alberta,
    Edmonton, September 16, 1907 -
    September 15, 1921
Supreme Court of Alberta, Appellate
    Division, Edmonton, September 15,
    1921 - July 26, 1924
Chief Justice of Alberta, Edmonton,
    September 15, 1921 - July 26, 1924

The Honourable David Lynch Scott was born in Brampton, Ontario on August 21, 1845. Educated at Brampton Grammar School, he received his legal education at Osgoode Hall. He practiced law in Orangeville, Ontario, from 1878 to 1882, serving as Mayor, 1879-1880. He also became a Lieutenant-Colonel commanding the 36th (Peel) Battalion. Scott moved to Regina in 1882, becoming its first Mayor that year. He married Mary McVittie of Barrie, Ontario, in 1883. Scott was resident Crown Counsel in *R. v. Riel*, which tried Louis Riel for treason following the North-West Rebellion of Métis and Aboriginals in 1885. He also appeared as Crown Counsel in the trials of Poundmaker, Big Bear,

and those tried for the Frog Lake massacre. Scott was the first person enrolled as an advocate of the NWT on January 11, 1885, and practiced in Regina with several partners including Hamilton, Robinson, and White, to 1896. He became resident at Edmonton when he was appointed to the newly-formed SCNWT in 1894. Scott died during the summer term on July 26, 1924, in his summer cottage at Cooking Lake, near Edmonton.

Scott's activity as a judge followed in the tradition he had set as a lawyer; he was active in precedent-setting cases both civil and criminal. In his first case on the bench, he set a precedent on the enforcement of by-laws in *R. v. Bank*s ([1894] 2 TLR 8). Other judgments included an expansive interpretation of the intent of parliamentary statute, and a broadening of the discretionary powers of the court *en banc* to hear all the circumstances of any case that came before it *R. ex Rel. Thompson v. Dinnin*, ([1898] 3 TLR 112). Scott became a master of the short, incisive judgment with pithy summaries of the legal issues. He remained an active member of the bench in writing opinions either in support of or in dissent from his brethren, both on the bench of the SCNWT and the SCA, where he became domiciled in Edmonton by 1907. This heavy activity, however, came to an end with the appointment of Horace Harvey as Chief Justice in 1910. Obviously displeased, he all but disappeared from the Court's judgments in the following decade, especially on cases *en banc*. Scott, like Justice Macleod, often wrote of the development of the "law of the west", a theme he came back to in his judgments during his last year on the bench as Chief Justice of Alberta, 1923-1924.

Scott became the centre of a judicial controversy when separate Appellate and Trial Divisions of the SCA were established in 1921 though the Supreme Court acts of 1919-1920. Scott was named Chief Justice of the AD and Chief Justice of Alberta, and the former Chief Justice of Alberta, Horace Harvey, became Chief Justice of the TD. Harvey claimed the right to retain his title as Chief Justice of Alberta, which was upheld in a reference case to the SCC in 1922, *Scott v. AG for Canada* ([1922] 64 SCR 135). Scott made his opposition very public. He appealed to the JCPC of Great Britain in 1924, represented by R.B. Bennett, and was reinstated as Chief Justice of Alberta. However, he died shortly thereafter.

Sellar, William

District Court of Southern Alberta, Calgary, August 30, 1962 - May 19, 1968

His Honour William Sellar was born in Montreal, Quebec on December 11, 1910. He attended McGill University where he graduated with a B.A. in 1932 and an LL.B. in 1935. Before being admitted to the Quebec bar in 1941, Sellar joined the Canadian Pacific Railway. He enlisted in the Royal Canadian Air Force during World War II and served overseas. After the war, he moved to Alberta, and was admitted to the Alberta bar on April 8, 1947. He practiced with the firm of Macleod, Riley, McDermid and Dixon before establishing his own firm in 1948. Sellar was with the Calgary firm of Sellar, Densmore and Eamon when he was appointed to the DC in 1962. He died in Calgary on May 19, 1968.

Shannon, Melvin Earl

Supreme Court of Alberta, Trial Division, May 18, 1973 - June 30, 1979
Court of Queen's Bench of Alberta, Calgary, May 18, 1973 -
Supernumerary Justice, Calgary, March 22, 1992 -

The Honourable Justice Melvin Earl Shannon was born near Harris, Saskatchewan, on March 22, 1927. He graduated from the University of Saskatchewan, receiving a B.A. with distinction in 1947, and an LL.B. with distinction in 1949. He articled in Calgary with R.H. Fenerty, QC, before being admitted to the Alberta bar on June 22, 1950. Shannon was with the firm of McLaws and Company from 1950 to 1953. He then founded the firm of Shannon and Cook, where he remained until his appointment to the bench at Calgary in 1973. Shannon was an unsuccessful provincial Liberal candidate in 1952, and served as an Alderman on Calgary City Council, 1953-1954. He was named QC on December 29, 1967. Shannon was President of the Law Society of Alberta in 1973. As a judge, he presided over *R. v. Beaulieu, Beaulieu and Pruneau* in 1987, the first trial conducted in French in Alberta.

Shannon only occasionally had his decisions published in the law reports in the 1970s and 1980s. They covered, however, a wide area, including employer-employee relations, insurance, family law, and criminal law. *Olympia & York Developments Limited v. Fourth Avenue Properties Limited, Switzer, Fishman, Fishman and Reichmann* ([1982] 20 ALR 2d 1187) concerned the right to trial by jury. An action for the specific performance of a contract for the sale of land, the plaintiff wanted its claim in tort tried by a jury. Shannon ruled that specific performance was a discretionary and equitable remedy, and was not suitable for juries. He used case law and legal treatises in a concise judgment to deny the request. And in *R. v. Wagner* ([1985] 36 ALR 2d 301), the accused owner of an video rental store was charged with the sale of obscene matter. Shannon takes the reader through an analysis of all the movies at issue, one by one, to convict for the "undue" exploitation of sex. He concluded that "social harm does result from repeated exposure to obscene films."

Shepherd, Simpson James

Supreme Court of Alberta, Trial
    Division, Lethbridge, November 3,
    1936 - February 6, 1952

The Honourable Simpson James Shepherd was born in Uttoxeter, Lambton County, Ontario, on February 6, 1877. Attending high school at Forest, Ontario, he travelled to the NWT with his brother-in-law in 1897. Shepherd settled first at Fort Walsh, then at Maple Creek, where he spent seven years working as a cowboy on the famous Y-Ranch. He also worked as a store clerk and on a survey party. He returned to Eastern Canada in 1903 to attend McGill University, graduating with a B.C.L. in 1906, and obtained

a travelling scholarship that took him to England and France for a year. Shepherd came to Alberta in 1908, and was admitted to the Alberta bar on April 19, 1909. He formed a partnership with the firm of W.G. Simmons in Lethbridge and ran unsuccessfully as a Liberal in the provincial election of 1911. After Simmons was appointed to the SCA in 1910, Shepherd went into partnership with Allen E. Dunlop, his brother-in-law. He continued to practice law in Lethbridge until his appointment to the bench in 1936. Shepherd was named KC on June 23, 1921. A devout member of the United Church, he was a Freemason and an active member of the Lethbridge Curling Club. Shepherd retired on February 6, 1952, and died on March 4, 1959.

As a local justice, Shepherd heard cases involving negligence, tenancy, contracts, and divorce. While he did not contribute to precedent, his short judgments reflect a willingness to go well beyond the strict letter of the law, and adherence to strict bureaucracy was not favoured in his court. He emphasized the facts of the case pertinent to the resolution of the dispute and tried to apply the law in the interests of local justice to the parties.

Sifton, Arthur Lewis

Supreme Court of the North-West
    Territories, Calgary, January 3, 1903
    - September 16, 1907
Chief Justice of the North-West
    Territories, Calgary, January 3, 1903
    - September 16, 1907
Supreme Court of Alberta, Calgary,
    September 16, 1907 - May 25, 1910
Chief Justice of Alberta, Calgary,
    September 16, 1907 - May 25, 1910

The Honourable Arthur Lewis Sifton was born in St. John's, Middlesex County, Ontario on October 26, 1859. He was educated in London, Ontario, and attended high school with his brother Clifford, who was deemed to be more popular and engaging. They moved with their family to Winnipeg when their father John won a large railway contract from the Liberal government of Alexander Mackenzie in 1874. The Sifton boys were nurtured and educated as staunch Methodists, steeped in temperance and reform politics. In 1875, Sifton articled with the A. Monkman firm of Winnipeg. He attended Victoria College in Toronto, a Methodist institution, and earned his B.A. in 1880. He was admitted to the Manitoba bar in 1883 and practiced in Brandon, Manitoba, with his brother Clifford until 1884, when he moved west to practice law at Prince Albert. At Brandon he organized a loan company, dealt in real estate, and was active in the temperance movement. He was also elected Alderman to the first Brandon City Council. At Prince Albert, besides practicing law, he wrote for the local newspaper and managed to earn an M.A. and LL.B. from Victoria College in Toronto in 1888. Sifton moved to Calgary in 1889 for his wife's health. In 1901, he was with the firm of Sifton, Short and Stuart, often acting as Crown Prosecutor. He was elected to the Territorial Legislature, 1898-1902, as a Liberal representative for Banff. Sifton was Treasurer and Commissioner of Public Works for the Haultain government, 1901-1903, and he was named KC in 1903. He was appointed Chief Justice of the SCNWT in 1903, replacing Thomas McGuire, and be-

came the first Chief Justice of the SCA in 1907. His appointment was widely regarded as crass Liberal patronage, a stigma he struggled to overcome. Calgary lacked a second resident judge following the death of Justice Rouleau in 1904, and thus Sifton remained in Calgary. Sifton received an honorary LL.D. from the University of Alberta in 1908. He resigned from the bench in May, 1910 to become Alberta's second Premier after the resignation of Alexander Rutherford in the aftermath of the Alberta and Great Waterways Railroad Company scandal.

As Premier, Sifton's government introduced prohibition and female suffrage in 1916, and women magistrates in 1913. Re-elected twice for Vermillion, he was also Minister of Public Works, Telephones and Railways, and Provincial Treasurer. One of his major setbacks, however, was the Supreme Court's disallowance of legislation to convert funds from a railway's bond issue to general revenues in *R. and the Provincial Treasurer of Alberta v. The Royal Bank of Canada* ([1912] 3 ALR 1st 249, [1913] 9 DLR 337). In 1917, he resigned to become a cabinet minister in the federal Union Government of Sir Robert Borden. His brother, Sir Clifford Sifton, had been Minister of the Interior, and was responsible for the federal immigration policy which transformed western Canada after 1900. On October 12, 1917, Sifton was appointed Minister of Customs, and in June, 1918, he was appointed Minister of Customs and Inland Revenue. In September, 1919, he was promoted to Minister of Public Works, and in December of that year he was appointed Secretary of State.

During the final months of World War I, Sifton, in his official capacity as Secretary of State, participated in the Paris Peace Conference. He died in Ottawa on January 21, 1921.

As a judge, Sifton was impassive, wearing a somewhat cynical, sphinx-like expression on the bench. He went through his court calendar rather quickly, and often gave his decisions immediately without a recess. In larger cases, however, the law in his judgments was more an instrument of common sense infused with a strong dose of social morality than a study of authorities. In *R. v. Clarke* ([1908] 1 ALR 1st 358), concerning an alleged conspiracy in restraint of trade by numerous lumber companies on the prairies, he depicted the defendant's acts as those of a criminal population, and warned businesses not interfere with the rights of the public in the province. Responding decisively to the growing problem of cattle rustling in southern Alberta, he heard numerous cases for theft of livestock, routinely sending offenders to three years hard labour. In *R. v. Lawrence* (1904) [unreported], for example, a prominent Maple Creek rancher was convicted of changing brands on cattle, partly on the testimony of a man he had recently testified against for the same offence. Sifton's sentence was merciless: four years at Stony Mountain Penitentiary. Working with established methods of the ranching community, Sifton ruled that cattle brands were admissable as evidence of ownership in *R. v. Dubois* ([1910] 12 WWR 560). According to the press, he had sent a message that would put fear in the hearts of the wicked. In criminal cases, his rather uncompromising

standards of morality nevertheless made him more sympathetic to the plight of the woman, as in *R. v. Lougheed* ([1903] 6 TLR 77), in which his conviction of a man for seduction under the promise of marriage was quashed on appeal. The Court *en banc* did not feel that the woman, who had sexual relations with the man for fifteen months prior to the complaint, was seduced. It could be said that Sifton also effectively served as justice for the northern frontier of the United States: he convicted as many Americans as Canadians. One of his most notable and spectacular criminal trials was *R. v. Cashel* (1904) [unreported], in which the "American Desperado" Ernest Cashel was convicted, allowed to escape, recaptured, and eventually executed for murder. When Sifton's decisions were appealed his brethren had difficulty in ruling on them because he rarely provided reasons for his judgments. Sitting on appeals himself, he often allowed the debate to run its course while he inclined in his chair, nonchalantly smoking his black cigar.

Simmons, William Charles

Supreme Court of Alberta, Calgary, October 12, 1910 - September 15, 1921

Supreme Court of Alberta, Trial Division, Calgary, September 15, 1921 - September 1, 1936

Supreme Court of Alberta, Trial Division, Chief Justice, Calgary, August 27, 1924 - September 1, 1936

The Honourable William Charles Simmons was born in the farming community of Tara, Arran Township, Bruce County, Ontario on February 25, 1865. Graduating with a B.A. from the University of Toronto in 1895, he moved west to accept the position of Principal of Schools in Lethbridge, teaching there for several years. He resigned his position in 1899 to article with R.B. Bennett in Calgary, where he acquired business skills and political instincts he used effectively later in his career. Simmons was admitted to the NWT bar on August 12, 1900, practicing first in Cardston and then in Lethbridge in partnership with S.J. Shepherd. He acquired a ranching clientele, and was elected as a Liberal MLA to the first Provincial Legislature in 1906, representing the Lethbridge constituency. He resigned his seat in 1908 to run as a Liberal candidate for Medicine Hat in the federal election and was defeated by Conservative Charles Magrath. Appointed to the SCA in 1910, Simmons moved to Calgary until he retired as Chief Justice of the TD on September 1, 1936. An active Presbyterian, he was a member of the Masonic Order, and was involved in a number of movements in Lethbridge aimed at raising the welfare and development of the town. His wife Mary founded the "Nursing Mission" for hungry children. The*Lethbridge Herald* hailed him as a leading exponent of progressive labour laws, and he was instrumental in the passage of provincial legislation in this area. A man of considerable energy and conviction, he was also a fine debater on the political hustings who lectured his constituents to stand up for themselves. While he was an outspoken critic of the Canadian Pacific Railway, the company was a party in none of his trials. Simmons died in Victoria, British Columbia on August 24, 1956.

On the bench, Simmons was perhaps overshadowed by his colleagues Harvey, Beck, and Stuart. His relatively few reported judgments over his long career are short but concise and carefully supported. His additional opinions on an appeal in *Alfred and Wickham v. Grand Trunk Pacific Railway Company* ([1911] 1 WWR 624) include a painstaking analysis of correspondence and calculations to find for the plaintiff regarding a breach of contract in a jury trial. Simmons also allowed an appeal in a negligence case involving a City of Calgary streetcar collision in *Harnovis v. City of Calgary* ([1913] 4 WWR 263), carefully distinguishing the case from an earlier Ontario decision, with Justice Walsh dissenting. In *Detro v. Detro* ([1922] 2 WWR 690), Simmons allowed an action for recovery of alimony, following the judgment by an American court. Generally, however, Simmons all but disappears from the reports in the last decade of his tenure on the bench.

Sinclair, William Robert

Supreme Court of Alberta, Trial Division, Edmonton, September 26, 1968 - January 25, 1973
Supreme Court of Alberta, Appellate Division, Edmonton, January 25, 1973 - February 22, 1979
Supreme Court of Alberta, Trial Division, Chief Justice, Edmonton, February 22, 1979 - June 30, 1979
Court of Queen's Bench of Alberta, Chief Justice, Edmonton, June 30, 1979 - February 24, 1984

Court of Queen's Bench of Alberta, Edmonton, February 24, 1984 - December 18, 1995

Supernumerary Justice, Edmonton, December 18, 1985 - December 18, 1995

The Honourable William Robert Sinclair was born on December 18, 1920. He attended the University of Alberta and graduated in 1941 with a B.Comm. At the outbreak of World War II, he enlisted in the Canadian Navy. He served as a landing craft officer and participated in the Dieppe raid in 1942. He also participated in the invasions of Algeria, Sicily, and Normandy. After being discharged from the Navy, Sinclair returned to the University of Alberta and received his LL.B. in 1948. He articled with S. Bruce Smith, later Chief Justice of Alberta, before being admitted to the Alberta bar on May 23, 1949. He began practice as a trial lawyer with Smith, Clement in Edmonton. He also lectured for four years on taxation for the University of Alberta Faculty of Law. Sinclair moved to Calgary in 1954 to join the Law Department of Canadian Gulf Oil Company, and later served as Gulf Oil's counsel for Western Canada. He returned to Edmonton in 1959, where he joined the firm of Emery, Jamieson, Chipman, Sinclair, Agrios and Emery. He was also with the successor firm of Emery, Jamieson, Chipman, Sinclair, Lambert and Agrios when he was appointed to the bench at Edmonton in 1968. He was named QC on December 30, 1963. Sinclair is one of the more prominent members of the Alberta judiciary of the last quarter of the twentieth century. After five years in the TD of the SCA, he was appointed to the Court Martial Appeal in 1972 and the AD and the CA of the NWT in 1973. Becoming Chief Justice of the QB in 1979, he also served as Deputy Judge of the NWT 1986-1989 prior to his retirement on December 18, 1995.

As a judge, Sinclair had a firm grasp of Canadian case law, and was a careful assessor of evidence. While he did not give many reported judgments, those that are reported are models of judicial analysis. In *Coopers & Lybrand Ltd. v. Symons General Insurance Co.* ([1988] 61 ALR 2d 214), the plaintiff was the second named payee on an insurance policy held by a restaurant that was gutted by fire while it was in the process of being sold. The plaintiff, appointed receiver, claimed an insurable interest. Sinclair wrote a long judgment which went through the chronology of events and documents with an exacting eye, including Canadian case law on relevant points along the way, and held for the plaintiff. In *Marcoux and Marcoux v. Martineau* ([1987] 52 ALR 2d 44), the plaintiff was left a quadripalegic at age fourteen in a car accident as a passenger. In a careful evaluation of the testimony of witnesses, statutes, and cases on negligence across the country, Sinclair held the defendant "grossly negligent." Later, when the same case came up ([1990] 70 ALR 2d 186) after the defendant failed to appear at the trial for damages, Sinclair awarded maximum damages plus accrued interest totalling over $200,000.

During his career on the bench, Sinclair served on many federal commissions, including the Federal Commission of Inquiry into Bilingual Air Traffic Services in Quebec from 1976 to 1979; Chairman of a Federal Commission of Inquiry on Canadian Sentencing in 1984; Chairman of the Federal Electoral Boundaries Commission for Alberta, 1986-1987. He was appointed by the Court of Appeal as Commissioner to the Nepoose Commission in 1991 and was Chairman of the Banff Refresher Course for the Legal Education Society of Alberta, 1988-1989, Chairman of the Federal Judicial Appointments Advisory Committee of Alberta, 1988-1990, and Chairman of the Advisory Committee on Judicial Activities at the Canadian Judges Conference, 1986-1991. His work on these significant government and judicial bodies is outstanding: Sinclair held a broad and driving commitment to the reform of Canadian law, public policy, and the administration of justice.

Sissons, John Howard

District Court of Southern Alberta, Lethbridge, October 30, 1946 - September 16, 1955
District Court of Southern Alberta, Chief Judge, Lethbridge, December 13, 1950 - September 16, 1955

The Honourable John Howard Sissons was born in Orillia, Ontario on July 14, 1892. His early education was intermittent, due largely to financial problems. Leaving school at age eighteen with his junior matriculation, he taught for three years, and moved west at Lethbridge and Edmonton where he continued his teaching. By 1913, he had saved enough money to continue his education at Queen's University in Kingston. He returned to Edmonton in 1914 to work as a clerk in the Department of Municipal Affairs and completed a year's course work by correspondence before completing his B.A. in 1917. Sissons articled with the Edmonton firm of Rutherford, Jamieson, Grant and Steer, working primarily under the supervision of Charles Grant. He passed his final examination in March, 1920, but had to wait until he completed his articles before being admitted to the Alberta bar on March 8, 1921. Sissons settled in Grande Prairie and practiced with the firm of Thomas, Wilson, Lawlor until he was appointed to the DC at Lethbridge in 1946.

One of Sissons' first major cases as a lawyer was a 1923 action against the CPR over the issue of freight rates. Representing the Town of Grande Prairie, he believed that the rates were out of proportion to distance, and that the Crowsnest Pass agreement rates should apply. While he and his associates won their case before the Railway Commission, Sissons claimed the reduction was so low that the decision by this biased institution was against "fundamental principles of justice". Sissons devoted much of the 1920s and 1930s to community affairs. He was a tireless supporter of the area's development, served on several community service clubs, and was an active member of the Liberal Party. In 1940, he was elected Liberal MP for Peace River, where he promoted northern development and Native rights. Defeated in the election of 1945, He impressed Prime Minister Mackenzie King, and was appointed to the DC the next year. Serving there for nearly a decade, he was appointed resident

Judge of the Territorial Court of the Northwest Territories at Yellowknife on September 16, 1955. Sissons retired on July 15, 1966, and died on July 11, 1969.

Sissons was a close relative of David Livingston, the famous African explorer. Countless stories of Livingston's exploits imbued him with a sense of adventure from his childhood days. Sissons was also influenced by his family's poverty, and the strong social morality of his Scots Presbyterian heritage. As he noted later in his memoirs, "I was taught to believe in law and order, but not necessarily in constituted authority". Justice required both a predilective mercy and an awareness of the local conditions under which it was to be administered.

As DC judge, Sissons authored numerous decisions concerning individual rights, the duties and obligations of governments and public bodies, and criminal prosecutions. He made his position clear in one of his early decisions in *Dwyer v. Staunton* ([1947] 2 WWR 22), where he said that "the regard for the public welfare is the highest law." In *Moody v. Canadian Corps of Commissionaires* ([1948] 1 WWR 69), a labour relations case, he held that the acceptance of a partial payment did not limit the individual's right to seek additional compensation for services rendered. In *Atwood v. Municipal District of Cochrane* ([1949] 1 WWR 858), he ruled that while the plaintiff's failure to comply with a statute constituted contributory negligence, this did not absolve the government of its duty to maintain public facilities properly. On the criminal law side, Sissons acquitted many individu-

als charged with hunting or fishing violations, arguing that game ordinances could not be applied to Aboriginal people because a 1763 Royal Proclamation granted them freedom to hunt for their livelihood. His position anticipated many rulings he made as Territorial judge after 1955. In *R. v. Zasadny* ([1948] 2 WWR 559), he held that a magistrate could not substitute a conviction on a lesser charge for an acquittal on a larger one. In *City of Lethbridge v. Oswald* ([1948] 2 WWR 815), he ruled that police could not use the claim of performing their duty to excuse them from negligent behaviour, and in his judgment highlighted the community's expectations that they should exercise restraint and common sense, and act alertly. And in *R. v. Parsons* ([1952] 7 WWR 359), he questioned whether the Crown had brought the proper charge, and found the accused not guilty because he had acted with adequate care under the circumstances prevailing at that time.

Sissons' greatest contributions and most important legal decisions were made as resident Judge of the Territorial Court of the Northwest Territories from 1955 to 1966. Rather than having parties, witnesses, and counsel travel to Yellowknife for their cases, he took the court out on circuit across the Arctic. He coerced Ottawa into appointing public defenders, enforced the right of accused to have trial by jury of their peers, and accepted Aboriginal concepts of justice and Inuit customs into his court proceedings. He upheld customs in *Re. Noah Estate* ([1961] 36 WWR 577), where he protected marriage rights under local Inuit customs. This followed his decision in 1958, where he ruled that Inuit adoptions as well as marriages were valid without government licences or church sanctions. In turn, he found that the *Child Welfare Ordinance* was unenforceable in the Northwest Territories because the government-imposed conditions bore no relationship to reality: *Re. Katie's Adoption Petition* ([1961] 38 WWR 100). Perhaps his most famous judgment, however, was *R. v. Sikyea* ([1962] 40 WWR 494) in which he held here that the *Migratory Birds Convention Act* (1917) was inapplicable because the *Bill of Rights* guaranteed pre-existing Native rights, and that the *Northwest Territories Act* of 1952 preserved unrestricted hunting and fishing rights for Aboriginals with respect to endangered species. Although parts of this decision were later reversed, it is still cited as precedent in Native land claims. Sissons' esteem among First Nations of the north was signified when he was named "Erkoktoyee" by the Inuit, meaning "he who listens."

Smith, Sidney Bruce

Supreme Court of Alberta, Trial
    Division, Calgary, January 8, 1959
    - April 7, 1960
Supreme Court of Alberta, Appellate
    Division, Calgary, April 7, 1960 -
    December 5, 1974
Chief Justice of Alberta, Calgary,
    March 15, 1961 - December 5, 1974

The Honourable Sidney Bruce Smith was born in Toronto, Ontario on December 5, 1899. He came to Alberta in 1914 and was educated in the Edmonton public schools. Attending the University of Alberta, he graduated with a B.A. in 1919 and an LL.B.

in 1922, for which he received the Gold Medal. He articled with Frank Ford before being admitted to the Alberta bar on June 29, 1921. Smith moved to Calgary and in 1929 he joined the law firm of A.A. McGillivray. He returned to Edmonton in 1931 and became a partner in the firm of H.H. Parlee, where he was engaged mainly in the practice of civil law. He was named KC on June 1, 1939 and was head of the Parlee firm by 1944. Smith established a reputation as one of the most competent lawyers in the province, and in his career served as counsel in many landmark cases before the SCA, SCC, and JCPC. He was also an active figure in Edmonton's development. He was a member of the Edmonton Public School Board from 1937 to 1941, and Chairman of the Rhodes Scholarship Committee for many years. A man of strong religious faith, he became Chancellor of the Anglican Diocese in Edmonton. Smith was dedicated to the growth of Alberta's legal community. A Bencher of the Law Society of Alberta from 1946 to 1958, he was President between 1956 and 1957, and Alberta Vice-President of the Canadian Bar Association. Smith was named Chairman of the Board of Transport Commission of Canada in 1958. Since his wife, however, was in poor health, he declined the invitation to go to Ottawa and remained in Alberta. He was head of the Parlee firm when he was appointed to the bench at Calgary in 1959. Elevated to the AD the next year, he became Chief Justice of Alberta in 1961. Smith was awarded an honorary LL.D. from the University of Alberta in 1962. He also became the first Chief Justice of the Northwest

Territories Court of Appeal when it was established as a separate court in 1971. Smith retired on December 5, 1974, and died in Calgary on April 19, 1984.

As a judge, Smith made many notable decisions in the areas of commercial law, family law, and industrial relations, and also on court rules and procedures affecting the administration of criminal law. Smith's decisions paid special attention to the needs of mothers and children. His judgments in several cases influenced the interpretation of the *Divorce Act*. In *Heikel v. Heikel* ([1970] 73 WWR 84), he allowed an appeal against a divorce decree which he thought was contrary to the Act. The husband was ordered to increase his support payments to ensure the financial well-bring of the family. He also influenced the interpretation of the *Fatal Accidents Act*. In *Ciniewicz v. Braden* ([1965] 52 WWR 111), he allowed an appeal by a widowed mother after an industrial accident claimed the life of her husband because the award was not sufficient to cover the costs of raising her family. And in *MacDonell v. Maple Leaf Mills* ([1972] 3 WWR 296), the deceased's employer appealed the sum it was ordered to pay the widow. Smith rejected it after a careful evaluation of her needs in raising five children.

On the criminal law side, Smith wrote important opinions on a number of procedural issues. For example, in *R. v. Latta* ([1972] 6 WWR 147), a convicted criminal appealed the jury's verdict because the trial judge had, to his mind, used inappropriate and prejudicial language in his instructions to the jury. Smith, while criticiz-

ing the judge's words, denied the appeal because there had been no breach of justice. And in *R. v. Sprague* ([1975] 1 WWR 22), he established the precedent which helped to establish the process by which cases may be appealed from a lower court, not only for an error in law, but also for an error in principle. This was due in part to Smith's belief that the law must continuously re-evaluate its procedures in order to serve social change as well as the evolution of the law.

Smith was renowned throughout his career for his research and his grasp of the law. His judgments used cases from all over the English-speaking world. He also referred to religious and family values in making awards. He was important as a jurist because he had a clear vision of the relationship between courts and legislatures in the law-making process, and by his death was regarded as one of the top judges in Canada. Smith also, however, became sanguine about the future course of society. Viewing what he considered to be the rise of vice and dysfunction and erosion of moral values, he was quick and severe in setting punishments for drug and alcohol-related offenses. In a speech delivered to the Boy Scouts of Edmonton on May 6, 1970, he said that "the two great principles of (civilization) are Christendom and Democracy. Some people are of the view that we are approaching the end of Christendom."

Smith, Vernor Winfield MacBriare

Court of Queen's Bench of Alberta, Edmonton, December 19, 1980 -

Supernumerary Justice, Edmonton,
    December 20, 1995 -

The Honourable Justice Vernor Winfield MacBriare Smith was born in Edmonton, Alberta on June 13, 1925. He attended the University of Alberta, where he graduated with an LL.B. in 1951 and was admitted to the Alberta bar on May 29, 1952. Smith became a partner in the Edmonton firm of Stanton and Smith. He was practicing in Edmonton with the firm of Duncan and Craig when he was appointed to the bench at Edmonton in 1980.

Stack, Luke Hannon

District Court of Southern Alberta,
    Calgary, October 2, 1945 -
    February 1, 1958

His Honour Luke Hannon Stack was born in Melrose, New Brunswick, on October 16, 1882. He received his B.A. from St. John's College at the University of New Brunswick and his LL.B. from Halifax College in Nova Scotia in 1912. He moved to Calgary that year, and was admitted to the Alberta bar on January 22, 1915. Stack practiced in Calgary until 1916, when he moved to Vulcan, Alberta. He was named KC on January 7, 1930. He continued to practice in Vulcan until he was appointed to the DC at Calgary in 1945. Stack retired on February 1, 1958 and died on March 15, 1972.

Steer, George Alexander Cameron

Supreme Court of Alberta, Trial
    Division, November 28, 1974 -
    June 30, 1979

Court of Queen's Bench of Alberta,
    June 30, 1979 - December 16, 1979

The Honourable George Alexander Cameron Steer was born in Edmonton on September 8, 1919. At the outbreak of World War II in 1939, he enlisted in the Canadian Army and was wounded in Italy. He was discharged with the rank of Major. Returning to Edmonton, Steer attended the University of Alberta, graduating with a B.A. in 1950 and an LL.B. in 1951 and was the Gold Medalist of his class. Articling with his father's firm of Milner Steer, he joined the firm after being admitted to the Alberta bar on May 30, 1952. Steer was a Lecturer on commercial law at the University of Alberta Faculty of Law for many years. He was named QC on December 30, 1965. Appointed to the bench at Edmonton in 1974, he was also appointed Deputy Judge of the SCYT February 9, 1978. Steer died in Edmonton of a sudden illness on December 16, 1979.

Stevenson, William Alexander

District Court of Northern Alberta,
    Edmonton, July 31, 1975 - October
    1,1975
District Court of Alberta, Edmonton,
    October 1, 1975 - June 30, 1979
Court of Queen's Bench of Alberta,
    Edmonton, June 30, 1979 - October
    23, 1980
Court of Appeal of Alberta,
    Edmonton, October 23, 1980 -
    September 17, 1990

The Honourable William Alexander Stevenson was born in Edmonton, Alberta on May 7, 1934. He attended the University of Alberta, receiving his B.A. in 1956 and his LL.B. in 1957 as a Gold Medal graduate. He was admitted to the Alberta bar on May 29, 1958. Stevenson became a partner in the Edmonton law firm of Morrow, Reynolds and Stevenson, where he practiced until 1968. He was admitted to the Northwest Territories bar in 1966, and the Yukon bar in 1967. Stevenson was a full-time law professor at the University of Alberta Faculty of Law from 1968 to 1970, and he acted as a Sessional Lecturer from 1962 to 1968, and from 1970 until 1990. Stevenson was the founding Chairman of the Legal Education Society of Alberta in 1975. He was with the firm of Hurlburt, Reynolds, Stevenson and Agrios from 1970 until his appointment to the DC in 1975. He received an Honorary LL.D. from the University of Alberta in 1992.

Stevenson is considered the pioneer of continuing education for Canadian judges. In 1986, he authored a report which led to the establishment of the Canadian Judicial Centre, which provides courses for judges and runs workshops for new appointees. He was also President of the Canadian Institute for the Administration of Justice, and Chairman of the Rules of Court Committee. He co-authored with Jean E.L. Côté the *Annotations of the Alberta Rules of Court* (1981), later called the *Civil Procedure Guide*, which became a standard legal text. Stevenson was a Deputy Judge of the SCNT, 1976-1980, and of the SCYT, 1978-1983. He served on the CANT, 1980-1990. In 1990, Stevenson was appointed to the SCC. He retired on June 6, 1992.

Stevenson was one of the most active writers of judgments for the CA in the 1980s, and his judgments dominate the pages of the law reports. He covered the entire ambit of the law, civil and criminal, and wrote on controversial matters such as professional and ethical practices, public utility rates, compensation for faulty goods, matrimonial property, and municipal zoning by-laws. For example, in *Mazurenko v. Mazurenko* ([1981] 15 ALR 2d 357), the husband appealed a division of property from the trial court on grounds that it included farming property given to him as a gift from his family. Stevenson wrote for an allowance in part, creating a very complex scale for the division of the various assets. In *Sembaliuk v. Sembaliuk* ([1985] 35 ALR 2d 193), a husband was accused of fraudulently conveying property to prevent his wife from acquiring his funds. Stevenson cited many historical statutes and cases in writing the Court's opinion, including the *Fraudulent Conveyances Act* of 1570. A final example is *Horsemen's Benevolent and Protective Association of Alberta and Fowling v. Alberta Racing Commission and Attorney General for Alberta* ([1990] 71 ALR 2d 210), an application challenging the constitutional validity of the Racing Commission's rules concerning the use of steroids in horses. Allowing the Commission's rules under statutory authority, Stevenson prepared a very short and cogent opinion on the cases and rulings at issue.

Stewart, John Douglas Reginald

District Court of Acadia, Hanna, November 6, 1919 - April 1, 1922
District Court of Hanna, Hanna, April 1, 1922 - October 4, 1931
His Honour John Douglas Reginald

Stewart was born in Georgetown, Prince Edward Island on March 18, 1879. After being admitted to the Prince Edward Island bar in 1900, he practiced in Charlottetown before moving to the NWT in 1904. Settling in Calgary, Stewart was admitted to the NWT bar on July 23, 1904, and to the Alberta bar on September 16, 1907. He practiced in Calgary for the next ten years. He enlisted in the Canadian Army in 1917 and served in France with the Canadian 9th Battalion before being discharged in 1919 with the rank of Colonel. He was appointed to the DC shortly thereafter. Stewart died on October 4, 1931.

Stratton, Joseph John Walter

Court of Queen's Bench of Alberta, Edmonton, October 23, 1980 - October 30, 1987

Court of Appeal of Alberta, Edmonton, October 30, 1987 - December 13, 1995

The Honourable Joseph John Walter Stratton was born in Calgary, Alberta, on September 9, 1925, and moved to Edmonton at an early age. During the last two years of World War II, Stratton served on H.M.C.S. *Peterborough* before returning to Edmonton. He attended the University of Alberta, earning a B.A. in 1947 and an LL.B. in 1948. He was admitted to the Alberta bar on June 1, 1949. Stratton joined the Calgary-based firm of Nolan Chambers and Company and was the partner responsible for its Edmonton office. He started his own firm, Stratton Lucas and Company, and remained a senior partner until his appointment to the bench at Edmon-

ton in 1980. Stratton was appointed to the CANT in 1987. He retired from the bench on December 13, 1995.

Stratton wrote numerous judgments for the QB and the CA in the 1980s relating to mortgages, landlord-tenant relations, mechanics liens, oil and gas law, trusts, and wardship, labour law, matrimonial disputes, and criminal law. In *Canadiana Gifts Limited v. Friedman et al.* ([1981] 15 ALR 2d 237), the plaintiff, lacking an agreement on a lease renewal, and in default of taxes, claimed that the lease was valid. Stratton, in a a clear and succinct judgment, held that it was valid because the default clause in the agreement was ambiguous. In *Lawrence v. Lindsey* ([1982] 21 ALR 2d 141), a common-law couple of twenty-four years held property in the husband's name. The plaintiff wife claimed part because of a constructive trust, but was disallowed. Stratton used a variety of legal sources in finding against her, citing what he considered to be her "unnecessary delay" in bringing the action. Finally, *Photinopoulos v. Photinopoulos* ([1989] 63 ALR 2d 193) concerned a wife who hired a third party to assault her husband and claimed immunity from a suit for damages because of her marital relationship. Stratton held for the husband, ruling that he was not barred in tort if he brought the action within a reasonable time after the grant of a divorce decree.

Stuart, Charles Allan

Supreme Court of the North-West Territories, District of Northern Alberta, Calgary, October 8, 1906 - September 16, 1907

Supreme Court of Alberta, Calgary,
    September 16, 1907 - September 15,
    1921
Supreme Court of Alberta, Appellate
    Division, Calgary, September 15,
    1921 - March 5, 1926

The Honourable Charles Allan
Stuart was born of English immigrants
in Caradoc, Middlesex County, Ontario on August 3, 1864. He received
his B.A. from the University of Toronto in 1891 with a Gold Medal in
classics, and his LL.B. from Osgoode
Hall in 1896. He was called to the
Ontario bar in 1896 and became a
lecturer in Constitutional History at
the University of Toronto. Later that
year, Stuart became seriously ill; he
was taken to Mexico, where he recovered the following year while practising some law there, and returned to
Canada. He moved to Alberta in 1897,
settling in Calgary, and was admitted
to the NWT bar on March 16, 1898. He
joined Peter McCarthy, KC, and
formed the firm of McCarthy and
Stuart in Calgary. In 1900, Stuart ran
against R.B. Bennett for the North-
West Territories Assembly for West
Calgary and was defeated. In 1901,
his partner Peter McCarthy died and
Stuart joined with Arthur L. Sifton
and James Short to form the firm of
Sifton, Short, and Stuart. He remained
with this firm until 1903. In 1905, he
was elected as a Liberal MLA for
Gleichen, where he had a small farm.
In the legislature, he was active in
committees on Privileges and Elections, Railways, Municipalities, and
Standing Orders. He also spoke on
the rights of the province with respect
to the Crown. Stuart left politics when
he was appointed to the SCNWT at

Calgary in 1906, and was one of the
inaugural members of the SCA in 1907,
moving to the AD in 1921. Stuart devoted a considerable part of his life to
the development of the University of
Alberta. He became the first Chancellor of the University in 1908 and
continued to serve until 1926. He died
on March 5, 1926.

Stuart was an activist on the bench
who did not hesitate to make new
law, delivering judgments which are
rich in legal and historical authorities.
In one of his famous judgments, *R. v.
Cyr (alias Waters)* ([1917] 3 WWR 849),
he rendered a liberal interpretation of
common law doctrine and held that
women could serve as Police Magistrates in Alberta, thereby upholding
the appointments of Alice Jamieson in
Calgary and Emily Murphy in Edmonton. His unique judgment traced
the history of female office-holding
from medieval England, and applied
it to Alberta's local circumstances.
Stuart had a firm vision of the law and
was not appreciative of those who
held a more circumscribed view,
blindly following precedent. Thus, in
R. v. Hartfeil ([1920] 16 ALR 1st 19), he
led the Court against Chief Justice
Harvey in holding that provincial
courts of appeal did not have to follow
previous decisions of such courts in
other provinces; further, he acknowledged historical reality when he
suggested that the criminal law of
Canada was not necessarily uniform
in its administration. Stuart also dis-
liked corporate lawyers and openly
sparred with them in court. In *The
International Coal and Coke Co. v. Trelle*
([1907] ALR 1st 178), Stuart systemati-
cally undermined virtually every argument put forward by R.B. Bennett

and Johnston, concluding that at least two-thirds of their authorities were irrelevant. Similarly, in the epic struggle between the Province of Alberta and the Royal Bank of Canada, Stuart found for the Province against Bennett's arguments in a relative short decision: *R. and the Provincial Treasurer of Alberta v. Royal Bank of Canada* ([1911] 3 ALR 1st 480). His judgment was eventually overturned by the JCPC.

Stuart's defence of local custom as an integral part of the common law was used not only in criminal, business, and corporate law, but also in the area of individual rights. One if his early "rights" cases was *Gallagher v. Armstrong* ([1911] 3 ALR 1st 443), where he gave judgment against the City of Edmonton for firing an employee without cause; and he commented acidly that the civic employee had been reduced to "the humblest navvy in the city sewers". Perhaps his most important judgment, however, was in *R. v. Trainor* ([1917] 1 WWR 415), in which the accused, who expressed joy at the sinking of the *Lusitania*, was convicted of uttering seditious words. Stuart made a thorough examination of English cases and treatises to find for the appeal. This landmark case of individual rights was a precursor of the "clear and present danger" doctrine enunciated shortly afterwards by the U.S. Supreme Court. Some of his other important decisions, moreover, were never reported. *R. v. Stoney Joe* ([1981] 1 CNLR 117) recognized an Aboriginals's right to hunt and take game irrespective of federal or provincial game laws in force. The decision was considered so controversial at the time that the federal government pressed to keep it out of the published reports, and consequently ineffective as case law, so as not to inflame federal-provincial relations. More than sixty years later it was unearthed and used extensively in Aboriginal land claims. Stuart's expansive and convincing historical review of English and colonial law also led him to dismiss an appeal which challenged the constitutional jurisdiction of the Alberta courts to decide divorce actions in *Board v. Board* ([1918] 2 WWR 633). Upheld by the JCPC, the judgment effectively established the basis for divorce law in Alberta for decades to come.

Sulatycky, Allen Borislaw Zenoviy

Court of Queen's Bench of Alberta, Edmonton/Calgary, November 4, 1982 -

The Honourable Justice Allen Borislaw Zenoviy Sulatycky was born in Hafford, Saskatchewan on June 13, 1938. He graduated from the University of Saskatchewan with a B.A. and an LL.B. in 1962. After being admitted to the Alberta bar on July 5, 1963, he practiced with the firm of Parlee, Cavanagh, Irving, Henning, Mustard and Rodney. Sulatycky was unsuccessful when he ran as a Liberal candidate in the Federal by-election for Jasper-Edson in 1967, but he was later elected to the House of Commons for the District of Rocky Mountain in the election of 1968. In 1971, Sulatycky was appointed Parliamentary Secretary to the Minister of Energy, Mines, and Resources and, in 1972, he became Parliamentary Secretary to the Minister of Indian Affairs and Northern Development. In 1972 he returned to the firm of Cavanagh, Irving, Henning, Mustard and Rodney, until his appointment to the bench at Edmonton in 1982. He transferred to Calgary in 1985.

Sulatycky authored few judgments in the QB, but many of them were significant. In *Re. Johannasen (No. 677)* ([1983] 48 AR 15), he defined the limitations of the *Dependent Care Act* in dismissing the compulsory care of an adult epileptic. In *P.V. Commodity v. Gen. Teamsters* ([1983] 53 AR 392), he dismissed the Alberta Labour Relations Board's certification of a union as the bargaining agent of the plaintiff's employees because the workers were solicited on the company's premises. And in *Dixon v. Patton and Patton Farms Ltd.* ([1986] 75 AR 73), he dismissed the plaintiff's suit for damages from a chemical spray that drifted over his lands destroying crops on the grounds that there were insufficient witnesses and scientific evidence. Sulatycky also contributed to the development of the law of tort. In *Kloeck v. Battenfelder* ([1985] 64 AR 98), a farmer hired a contractor to build a barn and manure pit and the pit collapsed. Sulatycky allowed damages against the contractor because of his failure to notify the farmer of deficiencies in the pit's components which he had provided. Throughout these cases and others, Sulatycky demonstrated a tight interpretation of the law which he was only willing to expand when the evidence before him was incontrovertible.

Tavender, Edward Rusling

District Court of Southern Alberta, Calgary, October 19, 1961 - October 1, 1975
District Court of Alberta, Calgary, October 1, 1975 - July 13, 1978

His Honour Edward Rusling Tavender was born in Chesley, Ontario on July 13, 1903. He graduated from the University of Alberta with a B.A. in 1925 and an LL.B. in 1927. After being admitted to the Alberta bar on June 30, 1927, Tavender practiced with the firm of Bennett Hannah and Sanford from 1927 to 1933. From 1933 to 1959, he went into partnership with Hugh C. Farthing and practiced in Calgary with the firm of Farthing and Tavender. He was with the Calgary firm of Tavender and Watkins from 1959 until he was appointed to the DC in 1961. Tavender retired on July 13, 1978.

Taylor, Hedley Clarence

District Court of Edmonton, Edmonton, November 21, 1907 - February 23, 1931

His Honour Hedley Clarence Taylor was born in Sheffield, New Brunswick on September 20, 1864. He received his B.A. in 1887 and his M.A. in 1880 from Mount Allison University, and his LL.B. in 1891 from the University of Michigan at Ann Arbor. Taylor articled in Saint John, New Brunswick, in 1891 at the firm of C.A. Stockton. He was called to the New Brunswick bar in 1891. He then moved to Edmonton, where he was admitted to the NWT bar on November 25,

1891. He formed the firm of Taylor and Taylor with his brother and practised with the firm of Taylor, Boyle and Parlee until he was appointed the first Judge of the DC at Edmonton in 1907. Taylor was active in the Edmonton community: he was a member of the Edmonton Public School Board from 1896 to 1908, and Chairman in 1897; he was Chairman of the Board of Alberta Colleges from 1903 to 1920; he served for two years on the Board of Governors of the University of Alberta and was also a member of the University's Senate. Taylor died on February 23, 1931.

Taylor was a controversial judge, and a number of his decisions were overturned on appeal. In *Martineau v. Grand Trunk Pacific Railway* ([1926] 22 ALR 1st 147), the plaintiff, perhaps intoxicated, was struck by an oncoming train while travelling to work on a handspeeder, and Taylor found for the plaintiff's family under the *Workmen's Compensation Act*. Justice Hyndman held on appeal that there was no evidence that the accident was work-related. In *Ringwood v. Kerr Bros. and Grand Trunk Pacific Railway* ([1914] 7 ALR 1st 227), Taylor awarded compensation under the same Act for a similar accident. Chief Justice Harvey held on appeal that there was no finding of fact to support the decision, and that the judgment was "not competent". Justices Simmons and Stuart were equally critical. Stuart held that Taylor used the wrong citation in *Sawyer-Massey Co. Ltd. v. Frank Weder and Robert Weder* ([1912] 5 ALR 1st 364), and Simmons contended that Taylor was ignorant of the law respecting notice of default in *Massey Harris Co. Ltd. v. Baptiste* ([1915] 9 ALR 1st 73).

Given his high political profile, Taylor was able to escape these censures throughout his tenure on the bench.

Travis, Jeremiah

Stipendiary Magistrate of the North West Territories, District of Alberta, Calgary, July 30, 1885 - February 17, 1887

The Honourable Jeremiah Travis was born in Saint John, New Brunswick in 1830. He received his LL.B. from Harvard University in Cambridge, Massachusetts in 1866, and practiced in Winnipeg before his appointment as a SM in 1885 resident in Calgary.

Travis was a recognized legal scholar. His Harvard Dissertation on "The Extent to which the Common Law is Applied in Determining What Constitutes a Crime" won the annual prize and was published in three issues of the *American Law Register* (1866-1877). His work in Saint John prompted the provincial legislature to make New Brunswick the first province to recognize a law degree for professional status. His partnership with Charles Duff, a future judge of the SCC, had the largest legal business in the province before Travis left it for the life of an entrepreneur which left him bankrupt. Later, practising before the SC of New Brunswick and of Canada, he became a famous advocate. A prohibitionist and stout supporter of temperance, this became his life's crusade. His legal writings on the constitutionality of prohibition denounced the SCC and the JCPC, and became quite controversial. The most notable of these writings is *Law Treatise on the Constitutional Powers of Parliament, and of the Local Legislatures, under the British North America Act, 1867*, which was published in Saint John in 1884. It was this quest, and Liberal patronage, which brought him to western Canada and earned him an appointment as SM at Calgary in 1885. After he left the court in 1887, Travis practiced real estate in Calgary and became quite wealthy. He died in Calgary in 1911.

The life of a Stipendiary Magistrate was not busy in this era, and Travis heard few cases on the Calgary court calendar. He sat on twenty criminal prosecutions in his official twenty months tenure, eleven of which were for theft and seven for assault. His brief judicial tenure was marked, however, by frequent and intense conflicts arising mainly from Travis' zealous and often high-handed campaign against lenient liquor trafficking. Declaring that the town was "lawless", he set about in speeches both on and off the bench to denounce public officials who opposed his efforts, eventually sentencing city councilman J.S. Clark to six months hard labour for resisting arrest in his saloon by NWMP without a warrant. When *Calgary Herald* Editor Hugh Cayley publicly condemned Travis' strict enforcement of the unpopular liquor laws, Travis had him jailed for contempt of court. He disbarred "drinking" attorneys and called his judicial colleague in Calgary Charles Rouleau an "incompetent drunkard". The controversy came to a head when Travis accused popular mayor George Murdoch of running the city with a "whiskey ring", declared a municipal election Murdoch had won invalid, and installed anti-liquor candidate James Reilly in his seat. NWMP Commissioner Herchmer had to arrest Travis and the Dominion government appointed a Commission to investigate his conduct in office. Travis was suspended and the Commission recommended dismissal, but this became unnecessary when the SMs were replaced by the SCNWT in 1887 - Travis was simply not appointed to the new court. He ended his legal career in Calgary with the publication of a two-volume *Commentaries on the Law of Sales* in 1892.

Trussler, Marguerite Jean

Court of Queen's Bench of Alberta, Edmonton, November 10, 1986 -

The Honourable Justice Marguerite Jean Trussler was born in Edmonton, Alberta on December 3, 1946. She graduated from the University of Alberta with a B.A. in 1969 and an LL.B. in 1970. She received an LL.M. from the University of Melbourne, Australia in 1974. Trussler was admitted to the Alberta bar on October 1, 1971, and the bar of the State of Victoria, Australia, in 1972. She was a partner with the Edmonton firm of Parlee, Irving, Henning, Mustard and Rodney from 1976 until her appointment to the bench in 1986.

Turcotte, Louis Sherman

District Court of Southern Alberta, Lethbridge, September 16, 1955 - October 1, 1975

District Court of Southern Alberta,
    Chief Judge, Lethbridge,
    September 24, 1969 - October 1,
    1975
District Court of Alberta, Associate
    Chief Judge, Lethbridge, October
    1, 1975 - December 1, 1975
Supernumerary Judge, Lethbridge,
    December 1, 1975 - June 30, 1979
Court of Queen's Bench of Alberta,
    Lethbridge, June 30, 1979 -
    September 10, 1979

The Honourable Louis Sherman
Turcotte was born in Grand'mere,
Quebec on October 10, 1904. The son
of the town's Mayor, a series of financial misfortunes caused the family to
move to Lethbridge, Alberta in 1912.
Educated at St. Basil's School and Bow-
man High School in Lethbridge,
Turcotte attended the University of
Alberta, graduating with a B.A. in
1921, and an LL.B. in 1924. After
articling in Edmonton, he was one of
the youngest lawyers ever admitted to the Alberta bar on December 18,
1925, at the age of twenty-one. He set
up practice in Vegreville, where he
remained for four years before moving to Cardston. Turcotte then settled
in Lethbridge, where he practiced for
the next nineteen years. He joined the
Canadian Reserve Army in 1941, and
attained the rank of Captain in 1943.
Active in the Liberal Party, he ran
unsuccessfully in the federal elections
of 1945 and 1949, and served as Treasurer for the Alberta Liberal Association. Turcotte was a major advocate
for the development of Lethbridge
and southern Alberta. He served nine
years on Lethbridge City Council, and
was elected Mayor, 1950-1953. He was
Secretary of the South Alberta Water

Conservation Council, Vice-President
of the Lethbridge Chamber of Commerce, President of the Lethbridge
Bar Association, and member of the
Rotary Club. He served for several
years on the Board of Governors of the
University of Lethbridge, and was
Chancellor from 1968 to 1983. Until he
was appointed to the DC there in
1955, Turcotte practiced with the firm
of Turcotte and Byrne. He received an
honorary LL.D. in 1972. He became a
Supernumerary Judge of the DC on
December 1, 1975, but returned
briefly to take up a position on the
new QB in Lethbridge when it was
formed on June 30, 1979, retiring finally on September 10, 1979, when he
reached the age of 75. He died in
Lethbridge on March 18, 1983.

Few of Turcotte's decisions were
published in the law reports, and most
of those date from the 1970s. This is
primarily due to the fact that he heard
cases from small towns. Having an
excellent memory, he was regarded
as a judge who, while working long
hours on the bench, could assimilate
facts with ease and never lose sight of
the legal issue in question. A number
of his judgments, however, were
significant. In *R. v. McCaugherty*
([1971] 2 WWR 579), he defined early
on the boundaries for the admissibility of breathalyzer evidence that
became widely used later in the prosecution of impaired driving. *Wood v.
Wood* ([1974] 5 WWR 18) involved the
legality in Canada of a divorce obtained by Canadians in the United
States, Turcotte holding that the *decree
nisi* was valid in Canada as long as the
reasons for the divorce were legiti-
mate. Finally, in *Royal Bank of Canada
v. Freeborn and Freedom* ([1983] 21 WWR

279), the plaintiff initiated a test case to determine its right to refuse mortgage payments from a person other than the mortgage holder. Turcotte held that the Bank could do so where there was an unauthorized transfer of title to another person. He chaired two commissions of inquiry into the government of the City of Calgary in 1959 and in 1970. Believing the role of the judiciary is to provide a conservative reformation of legal norms, Turcotte relied heavily on Canadian case law and practical experience in community life to shape his decisions.

Tweedie, Thomas Mitchell March

Supreme Court of Alberta, Trial
  Division, Calgary, September 15,
  1921 - October 4, 1944
Supreme Court of Alberta, Trial
  Division, Chief Justice, Calgary,
  August 16, 1944 - October 4, 1944

The Honourable Thomas Mitchell March Tweedie was born in River John, Nova Scotia on March 3, 1872. He received his B.A. from Mount Allison University and his LL.B. from Harvard University in 1905. He was admitted to the Nova Scotia bar in 1905. Tweedie moved to Alberta in 1907 and was one of the last advocates admitted to the North-West Territories bar on July 10, 1907. He settled in Calgary and practiced there for the next fourteen years, much of the time in partnership with Alexander A. McGillivray. He was with the firm of Tweedie and McGillivray when he was appointed to the bench in 1921. Tweedie, a staunch Conservative, was elected MLA for Calgary in 1911 and

was re-elected in 1913. When he was defeated in the 1917 provincial election in 1917, he ran in the federal election in the same year and was elected MP for Calgary. He was named KC on March 19, 1913. Proud of his British ancestry, Tweedie served as President of the Southern Alberta Branch of the Canadian Patriotic Fund and as a member of its Dominion executive. A devout member of the United Church, he headed many of its volunteer organizations, and was Vice-President of the Alberta Chapter of the Canadian Red Cross. He was also President of the Maritime Provinces Association in Calgary. A bachelor, he lived at the Ranchmen's Club. Appointed Chief Justice of the Trial Division in August 1944, Tweedie presided only over the summer term: he died in Lethbridge after attending a dinner in his honour given by the Lethbridge Bar Association on October 5, 1944.

As a judge, Tweedie drew on a wealth of legal skills and experience. His written judgments demonstrated strength specifically in civil actions involving business contracts, bankruptcy, and torts. For example, in both *Canadian Credit Men's Trust Association v. Umbel and Gillespie Grain Co. Ltd.* ([1931] 3 WWR 145), and *Saker & Saker v. The Canadian Men's Trust Association* ([1931] 3 WWR 175), he interpreted the *Exemptions Act* in favour of bankrupt companies being sued by their creditors. Later, in *Colton v. Canadian Bakeries Ltd. and Dingle* ([1939] 2 WWR 315), he explored the law of tort for negligence questions where people were injured at work. In *Blatchford v. AG of Alberta and Van Ruyen* ([1933] 3 WWR), the plaintiff, a potential beneficiary of her estranged husband's estate, applied to set aside a *decree absolute* in a previous divorce action because it had been obtained through her husband's perjured testimony. Tweedie broke precedent first by allowing the appeal, and then by setting aside the divorce decree. In addition to his contributions to the bench, Tweedie also served as a member of the Alberta Natural Resources Commission, 1934-1935.

Veit, Joanne Barbara

Court of Queen's Bench of Alberta, Edmonton, June 18, 1981 -

The Honourable Justice Joanne Barbara Veit was born on September 9, 1942. She graduated with an LL.B. from the University of Ottawa in 1964, winning the Governor General's Medal. After being called to the Ontario bar with honours in 1966, she spent a year as a law clerk to Chief Justice Porter of the High Court of Ontario. Veit then practiced briefly with the well-known Ottawa firm of Gowling and Henderson before attending the London School of Economics, where she obtained a LL.M.. She came to Alberta in 1970 and was admitted to the Alberta bar on January 27, 1971. Veit was a solicitor with the AG's Department and was an Associate Professor of Law at the University of Alberta. She was also an official with the Alberta Securities Commission, and was the Director of the Commission when she was appointed to the bench at Edmonton in 1981.

Veit wrote a number of major opinions in the 1980s. Most of her decisions involved criminal prosecutions, native rights, and family law. In *R. v. Linn* ([1983] 39 ALR 2d 584), the accused appealed a conviction for impaired driving, and the appeal was dismissed because he had failed to establish grounds for the appeal, even though he may not have been the driver. In *R. v. Crane et al.* ([1985] 59 ALR 2d 250), five Treaty Indians were accused of selling fish contrary to the provincial fishing regulations. Veit held that the provincial statute was *ultra vires* the federal government's power to legislate, but was not invalid of itself, and thus upheld the Crown's conviction. A similar case of *R. v. Steinhauer* ([1985] 63 ALR 2d 381) concerned the appeal by an Aboriginal who was convicted of fishing with a net and without a licence. Veit held, through a close reading of Treaty 6, that it did not forbid licencing, and through interpretation of the *Canadian Charter of Rights and Freedoms* that his rights were not contravened. Thus the appeal was dismissed. Finally, with regard to estates and maintenance, *Wyant Estate v. St. Arnault et al.* ([1985] 63 ALR 2d 91) stemmed from an automobile accident in 1973 where discovery did not take place until 1978 and the plaintiff did not proceed to trial until 1984. Veit held that the defendant was allowed a dismissal due to the delay which had prejudiced his defence. And in *Fenwick v. Fenwick* ([1989] 89 ALR 2d 372), Veit quashed the continuation of a maintenance order due to the financial problems of the husband. Veit wrote finely-reasoned judgments which draw on balanced interpretations of case law and contemporary jurisprudence.

Virtue, Charles Gladstone

Court of Queen's Bench of Alberta,
   Calgary, October 9, 1985 -

The Honourable Justice Charles Gladstone Virtue was born in Lethbridge, Alberta, on May 30, 1926. He earned his B.A. at McMaster University in Hamilton, Ontario in 1947, and his LL.B. from the University of Alberta in 1920, where he graduated as Silver Medallist. He was admitted to the Alberta bar on June 18, 1951 and was named QC on December 27, 1968. From 1950 until his appointment to the bench at Calgary in 1985, Virtue practiced in the Lethbridge firm his father had established, Virtue and Company. Active in the community, Virtue was Chairman of the Lethbridge Municipal Hospital 1968-1969. He was also President of the Alberta Hospitals Association in 1970 and was President of the Canada Winter Games in 1975. Virtue was President of the Law Society of Alberta, 1984-1985, and served as Chairman of the Alberta Law Foundation. He was also appointed Deputy Justice of the SCNT on October 4, 1985.

Wachowich, Allan Harvey Joseph

District Court of Northern Alberta,
   Edmonton, December 20, 1974 -
   October 1, 1975
District Court of Alberta, Edmonton,
   October 1, 1975 - June 30, 1979
Court of Queen's Bench of Alberta,
   Edmonton, June 30, 1979 -
Court of Queen's Bench of Alberta,
   Associate Chief Justice, Edmonton,
   February 1, 1993 -

The Honourable Justice Allan Harvey Joseph Wachowich was born in Opal, Alberta on March 8, 1935. His parents immigrated to Canada from Poland in 1904 and were among the first five Polish families to settle in Alberta. Educated in Opal and Edmonton, Wachowich attended the University of Alberta, graduating with a B.A. in 1957 and an LL.B. in 1958. After being admitted to the Alberta bar on May 29, 1959, Wachowich joined the Edmonton firm of Kosowan and Wachowich where he remained a partner until his appointment to the DC in 1974. He was admitted to the bars of the Northwest Territories in 1963 and of the Yukon Territory in 1964. Wachowich has lectured at the University of Alberta Faculty of Law in insurance law and professional responsibility. Currently, he is the Chair of the Alberta Automobile Insurance Board and is also on the Board of Governors of the International Insurance Society. Active in community affairs, Wachowich has served as judicial advisor to the St. Thomas Moore Lawyer's Guild, arbitrator for the Canadian Football League, President of the Canadian Catholic Organization for Development and Peace, an international Aid Organization, a Director of the United Way of Edmonton, President of Catholic Charities in Edmonton, and Chair of the Henry Singer Memorial Scholarship Fund. Appointed to the QB in 1979, he was named Associate Chief Justice in 1993 and is also the bankruptcy judge of the QB. He has also been a member of the Board of Directors of the Curriculum Committee of the Cambridge Conference of the Canadian Institute for Advanced Legal Studies.

Wachowich has been a frequent contributor to the judgments of the courts since his appointment to the QB in 1979. His decisions generally have been in the areas of civil procedure, corporate law, banking, and criminal law. For example, in *Rafael v. Allison et al.* ([1987] 56 ALR 2d 79, 328), Wachowich ruled that the *Federal Interest Act*, which placed a limit of five per cent interest on judgments awarded in western provinces and territories, was discriminatory and upheld a claim for a higher return. Following a precedent set by Chief Justice Laycraft, the Act was interpreted as violating the *Charter of Rights and Freedoms*. In *Re. Canadian Commercial Bank; Canadian Deposit Insurance Corporation v. Canadian Commercial Bank* ([1987] 50 ALR 2d 1), Wachowich used a plethora of cases from across the country to determine the priority of costs in a sale of assets of little value containing indemnity provisions. A similar search of case law was involved in *Ed Miller Sales and Rentals Ltd. v. Caterpillar Tractor Company et al.* ([1988] 57 ALR 2d 182, 187), where the plaintiff applied to have the defendant's officer in discovery to list its authorized dealers for a combines investigation. Wachowich dismissed the application, holding that the application was improper for anticipated or pending litigation. In the earlier case of *Two Hills Rental Properties Ltd. and Bahnuik v. First Calgary Trust Co.* ([1982] 18 ALR 2d 82), Wachowich ruled that the defendant acted in bad faith in giving the plaintiff assurances that funds would be advanced, but was not legally obliged to advance them. No damages were to be paid, but the commitment fee plus interest and plaintiff's costs were to be paid by the defendant. He was asked to prepare the judgment in *Canadian Commercial Bank and Price Waterhouse Ltd. v. McLaughlan* ([1988] 62 ALR 2d), where the plaintiffs sought damages of close to $300 million for misrepresentation, fraud, and wilful default, while the defendant sought the documentation on which such allegations were made. The application was dismissed on condition that the plaintiffs be given one year to deliver the documents. Wachowich also was one of several judges dealing with applications relating to the liquidation of the failed Canadian Commercial Bank in 1987. These cases demonstrate Wachowich's adept navigation of complex legal and financial issues with strong arguments on both sides. They also reveal the applicability of his judgments to future case law.

Waite, John Hilary

Supreme Court of Alberta, Trial
    Division, Calgary, February 2, 1978
    - June 30, 1979
Court of Queen's Bench of Alberta,
    Calgary, June 30, 1979 -
Supernumerary Justice, Calgary, May
    30, 1993 -

The Honourable Justice John Hilary Waite was born in Schamacher, Ontario, on April 12, 1928. Educated in Schamacher, he attended Queen's University, where he received a B.A. in Political Science. He studied law at the University of Toronto, obtaining his LL.B. in 1953. Waite moved to Calgary in 1954 and was admitted to the Alberta bar on June 17, 1954. He practiced in Calgary for the next twenty-three years, and was a partner in the firm of Harradence and Company when he was appointed to the bench in 1978. He was named QC in 1976 and was a Sessional Lecturer at the University of Calgary Faculty of Law. He was also an active member of Calgary's theatrical community, and has served on the Board of Directors of Alberta Theatre Projects. He has been a member of the Alpine Club of Canada, and is a life member of the Trail Riders of the Canadian Rockies.

Waite's numerous report judgments span both civil and criminal law, but he has been particularly active in the areas of the environment, health, and family law. In *Old Cabin Crafts v. R.* ([1980] 12 ALR 2d 197), he dismissed an appeal of a conviction for converting and selling parts of birds of prey, citing a large array of statutes to hold that the prohibition was fundamental. In *Herman v. Smith* ([1984] 34 ALR 2d 90), he allowed the wife of a common law marriage compensation from the trustee of her husband's estate even though she had not contributed materially to the marriage. Waite determined her value through that of the labour of a house keeper less the value of the material benefits of her cohabitation. In *Montaron v. Wagner* ([1988] 57 ALR 2d 273), the defendant performed ear surgery on the plaintiff who claimed negligence. Waite awarded damages for loss of work on the grounds that the plaintiff was not properly informed of the risks of the operation, not that the results of the operation comprised negligence. And, in *Tuck v. Lam and Calgary General Hospital* ([1988] 57 ALR 2d 323), the plaintiff was denied access to medical records concerning

confinement to a psychiatric ward on the advice of his psychiatrist on the grounds that the legislation does not provide an absolute and unqualified right of access to them. Waite made a careful review of legislation, case law, and individual circumstances in reaching his decisions and writing his judgments.

Walsh, William Legh

Supreme Court of Alberta, Calgary, April 3, 1912 - September 15, 1921
Supreme Court of Alberta, Trial Division, Calgary, September 15, 1921 - January 27, 1931
Supreme Court of Alberta, Appellate Division, Calgary, January 27, 1931 - May 1, 1931

The Honourable William Legh Walsh was born in Simcoe, Ontario, on January 28, 1857. The son of a pioneer legislator of Upper Canada, he attended the University of Toronto, receiving his LL.B. in 1878. After being admitted to the Ontario bar in 1880, Walsh began practicing law in Simcoe, but later moved to Orangeville, where he became a partner in the firm of D'Alton McCarthy. He remained in Orangeville for the next nineteen years, serving on the school board, and was elected Mayor three times. He also ran as a Conservative in a provincial election, but lost. In 1900, attracted by the Yukon gold rush, Walsh travelled to Dawson City where he practiced law and was named KC there in 1903. He left the far north with the economic decline in 1904 and settled in Calgary where he was admitted to the North-West Territories bar on June 14, 1904. Walsh was the first

President of the Alberta Conservative Association in 1905 and he was the Party's chief organizer for several years thereafter. He was defeated, however, in a provincial election in Gleichen. Walsh was senior partner in the law firm of Walsh, McCarthy and Carson until he was appointed to the bench at Calgary in 1912. He left the court on May 1, 1931, to become the fourth Lieutenant-Governor of Alberta, a post he held until 1936. Walsh was a man of many interests. An avid sportsman, he was a noted lacrosse and cricket player in Orangeville, and took up curling in the Yukon. He became a competent golfer in Calgary, and played on Canadian Seniors events. A devout Anglican, Walsh served as Chancellor of the Anglican Diocese of Calgary for nineteen years. He was one of the Church's major supporters for nearly three decades, and was also the first non-Aboriginal man to be made an Honorary Chief of the Blood Indian Tribe, becoming Chief Sitting Eagle in 1931. His son Legh was a prominent lawyer and Secretary of the Law Society of Alberta. Walsh died in Victoria, British Columbia on January 13, 1938.

Walsh possessed great conviction, energy, and enthusiasm for the law. Handling a wide variety of cases on the SCA, he was especially active in criminal law cases. A strong supporter of capital punishment, he believed that punishment was an effective deterrent to criminality. He was reported to have sentenced eighteen men and women to be hanged. Walsh's most famous criminal case was *R. v. Picariello and Lassandro* ([1922] 2 WWR 872). Picariello, a wealthy and powerful rumrunner, was tried with his fe-male accomplice for the murder of a police constable in the Crowsnest Pass. The jury found them guilty, and Walsh sentenced them to death. In spite of some thirty-three points of trial misconduct alleged against Walsh, appeals to the SCA ([1922] 2 WWR 872) and the SCC failed. Walsh also allowed rather loose interpretations of "nightwalker" and "prostitute" to sustain convictions of women who had not given satisfactory accounts of themselves when found in the company of prostitutes or the vicinity of bawdy houses, as in *Re. Brady* ([1913] 5 ALR 1st 400), and *R. v. Jackson* ([1914] 5 WWR 1286).

Walsh did not take his court lightly. A firm believer in decorum, he often included ad hoc comments in his judgments on the way in which counsel conducted business before him. For example, in *Muirhead v. Newman* ([1930] 3 WWR 589), concerning the plaintiff's appeal of a judgment he had won, the justice rebuked him vigorously for wasting the Court's time with a "nuisance" appeal. In *Powell v. Thomas, Jamieson and MacKenzie, Ltd.* ([1918] 3 WWR 901), Walsh dismissed the plaintiff's action for damages from an accident while employed under the *Workmen's Compensation Act* and, while expressing sympathy for the plight of the injured worker, used the words of an English judge to explain his view of the proper judicial attitude: "human sympathy can never work less worthily than in warping the judgments of judicial tribunals." Walsh had a strong belief in English common law and precedent. He was also a firm supporter of English culture and society, of the British Empire, and of Canada's colonial ties to Great

Britain. When asked to comment on the idea of abolishing appeals to the JCPC in 1931, he replied that judicial appeals to Great Britain should be strengthened and not severed.

Wetmore, Edward Ludlow

Supreme Court of the North-West
    Territories, District of Eastern
    Assiniboia, Moosomin, February
    18, 1887 - August 16, 1897
Supreme Court of the North-West
    Territories, District of
    Saskatchewan, Fort Battleford,
    August 16, 1897 - September 16,
    1907

The Honourable Edward Ludlow Wetmore was born in Fredericton, New Brunswick on March 24, 1841. His father was a barrister, and Clerk of the New Brunswick Legislature for over fifty years. Educated at grammar schools in Fredericton and Georgetown, Wetmore graduated from the University of New Brunswick (then King's College) with a B.A., and an LL.B. with Honours in 1959. He was called to the New Brunswick bar in 1864. Wetmore practiced law in Fredericton for a time and joined the firm of Fraser and Winslow in 1877. In 1881, he became Deputy Clerk of the Crown and a QC. He was Mayor of Fredericton from 1874 to 1876, and a Conservative member of the Legislative Assembly for York County from 1883 to 1886, where he was the Leader of the Opposition. He served as President of the Barristers" Society from 1886 to 1887.

Wetmore was appointed Commissioner to consolidate the statutes of New Brunswick in 1887 when he re-ceived an appointment to the SCNWT for the Eastern Assiniboia District at Moosomin. He rode this large circuit for a decade until he was appointed to the Saskatchewan Judicial District at Battleford in 1897. As a member of the SCNWT, he often travelled to what is now southern Alberta to hear cases *en banc* at Fort Macleod and Calgary. Moosomin became his family home, and he was an Anglican Church official at the parish church of St. Albans. He enjoyed cricket, fishing, and shooting, and was a member of the Assiniboia Club. He also served as a member of the District's Board of Education, and was a Commissioner for consolidating the *Ordinances of the NWT* in 1898. Wetmore was appointed Chief Justice of the first Supreme Court of Saskatchewan at Regina in 1907. There he was also appointed Chairman of the Commission to consolidate the laws of Saskatchewan in 1908, and was the administrator of the provincial government on three occasions. He also served as Chancellor of the University of Saskatchewan from 1907 to 1912. Wetmore retired on October 15, 1912, and died in Victoria, British Columbia, on January 19, 1922. He was buried in Moosomin, Saskatchewan.

Wetmore was known as an outstanding jurist who brought dignity, prestige, and credibility to the superior court of the frontier. His decisions were voluminous. While he wrote judgments on virtually every aspect of the law, he was particularly interested in questions of procedure, in the interpretation of statutes, and in criminal and constitutional law. Writing for the majority, he was usually short, clear, and cogent. His judgments in dissent were equally forceful. Wetmore made many rulings in matters of civil procedure, and Volume III of the *Territories Law Reports*, for example, consists mainly of his decisions. He often ruled on the applicability of various English precedents and statutes. For example, in *R. v. Nan-e-quis-a-ka* ([1889] 1 TLR 211), he held that the forms and ceremonies of English marriage law were not applicable to the Territories, and that marriages by Indian custom were valid. In *R. v. Howson* ([1894] 1 TLR 492), he held that an individual whose mother was Aboriginal possessed all the rights of Indian status. His dissenting opinion in *Conger v. Kennedy* ([1895] 2 TLR 186), formed the basis of the SCC's reversal of the SCNWT's decision that the *Married Women's Property Ordinance* was *ultra vires* the Legislative Assembly.

Wetmore provided judgments on a series of Territorial ordinances, including those concerning judicature, prairie fires, workmen's compensation, and the medical profession. He ran a tight court, and one that was unusually punctual for the era. He also did not tolerate legal chicanery. When a defendant appealed to set aside a statement of claim because it lacked full compliance with technical rules in *Clark v. Brownlie* ([1893] 3 TLR 194), he rejected the application and accused counsel of "gross ignorance or gross carelessness." An examination of approximately 100 cases which he decided reveals that only twenty were appealed, and only four of those were reversed. Wetmore also served on several government commissions. One of the most famous was his commission to investigate charges against Commissioner Herchmer of the NWMP in 1891. While some 137 complaints were preferred, Wetmore exonerated Herchmer in view of the context of conditions and circumstances of Herchmer's tenure. He had an impressive knowledge of jurisprudence and an unassuming style.

Whittaker, Bruce Cavanagh

District Court of Northern Alberta, Edmonton, September 26, 1963 - October 1, 1975
District Court of Alberta, Edmonton, October 1, 1975 - March 23, 1978

His Honour Bruce Cavanagh Whittaker was born in Edmonton, Alberta on June 20, 1914. He attended the University of Alberta, graduating with an LL.B. in 1936 with the Gold Medal in law. He was admitted to the Alberta bar on June 21, 1937. Whittaker practiced first with the firm of Clement and Whittaker, and then with the Edmonton firm of Clement, Parlee, Whittaker, Irving, Mustard, and Rodney, where he specialized in corporate and insurance law as well as litigation. He was named QC on December 31, 1957. From 1956 to 1961, Whittaker was a member of the Board of Governors of Royal Alexandra Hospital in Edmonton, and was its Chairman for two years. He was a member of the Board of Governors of the University of Alberta, 1969-1972. Appointed to the DC in 1963, he retired on March 23, 1978.

Wilson, Ernest Brown

Supreme Court of Alberta, Trial Division, Edmonton, June 27, 1952 - December 10, 1958

The Honourable Ernest Brown Wilson was born in Innisfail, Alberta, on March 2, 1904. Educated in Edmonton public schools, he joined the 19th Alberta Dragoons in 1921 and rose to the rank of Lieutenant. He also attended the University of Alberta, graduating with a B.A. in 1925 and an LL.B. in 1927. After being admitted to the Alberta bar on November 23, 1928, he began practice with R.D. Tighe. He was practicing with the firm of Cairns, Ross, Wilson and Wallbridge at Edmonton when he was appointed to the bench there in 1952. Wilson was named KC in 1939. At the outbreak of World War II, he enlisted in the Canadian Army and was placed second in command of the Loyal Edmonton Regiment as they were mobilized overseas in 1939. By the end of the war, he held a senior staff appointment at the Canadian Military Headquarters in London, England, with the rank of Brigadier. Wilson was given the Canadian Efficiency Decoration for his long service in the armed forces and was made an Officer of the Order of the British Empire. Active in welfare work, he was elected President of the Edmonton Council of Social Agencies, 1947-1948, and served as President of the Men's Canadian Club in 1947. He was President of the Edmonton Liberal Association and was active in the Freemasons and the United Service Institute. He was the first native Albertan and graduate of the University of Alberta Law School to be appointed to the SCA in 1952. He died in Edmonton on December 10, 1958.

As a judge, Wilson was known to pay meticulous care and attention to details, was helpful to all legal counsel before him, and was quick to dispatch a case. He also handled a number of bizarre cases. For example, in *Russell v. Russell* ([1953] 10 WWR 62), both husband and wife had committed adultery. Scanning the case law for England and Canada, Wilson held that the husband's claim was not well plead because of his circumstances and that both parties were at fault. Since the husband was more blameworthy, he awarded maintenance payable to his wife. Similarly, in *McKeever v. McKeever and Connolly* ([1955] 18 WWR 428), the wife sued her husband for divorce on grounds of adultery, and a judicial separation on grounds of mental cruelty. Wilson, using a similar survey of the case law, held that there was no evidence for the wife's adultery, nor convincing evidence for the husband's, but evidence for mental cruelty and thus a judicial separation was awarded. Many of his cases were on appeal from Police Magistrates, and in general he upheld their discretionary powers. Wilson was most effective in distilling clarity and order from complex cases. For example, in *Schlaut v. Northern Trusts Company et al.* ([1954] 1 WWR 20), Wilson deftly unravelled and dismissed a claim of title by the original landowner to a successful oil well in a case involving mineral rights, two sales and transfers of land with default in taxes and abandonment, an oil and gas lease with some prior rights reserved, and gaps in much of the evidence.

Winter, William Roland

District Court of Lethbridge,
    Lethbridge, November 21, 1907 -
    December 13, 1913

District Court of Calgary, Calgary,
December 13, 1913 - March 13, 1926

His Honour William Roland
Winter was born of English parent-
age in Messina, Sicily, and educated
in England and France. He was admitted to the English bar and practiced in
England until 1893, when he came to
Calgary, being admitted to the bar of
the North-West Territories on October 30, 1893. Winter was a Police
Magistrate in NWT, 1895-1897 and
Registrar of Land Titles, 1897-1907.
He moved to the DC in Lethbridge in
1907 but returned to Calgary in 1913,
where he served on the DC until his
retirement. Winter was a gentleman
of refinement, and worked to upgrade
the culture of Calgary. A known
patron of music, literature, and drama,
he was an active financial backer of
amateur theatricals and a supporter
of the Calgary Amateur Association.
A talented cellist, his house was a
place of music, and his lawns were
placed at the disposal of the Calgary
Lawn Bowling Club. His wife Lydia
Winter became one of Calgary's best
known citizens. The former actress of
the London and European stage became known as Calgary's mother of
the arts in the early twentieth century.
Winter retired on March 13, 1926, and
died on February 22, 1929.

Winter was one of Calgary's
pioneer solicitors, and the first barrister to be appointed to the DC when
Alberta was organized as a province.
While there are no reported decisions
of his in the published law reports,
Justice Harvey considered him an
expert on probate matters. A strong
Liberal, he authored several small articles on legal reform.

Yanosik, Clarence George

District Court of Southern Alberta,
Lethbridge, September 24, 1969 -
October 1, 1975
District Court of Alberta, Lethbridge,
October 1, 1975 - June 30, 1979
Court of Queen's Bench of Alberta,
Lethbridge, June 30, 1979 -
Supernumerary Justice, Lethbridge,
April 20, 1991 -

The Honourable Justice Clarence
George Yanosik was born in Lethbridge, Alberta on April 20, 1926.
Educated in Lethbridge, he enlisted
in the Canadian Navy in 1943. Following the war, Yanosik attended the
University of British Columbia, where
he graduated with a B.A. in 1951, and
an LL.B. in 1952. He was admitted to
the Alberta bar on June 8, 1953. Yanosik
was a member of the Lethbridge firm
of Moscovich, Moscovich, Spanos,
Matisz, and Yanosik until 1964, when
he joined the Lethbridge firm of Rice,
Paterson, Prowse, MacLean, and
Yanosik. He remained with this firm
for over five years until his appointment to the DC in 1969. His was the
first appointment of a native of
Lethbridge as federally appointed
judge.

Yanosik wrote a number of reported judgments, and many of them
were quite extensive. For example, in
Millar v. Province of Alberta ([1981] 25
ALR 2d 561), the plaintiff sued for
wrongful dismissal. In a very lengthy
opinion on a somewhat simple matter
involving an employee backstamping
a government report, Yanosik found
for the plaintiff. *Bank of Nova Scotia v.
Guenette* ([1986] 68 ALR 2d 368), which
involved countersuits, concerned the

defendant's wife, who was sued by the Bank for transferring funds to a third party for a loan agreement on which she had not signed. Neither party was held liable. In a very curious case, *Weaver v. Buckle* ([1982] 35 ALR 2d 97), plaintiffs brought an action for damages on behalf of an infant who was struck and injured by the defendant's car. Following lengthy recitation of facts, evidence, and interpretation, Yanosik held that the infant was forty per cent at fault, and then ruled that the defendant was liable for $70,000 in his share of fault.

Court Lists

Stipendiary Magistrates of the North-West Territories
January 1, 1876 - February 17, 1887

Macleod, James Farquharson, January 1, 1876 - February 17, 1887
Ryan, Matthew, January 1, 1876 - July 1881
Richardson, Hugh, July 22, 1876 - 17 February 1887
Rouleau, Charles Borromée, September 28, 1883 - February 17, 1887
Travis, Jeremiah, July 30, 1885 - February 17, 1887

Supreme Court of the North-West Territories
February 18, 1887 - September 16, 1907

Macleod, James Farquharson, February 18, 1887 - September 5, 1894
Richardson, Hugh, February 18 1887 - 12 November 1903
Rouleau, Charles Borromée, February 18, 1887 - August 25, 1901
Wetmore, Edward Ludlow, February 18, 1887 - September 16, 1907
McGuire, Thomas Horace, April 25, 1887 - January 3, 1903;
   Chief Justice, February 18, 1902 - January 3, 1903
Scott, David Lynch, September 28, 1894 - September 16, 1907
Prendergast, James Emile Pierre, February 18, 1902 - September 16, 1907
Sifton, Arthur Lewis, Chief Justice, January 3, 1903 - September 16, 1907
Newlands, Henry William, January 19, 1904 - September 16, 1907
Harvey, Horace, June 27, 1904 - September 16, 1907
Johnstone, Thomas Cook, October 8,1906 - September 16, 1907
Stuart, Charles Allan, October 8, 1906 - September 16, 1907

Supreme Court of Alberta
September 16, 1907 - September 15, 1921

Harvey, Horace, September 16, 1907 - September 15, 1921;
   Chief Justice, October 12, 1910 - September 15, 1921
Scott, David Lynch, September 16, 1907 - September 15, 1921
Sifton, Arthur Lewis, Chief Justice, September 16, 1907 - May 25, 1910
Stuart, Charles Allan, September 16, 1907 - September 15, 1921
Beck, Nicholas Du Bois Dominic, September 23, 1907 - September 15, 1921
Simmons, William Charles, October 12, 1910 - September 15, 1921
Walsh, William Legh, April 3, 1912 - September 15, 1921
Hyndman, James Duncan, July 11, 1914 - September 15, 1921
Ives, William Carlos, July 11, 1914 - September 15, 1921
McCarthy, Maitland Stewart, July 11, 1914 - September 15, 1921

Local District Courts
November 21, 1907 - August 3, 1935

Acadia

Stewart, John Douglas Reginald, November 6, 1919 - October 4, 1931

Athabasca

Noel, Joseph Camillien, July 6, 1909 - March 16, 1920

Calgary

Mitchell, Charles Richmond, November 21, 1907 - May 31, 1910
Carpenter, Arthur Allan, November 12, 1910 - November 15, 1915
Jennison, John Leslie, November 16, 1915 - December 1, 1919
Winter, William Roland, March 19, 1913 - March 13, 1926
McNeill, Edward Peel, October 6, 1920 - August 3, 1935
MacDonald, William Alexander, March 13, 1926 - August 3, 1935

Edmonton

Taylor, Hedley Clarence, November 21, 1907 - February 1930
Crawford, John Lyndon, March 19, 1913 - August 3, 1935
Dubuc, Lucien, January 25, 1922 - August 3, 1935

Hanna

Stewart, John Douglas Reginald, April 1, 1922 - October 4, 1931

Lethbridge

Winter, William Roland, November 21, 1907 - March 19, 1913
Jackson, John Ainslie, March 19, 1913 - August 3, 1935

Macleod

Carpenter, Arthur Allan, November 21, 1907 - November 12, 1910
Crawford, John Lyndon, November 25, 1910 - March 19, 1913
McNeill, Edward Peel, March 19, 1913 - September 15, 1921
McDonald, Angus Marcellus, September 15, 1921 - August 3, 1935

Medicine Hat

Greene, George Wellington, December 18, 1915 - August 3, 1935

Peace River

Dubuc, Lucien, October 6, 1920 - March 29, 1934
Matheson, Joseph Duncan, March 29, 1934 - August 3, 1935

Red Deer

Mahaffy, James Jeffers, December 18, 1915 - August 3, 1935

Stettler

Morrison, Frederic Augustus, October 7, 1916 - February 25, 1929

Westaskiwin

Lees, William Andrew Dickson, July 6, 1909 - August 27, 1934
Noel, Joseph Camillien, November 21, 1907 - July 6, 1909

Supreme Court of Alberta, Appellate Division
September 15, 1921 - June 30, 1979

Beck, Nicholas Du Bois Dominic, September 15, 1921 - May 14, 1928
Hyndman, James Duncan, September 15, 1921 - January 15, 1931
Clarke, Alfred Henry, September 15, 1921 - January 30, 1942
Scott, David Lynch, Chief Justice of Alberta, September 15, 1921 -
        July 26, 1924
Stuart, Charles Allan, September 15, 1921 - March 5, 1926
Harvey, Horace, Chief Justice of Alberta, August 27, 1924 -
        September 9, 1949
Mitchell, Charles Richmond, March 13, 1926 - November 3, 1936
Lunney, Henry William, May 23, 1928 - October 6, 1944
Walsh, William Legh, January 27, 1931 - May 1, 1931
McGillivray, Alexander Andrew, May 8, 1931 - December 12, 1940
Ford, Frank C., November 3, 1936 - October 13, 1954
Ewing, Albert Freeman, January 13, 1941 - August 28, 1946
Howson, William Robinson, May 6, 1942 - October 20, 1944
MacDonald, William Alexander, October 20, 1944 - January 17, 1957
Parlee, Harold Hayward, April 9, 1945 - February 28, 1954
O'Connor, George Bligh, October 30, 1946 - January 13, 1957;
        Chief Justice of Alberta, January 25, 1950 - January 13, 1957

Ford, Clinton James, January 25, 1950 - March 1, 1961;
    Chief Justice of Alberta, January 17, 1957 - March 1, 1961
Porter, Marshall Menzies, September 1, 1954 - October 12, 1969
Johnson, Horace Gilchrist, December 16, 1954 - December 20, 1973
MacDonald, Hugh John, January 17, 1957 - March 2, 1965
McBride, James Boyd, January 17, 1957 - January 2, 1960
Smith, Sidney Bruce, April 7, 1960 - December 5, 1974;
    Chief Justice of Alberta, March 1, 1961 - December 5, 1974
Kane, Edward William Scott, March 1, 1961 - April 29, 1974
McDermid, Neil Douglas, August 14, 1963 - June 30, 1979
Cairns, James Mitchell, February 15, 1965 - October 25, 1977
Allen, Gordon Hollis, May 12, 1966 - May 28, 1978
Clement, Carlton Ward, February 12, 1970 - June 30, 1979
Prowse, David Clifton, September 1, 1972 - June 30, 1979
Sinclair, William Robert, January 25, 1973 - February 22, 1979
Moir, Arnold Fraser, May 18, 1973 - June 30, 1979
Haddad, William Joseph, November 29, 1974 - June 30, 1979
McGillivray, William Alexander, Chief Justice of Alberta, December 5, 1974 -
    June 30, 1979
Morrow, William George, May 28, 1976 - June 30, 1979
Lieberman, Samuel Sereth, December 23, 1976 - June 30, 1979
Harradence, Asa Milton, March 26, 1979 - June 30, 1979
Laycraft, James Herbert, March 26 1979 - June 30, 1979

Supreme Court of Alberta, Trial Division
September 15, 1921 - June 30, 1979

Harvey, Horace, September 15, 1921 - August 27, 1924
Ives, William Carlos, September 15, 1921 - August 16, 1944;
    Chief Justice, September 25, 1942 - August 16, 1944
McCarthy, Maitland Stewart, September 15, 1921 - May 3, 1926
Simmons, William Charles, September 15, 1921 - September 1, 1936;
    Chief Justice, August 27, 1924 - September 1, 1936
Tweedie, Thomas Mitchell, September 15, 1921 - October 4, 1944;
    Chief Justice, August 16, 1944 - October 4, 1944
Walsh, William Legh, September 15, 1921 - January 27, 1931
Boyle, John Robert, August 27, 1924 - February 15, 1936
Ford, Frank, May 3, 1926 - November 3, 1936
Ewing, Albert Freeman, January 27, 1931 - January 13, 1941
Howson, William Robinson, March 2, 1936 - May 6, 1942;
    Chief Justice, October 20, 1944 - June 15, 1952
Mitchell, Charles Richmond, Chief Justice, November 3, 1936 -
    August 16, 1942
Shepherd, Simpson James, November 3, 1936 - February 6, 1952

O'Connor, George Bligh, January 13, 1941 - October 30, 1946

MacDonald, William Alexander, May 6, 1942 - October 20, 1944

McLaurin, Colin Campbell, September 23, 1942 - September 1, 1968;
      Chief Justice, June 27, 1952 - September 1, 1968

MacDonald, Hugh John, October 20, 1944 - January 17, 1957

Parlee, Harold Hayward, December 19, 1944 - April 19, 1945

Ford, Clinton James, April 19, 1945 - January 25, 1950

McBride, James Boyd, October 30, 1946 - January 17, 1957

Egbert, William Gordon, January 25, 1950 - February 8, 1960

Cairns, James Mitchell, March 4, 1952 - February 15, 1965

Wilson, Ernest Brown, June 27, 1952 - December 10, 1958

Primrose, Neil Phillip, September 1, 1954 - September15, 1965

Greschuk, Peter, January 17, 1957 - June 30, 1979

Riley, Harold William, January 17, 1953 - January 1, 1973

Smith, Sidney Bruce, January 8, 1959 - April 7, 1960

Manning, Marshall Edward, August 18, 1959 - June 30, 1979

Milvain, James Valentine Hogarth, August 18, 1959 - February 14, 1979;
      Chief Justice, September 26, 1968 - February 14, 1979

Farthing, Hugh Cragg, April 7, 1960 - July 18, 1967

Kirby, William John Cameron, October 18, 1960 - June 30, 1979

Dechene, André Miville, February 15, 1965 - June 30, 1979

O'Byrne, Michael Brien, September 19, 1967 - June 30, 1979

MacDonald, Hugh John, March 25, 1968 - 30 June 1979

Sinclair, William Robert, September 26, 1968 - January 25, 1973;
      Chief Justice, February 22, 1979 - June 30, 1979

Cullen, Alan Joseph, February 12, 1970 - April 23, 1975

Lieberman, Samuel Sereth, February 12, 1970 - April 23, 1975

Bowen, Donald Haines, January 20, 1972 - June 30, 1977

Moore, William Kenneth, January 20, 1972 - June 30, 1979

Cavanagh, James Creighton, May 18, 1973 - June 30, 1979

Shannon, Melvin Earl, May 18, 1973 - June 30, 1979

McDonald, David Cargill, January 1, 1974 - June 30, 1979

Quigley, Francis Hugh, November 29, 1974 - June 30, 1979

Steer, George Alexander Cameron, November 28, 1974 - June 30, 1979

Laycraft, James Herbert, July 31, 1975 - March 26, 1979

Brennan, William Robert, April 8, 1976 - June 30, 1979

Moshansky, Virgil Peter, May 27, 1976 - June 30, 1979

Miller, Tevie Harold, July 8, 1976 - June 30, 1979

Hope, John McIntosh, December 23, 1976 - June 30, 1979

McClung, John Wesley, December 22, 1977 - June 30, 1979

Waite, John Hilary, February 2, 1978 - June 30, 1979

MacLean, Lawrence David, December 21, 1978 - June 30, 1979

Forsyth, Gregory Rife, March 26, 1979 - June 30, 1979

Regional District Courts
August 3, 1935 - October 1, 1975

District Court of Northern Alberta

Bury, Ambrose Upton Gledstanes, August 3, 1935 - December 19, 1944
Crawford, John Lyndon, August 3, 1935 - September 2, 1946
Dubuc, Lucien, August 3, 1935 - September 13, 1949
      Chief Judge, March 18, 1944 - September 13, 1949
Mahaffy, James Jeffers, August 3, 1935 - October 6, 1944
Matheson, Joseph Duncan, August 3, 1935 - February 24, 1948
McIsaac, Joseph Patrick, November 5, 1943 - August 20, 1963
McDonald, John Cameron, March 18, 1944 - September 15, 1951
Fraser, Harry Blackwood, December 19, 1944 - August 28, 1963
McBride, James Boyd, December 19, 1944 - October 30, 1946
Kerr, Stanley Chandos Staveley, February 5, 1947 - May 19, 1953;
      Chief Judge, September 13, 1949 - May 19, 1953
Cross, Thomas Lynde, February 24, 1948 - October 1, 1975
Gariepy, Charles Edouard, September 13, 1949 - March 19, 1963
Buchanan, Nelles Victor, March 4, 1952 - January 23, 1965;
      Chief Judge, October 14, 1953 - January 23, 1965
Greschuk, Peter, October 14, 1953 - January 17, 1957
Cairns, Laurence Yeomans, September 24, 1957 - September 1, 1965
Gardiner, Duncan McIntyre, November 20, 1961 - March 10, 1969
Cormack, John Spiers, March 19, 1963 - October 1, 1975
Dechene, André Miville, August 21, 1963 - February 15, 1965
Whittaker, Bruce Cavanagh, September 26, 1963 - October 1, 1975
Decore, John Nickolas, Chief Judge, March 29, 1965 - September 30, 1975
Haddad, William Joseph, August 18, 1965 - November 29, 1974
Legg, Sidney Vincent, December 22, 1965 - October 1, 1975
Lieberman, Samuel Sereth, November 1, 1966 - February 12, 1970
Belzil, Roger Hector, June 5, 1969 - October 1, 1975
Kerans, Roger Philip, February 12, 1970 - October 1, 1975
Feehan, Joseph Bernard, September 13, 1974 - October 1, 1975
Crossley, Arthur William, November 1, 1973 - October 1, 1975
Miller, Tevie Harold, December 20, 1974 - October 1, 1975
Wachowich, Allan Harvey Joseph, December 20, 1974 - October 1, 1975
Bracco, John David, July 31, 1975 - October 1, 1975
Stevenson, William Alexander, July 31, 1975 - October 1, 1975

District Court of Southern Alberta

Greene, George Wellington, August 3, 1935 - July 14, 1936
Jackson, John Ainslie, August 3, 1935 - October 2, 1945
MacDonald, Angus Marcellus, August 3, 1935 - October 2, 1945

MacDonald, William Alexander, August 3, 1935 - May 6, 1942
McNeill, Edward Peel, August 3, 1935 - May 24, 1940
McDonald, John Walter, May 24, 1940 - November 8, 1950;
    Chief Judge, March 18, 1944 - November 8, 1950
Ford, Clinton James, May 6, 1942 - April 19, 1945
Edmanson, Roy Manning, March 18, 1944 - November 5, 1960
Fairbairn, Lynden Eldon, April 19, 1945 - January 23, 1946
Feir, Elmor Best, October 2, 1945 - August 17, 1969;
    Chief Judge, September 16, 1955 - August 17, 1969
Stack, Luke Hannon, October 2, 1945 - February 1, 1958
Sissons, John Howard, October 30, 1946 - September 16, 1955;
    Chief Judge, December 13, 1950 - September 16, 1955
Edwards, Manley Justin, January 1, 1951 - May 28, 1962
Turcotte, Louis Sherman, September 16, 1955 - October 1, 1975;
    Chief Judge, September 24, 1969 - October 1, 1975
Farthing, Hugh Cragg, February 1, 1958 - April 7, 1960
Beaumont, Arthur, December 24, 1958 - March 17, 1964
Patterson, Henry Stuart, April 7, 1960 - October 1, 1975
Tavender, Edward Rusling, October 19, 1961 - October 1, 1975
Sellar, William, August 30, 1962 - May 19, 1968
Cullen, Alan Joseph, August 1, 1964 - February 12, 1970
Kidd, James George, October 31, 1968 - October 1, 1975
Yanosik, Clarence George, September 24, 1969 - October 1, 1975
Quigley, Francis Hugh, February 12, 1970 - November 29, 1974
Rowbotham, Henry Slater, February 12, 1970 - October 1, 1975
Medhurst, Donald Herbert, November 28, 1974 - October 1, 1975

District Court of Alberta
October 1, 1975 - June 30, 1979

Belzil, Roger Hector, October 1, 1975 - June 30, 1979
Bracco, John David, October 1, 1975 - June 30, 1979
Cormack, John Spiers, October 1, 1975 - June 30, 1979
Cross, Thomas Lynde, October 1, 1975 - July 1, 1977
Crossley, Arthur William, October 1, 1975 - June 30, 1979
Decore, John Nickolas, Chief Judge, October 1, 1975 - June 30, 1979
Feehan, Joseph Bernard, October 1, 1975 - June 30, 1979
Kerans, Roger Philip, October 1, 1975 - June 30, 1979;
    Associate Chief Judge, December 19, 1975 - June 30, 1979
Kidd, James George, October 1, 1975 - June 30, 1979
Legg, Sidney Vincent, October 1, 1975 - June 30, 1979
Medhurst, Donald Herbert, October 1, 1975 - June 30, 1979
Miller, Tevie Harold, October 1, 1975 - July 8, 1976
Patterson, Henry Stuart, October 1, 1975 - June 30, 1979

Rowbotham, Henry Slater, Calgary, October 1, 1975 - June 30, 1979
Stevenson, William Alexander, October 1, 1975 - June 30, 1979
Tavender, Edward Rusling, October 1, 1975 - July 13, 1978
Turcotte, Louis Sherman, October 1, 1975 - June 30, 1979
     Associate Chief Judge, October 1, 1975 - December 1, 1975
Wachowich, Allan Harvey Joseph, October 1, 1975 - June 30, 1979
Whittaker, Bruce Cavanagh, October 1, 1975 - March 23, 1978
Yanosik, Clarence George, October 1, 1975 - June 30, 1979
McFadyen, Elizabeth Ann, January 5, 1976 - June 30, 1979
Holmes, Jack Kenneth, April 8, 1976 - June 30, 1979
McClung, John Wesley, December 23, 1976 - December 22, 1977
Dea, John Berchmans, February 2, 1978 - June 30, 1979
Hetherington, Mary Margaret McCormick, December 21, 1978 - June 30, 1979
Foisy, Rene Paul, March 26, 1979 - June 30, 1979

Court of Appeal of Alberta
June 30, 1979 - December 31, 1990

Clement, Carlton Ward, June 30, 1979 - January 7, 1982
Haddad, William Joseph, June 30, 1979 - November 26, 1990
Harradence, Asa Milton, June 30, 1979 - April 23, 1997
Laycraft, James Herbert, June 30, 1979 - December 31, 1991
     Chief Justice of Alberta, February 20, 1985 - December 31, 1991
Lieberman, Samuel Sereth, June 30, 1979 -
McDermid, Neil Douglas, June 30, 1979 - June 5, 1986
McGillivray, William Alexander, Chief Justice, June 30, 1979 - December 16, 1984
Moir, Arnold Fraser, June 30, 1979 - September 24, 1987
Morrow, William George, June 30, 1979 - August 13, 1980
Prowse, David Clifton, June 30, 1979 - July 26, 1988
Kerans, Roger Philip, October 23, 1980 -
Stevenson, William Alexander, October 23, 1980 - September 17, 1990
McClung, John Wesley, December 19, 1980 -
Belzil, Roger Hector, June 18, 1981 - December 26, 1996
Irving, Howard Lawrence, February 15, 1985 -
Hetherington, Mary Margaret McCormick, October 4, 1985 -
Foisy, René Paul, January 1, 1987 -
Côté, Jean Edouard Leon, October 30, 1987 -
Stratton, Joseph John Walter, October 30, 1987 - December 13, 1995
Bracco, John David, December 31, 1987 -

Court of Queen's Bench of Alberta
June 30, 1979 - December 31, 1990

Belzil, Roger Hector, June 30, 1979 - June 18, 1981
Bowen, Donald Haines, June 30, 1979 - September 14, 1986
Bracco, John David, June 30, 1979 - December 31, 1987
Brennan, William Robert, June 30, 1979 -
Cavanagh, James Creighton, June 30, 1979 - December 31, 1990
Cormack, John Spiers, June 30, 1979 - February 21, 1985
Crossley, Arthur William, June 30, 1979 - September 9, 1991
Dea, John Berchmans, June 30, 1979 -
Dechene, André Miville, June 30, 1979 - March 25, 1987
Decore, John Nickolas, June 30, 1979 - April 9, 1984
Feehan, Joseph Bernard, June 30, 1979 -
Foisy, René Paul, June 30, 1979 - January 1, 1987
Forsyth, Gregory Rife, June 30, 1979 -
Greschuk, Peter, June 30, 1979 - November 14, 1983
Hetherington, Mary Margaret McCormick, June 30, 1979 - October 4, 1985
Holmes, Jack Kenneth, June 30, 1979 -
Hope, John McIntosh, June 30, 1979 - February 26, 1992
Kerans, Roger Philip, June 30, 1979 - October 23, 1980
Kidd, James George, June 30, 1979 - April 4, 1985
Kirby, William John Cameron, June 30, 1979 - January 12, 1984
Legg, Sidney Vincent, June 30, 1979 - September 22, 1984
MacDonald, Hugh John, June 30, 1979 - 11 April 1986
MacLean, Lawrence David, June 30, 1979 -
Manning, Marshall Edward, June 30, 1979 - December 28, 1979
McClung, John Wesley, June 30, 1979 - December 19, 1980
McDonald, David Cargill, June 30, 1979 - January 1, 1996
McFadyen, Elizabeth Ann, June 30, 1979 - February 1, 1993
Medhurst, Donald Herbert, 30 June 1979 -
Miller, Tevie Harold, June 30, 1979 - August 21, 1996;
    Associate Chief Justice, February 24, 1984 - August 21, 1996
Moore, William Kenneth, June 30, 1979 -
    Associate Chief Justice, April 28, 1981 - February 24, 1984
    Chief Justice, February 24, 1984 -
Moshansky, Virgil Peter, June 30, 1979 -
O'Byrne, Michael Brien, June 30, 1979 -
Patterson, Henry Stuart, June 30, 1979 - November 3, 1988
Quigley, Francis Hugh, June 30, 1979 -
Rowbotham, Henry Slater, June 30, 1979 -
Shannon, Melvin Earl, June 30, 1979 -
Sinclair, William Robert, June 30, 1979 - December 18, 1995;
    Chief Justice, June 30, 1979 - February 24, 1984
Steer, George Alexander Cameron, June 30, 1979 - December 16, 1979

Stevenson, William Alexander, June 30, 1979 - October 23, 1980
Turcotte, Louis Sherman, June 30, 1979 - September 10, 1979
Wachowich, Allan Harvey Joseph, June 30, 1979 -
    Associate Chief Justice, February 1, 1993 -
Waite, John Hilary, June 30, 1979 -
Yanosik, Clarence George, June 30, 1979 -
Cawsey, Robert Allan, November 27, 1979 -
Egbert, William Gordon Neil, November 27, 1979 -
Power, Peter Charles Garneau, November 27, 1979 -
Prowse, Hubert Samuel, November 27, 1979 -
Agrios, John Andrew, July 3, 1980 -
Kryczka, Joseph Julius, July 3, 1980 - January 11, 1991
Purvis, Stuart Somerville, July 3, 1980 - September 25, 1986
Dixon, Russell Armitage, October 23, 1980 -
Stratton, Joseph John Walter, October 23, 1980 - September 29, 1987
MacNaughton, Frederick Richards, December 19, 1980 - July 17, 1987
Smith, Vernor Winfield MacBriare, December 19, 1980 -
Lomas, Melvin Earl, April 28, 1981 -
Girgulis, William James, June 18, 1981 -
Veit, Joanne Barbara, June 18, 1981 -
Chrumka, Paul Stephan, January 28, 1982 -
Lutz, Arthur Morton, November 4, 1982 -
Montgomery, Robert Archibald Fraser, November 4, 1982 -
Sulatycky, Allen Borislaw Zenoviy, November 4, 1982 -
Decore, Lionel Leighton, August 1, 1983 - March 5, 1984
MacCallum, Edward Patrick, December 22, 1983 -
MacKenzie, John Horace, December 22, 1983 -
McBain, Ross Thomas George, December 22, 1983 -
O'Leary, Willis Edward, December 22, 1983 - September 27, 1994
Foster, Nina Leone, April 18, 1984 -
Gallant, Tellex William, June 21, 1984 -
MacPherson, Jack Leon, March 7, 1985 - April 2, 1991
Matheson, Douglas Randolph, March 15, 1985
Andrekson, Alexander, August 22, 1985 -
Berger, Ronald Leon, August 22, 1985 - June 20, 1996
Hutchinson, Ernest Arthur, September 30, 1985 -
Mason, David Blair, August 22, 1985 -
Hetherington, Mary Margaret McCormick, October 4, 1985 -
Virtue, Charles Gladstone, October 4, 1985 -
Picard, Ellen Irene, January 1, 1987 - April 27, 1995
Marshall, Ernest Arthur, June 16, 1986 -
Conrad, Carole Mildred, November 10, 1986 - June 24, 1992
Cooke, Alan Thomas, November 10, 1986 -
Trussler, Marguerite Jean, November 10, 1986 -
Murray, Alec Thirlwell, October 30, 1987 -

Deyell, Roy Victor, December 18, 1987 -
Roslak, Yaroslaw, December 31, 1987 - May 3, 1995
Fraser, Catherine Anne, March 7, 1989 - March 1, 1991
Rawlins, Bonnie Leigh, March 8, 1989 -
Perras, Delmar Walter Joseph, October 4, 1989 -
MacLeod, Donald Ingraham, March 14, 1990 -
Bielby, Myra Beth, December 24, 1990 -

Bibliography

Secondary Sources

Bowker, W.F. "The Honourable Horace Harvey, Chief Justice of Alberta."
Canadian Bar Review 32 (1954): 933-981, 1118-1139.

Bowker, W.F. "Three Alberta Judges." *Alberta Law Review* 4 (1962-1964): 5-10
[Frank Ford, Clinton Ford, Hugh John Macdonald].

Bowker, W.F. "Stipendiary Magistrates and the Supreme Court of the Northwest
Territories, 1876-1907." *Alberta Law Review* 26 (1988), 245-286.

Bucknall, Brian O. "John Howard Sissons and the Development of Law in
Northern Canada." *Osgoode Hall law Journal* 5 (1967): 159-171.

Decore, J.N. "The District Court of Alberta." *Alberta Law Review*, 25th
Anniversary Issue (1980): 23-24.

Harvey, Horace. "The Early Administration of Justice in the North West." *Alberta
Law Quarterly* 1 (1934): 1-15.

Harvey, Horace. "Some Notes on the Early Administration of Justice in Canada's
Northwest." *Alberta History* 1 (Autumn 1953): 5-20.

Jamieson, F.C. "Edmonton Courts and Lawyers in Territorial Times." *Alberta
History* 4 (Winter 1956): 3-9.

Knafla, Louis A. "From Oral to Written Memory: The Common Law Tradition in
Western Canada," in *Law & Justice in a New Land. Essays in Western Canadian
Legal History*. Toronto, Calgary & Vancouver: Carswell, 1986. Pp. 31-77.

Knafla, Louis A. "Charles Borromée Rouleau." In *Dictionary of Canadian
Biography, Vol. XIII 1900 to 1910* (Toronto: University of Toronto Press, 1994).
Pp. 907-909.

Macleod, R.C. "James Farquharson Macleod." In *Dictionary of Canadian Biography,
Vol. XII 1891 to 1900* (Toronto: University of Toronto Press, 1990). Pp. 672-674.

McCaul, C.C. "Precursors of the Bench and Bar in the Western Provinces."
Canadian Bar Review 3 (1925): 25-40.

Morrow, W.G. "An Historical Examination of Alberta's Legal System: The First
Seventy-Five Years." *Alberta Law Review* 19 (1981): 148-170.

Morrow, W.G. "Some Legal Legends." *Alberta Law Review, 25th Anniversary Issue* (1980): 15-22.

Morrow, W.H. (ed). *Northern Justice*. The Memoirs of Mr. Justice William G. Morrow. Toronto: The Osgoode Society and the Legal Archives Society of Alberta, 1995.

Patterson, H.S. "The District Court of Southern Alberta." *Alberta Law Review*, 25th Anniversary Issue (1980): 25-29.

Sissons, John Howard. *Judge of the Far North: Memoirs of Jack Sissons*. Toronto: McClelland and Stewart, 1968.

Smith, S.B. "The Superior Courts of Alberta." *Alberta Law Review*, 25th Anniversary Issue (1980): 8-14.

Thorner, Thomas, and Neil B. Watson. "Keeper of the King's Peace: Colonel G. E. Sanders and the Calgary Police Magistrate's Court, 1911-1932." *Urban History Review* 12 (February 1984): 45-55.

Primary Sources

Legal Archives Society of Alberta

Law Society of Alberta fonds, Members' files, Fonds 05-00-01, 1907-1983 (Restricted) A.H. Clarke,

William Carlos Ives fonds, Fonds 10-00-00, 1940-1944 (Open)

Arthur L. Sifton fonds, Fonds 11-00-00, 1903-1906 (Open)

Nicholas D. Beck fonds, Fonds 12-00-00, 1907-1928 (Open)

Ernest B. Wilson fonds, Fonds 19-00-00, 1952-1958 (Restricted)

James Herbert Laycraft fonds, Fonds 20-00-00, 1975-1991 (Restricted)

Yaroslaw Roslak fonds, Fonds 23-00-00, 1975-1995 (Restricted)

Edward Patrick MacCallum fonds, Fonds 25-00-00, 1984-1992 (Restricted)

Melvin E. Shannon fonds, Fonds 28-00-00, 1959-1993 (Restricted)

Frank Ford fonds, Fonds 43-00-00, 1927-1942 (Open)

Wilbur F. Bowker fonds, Fonds 44-00-00, 1934-1938 (Open)

Allan H.J. Wachowich fonds, Fonds 45-00-00, 1974-1975 (Restricted)

James V. H. Milvain fonds, Fonds 47-00-00, 1972-1990 (Restricted)

Alexander McGillivray fonds, Fonds 49-00-00, 1931-1939 (Open)

Louis D. Hyndman fonds, Collected source material for legal history, Fonds 53-00 02, 1970-1985 (Open)

David Lynch Scott fonds, Fonds 54-00-00, 1923-1924 (Open)

William J. Haddad fonds, 1965-1968, Accession 96006 (Restricted)

Edward W. S. Kane fonds, 1970-1971, Accession 96003 (Restricted)

David C. MacDonald fonds, 1955-1996, Accession 96004, 96022, 96023, 96024 (Restricted)

Provincial Archives of Alberta

Attorney-General's Department fonds

Administration Branch Records, 1921-1979, Accessions 84.130, 84.267, 89.176

Alberta Inspector of Legal Offices, 1909-1947, Accession 73.322

Supreme and District Courts, Civil and Criminal Case Files and Records:

Edmonton, 1881-1975, Accessions 69.305, 83.1, 87.95, 89.79, 88.469

Calgary, 1883-1971, Accessions 79.266, 79.285, 85.249, 87.246, 88.471, 70.364

Fort Macleod, 1880-1972, Accessions 78.235, 87.94, 68.18, 68.96, 75.114

Medicine Hat, 1906-1968, Accessions 83.238, 82.60, 77.318, 83.238, 82.60, 83.168

Wetaskiwin, 1907-1979, Accessions 81.198, 86.13, 88.600

Drumheller, 1926-1959, Accessions 85.61, 79.292

Vegreville, 1928-1972, Accessions 83.169

Grande Prairie, 1917-1980, Accessions 84.255, 85.183

Peace River, 1919-1972, Accessions 80.320, 81.34

Hanna, 1916-1972, Accessions 79.126, 85.377

Red Deer, 1907-1977, Accessions 79.153, 79.220

Stettler, 1914-1936, Accession 87.395

Charles B. Rouleau fonds, 1886-1901, Accession 68.302

Horace Harvey fonds, 1904-1950, Accessions 68.302, 73.182

David Lynch Scott fonds, 1904-1950, Accession 69.310

S. Bruce Smith fonds, 1959-1964, Accession 74.518

Nelles V. Buchanan fonds, 1952-1974, Accession 87.55

André M. Dechene fonds, 1968-1985, Accession 87.156

James Duncan Hyndman fonds, 1914-1931, Accession 86.285

National Archives of Canada:

Horace Harvey Records, M30, E87, 1887-1949

Glenbow-Alberta Institute Archives

Rouleau Family fonds, 1896-1985

William G. Morrow fonds, 1939-1980

University of Calgary, Special Collections

William G. Morrow fonds, 1913-1980

Reference Works

Canada.*The Canada Gazette, Part I.* Ottawa: Queen's Printer, 1867-

*Dictionary of Canadian Biography.*Vol. 1-13. Ed. George W. Brown, Frances
    Halpenny. Toronto: University of Toronto Press, 1966 -

Table of Cases

A

D

E

F

G

H

I

J

K

N

O

P

Index of Personal Names